Adventures of a Southern Boyhood

Walking with Giants

To Caroline —
Love forever —
From your
cousin —
Will
May 31, 2014

Also by William E. Dunstan

FICTION

The Runaway Detectives

NONFICTION

The Ancient Near East

Ancient Greece

Ancient Rome

ADVENTURES OF A SOUTHERN BOYHOOD

Volume Two: *Running with the Grim Reaper*

Volume Three: *Budding as a Young Scientist*

Volume Four: *Spinning Mischief Galore*

Volume Five: *Chasing Profit and Pleasure*

Volume Six: *Finding My Way*

Adventures of a Southern Boyhood

Volume One

Walking with Giants

William E. Dunstan

Adventures of a Southern Boyhood/William E. Dunstan

Volume 1: Walking with Giants
Copyright © 2013 by William E. Dunstan

All rights reserved. No part of this publication may be reproduced or used in any manner whatsoever without prior written permission from the author, except for brief quotations embodied in critical articles and reviews. The information in this publication is true and complete to the best of the author's knowledge and is offered without guarantee on his part. The author assumes no responsibility for errors or omissions in this book and disclaims any liability in connection with the use of information contained herein.

Memoir / After introducing the author's noteworthy ancestors in Virginia and North Carolina, this six-volume series focuses on his remarkable boyhood in Elizabeth City, North Carolina.

ISBN-13: 978-1493695546
ISBN-10: 1493695541
CreateSpace, Charleston, South Carolina

Cover Images

Front cover (from top, left):

> Garland Herrington Dunstan (born 1916), Forrest Vaughan Dunstan (born 1914), and William Edward Dunstan II (born 1908), circa 1918
>
> Ida Powell Fuller (the future Ida Powell Fuller Dunstan, born 1914), November 1938
>
> William E. Dunstan House, Elizabeth City, North Carolina (built circa 1895, destroyed by fire 1966); photograph, circa 1948, by Edmund Fleetwood Dunstan, courtesy of Ethan Andrew Dunstan

Back cover (from top, left):

> Rebecca Vaughan House, Southampton County, Virginia (built circa 1795), pen-and-ink drawing by Kyle Keeter, capturing the essence of the original design
>
> Walnut Hill, Southampton County, Virginia (built circa 1815, demolished early twenty-first century), pen-and-ink drawing by Kyle Keeter, capturing the essence of the original design
>
> Edmund Fleetwood Dunstan (born 1896), September 25, 1900
>
> Annie Elizabeth Mangum (the future Annie Elizabeth Mangum Fuller, born 1875), circa 1892
>
> Mary Susan Fuller (the future Mary Susan Fuller Woodall, born 1907), circa 1925; photograph courtesy of Wilbur and Charlotte Woodall
>
> William Edward Dunstan II (born 1908), circa 1922

Contents

Cover Images v

Preface to the Series ix

Acknowledgements xiii

1. Death and Devotion 1
2. Will and Emma 31
3. Will as Husband, Father, Poet, Business Trailblazer, and Civic Leader 47
4. Edward and His Circle 69
5. Edward Retreats from Wall Street and Wrestles with the *Independent* 97
6. Edward Mesmerized by Miss Ida Powell Fuller 131
7. David and Zenobia and Miss Annie 143
8. Miss Annie Shows Grit and Becomes a Power in Franklin County 159
9. Ida Denied a Career in Music 173
10. Edward and Ida 185
11. Ida's Carefully Concealed Secret 197

About the Author 225

Preface to the Series

This six-volume series, *Adventures of a Southern Boyhood*, springs from persistent requests by friends, relatives, and college students to chronicle my fledgling escapades in northeastern North Carolina, focusing on my not-so-sleepy hometown of Elizabeth City, beautifully linked by fragile swamps, ragged fingers of land, and grand watercourses to the tempestuous Atlantic. I finally agreed to pen my boyhood adventures but decided to enhance the tapestry in two ways. First, I introduced the exploits of three generations of my ancestors and described their imprints on the nineteenth and twentieth centuries. Second, I marched into a panorama of historical events and thickets shaping the fabric of human life, from the early nineteenth century through my graduation from high school in the twentieth. Accompanied by stunning twists and revelations, the many-layered developments headlined in these books touch both my immediate circle and the wider world beyond. Powerful women, men, and children tramp through every chapter, yet they wrestle with forces beyond their control and struggle vainly to outwit their destiny. Their lives send infinite ripples across the globe. Readers will find unforgettable tales, surging passions, warm friendships, and strong family bonds permeating the six volumes of this series: *Walking with Giants, Running with the Grim Reaper, Budding as a Young Scientist, Spinning Mischief Galore, Chasing Profit and Pleasure*, and *Finding My Way*.

The story begins on my father's side, in 1831, when eight-year-old Mary Louisa Vaughan, my great-grandmother, survives the blood-drenched Nat Turner slave revolt in Southampton County, Virginia, but hears the tormented shrieks of her perishing loved ones. Later, she marries my great-grandfather, Edmund Fleetwood Dunstan, a prosperous planter of Bertie and Hertford Counties, North Carolina. Edmund suffers an untimely death before the outbreak of the Civil War, but his astonishing widow, children, and grandchildren embark upon near-epic adventures. Mary Louisa's gifted sixth child, William Edward Dunstan, my grandfather and namesake, lives through the dismal Civil War and then travels by train as a fourteen-year-old boy to Poughkeepsie, New York, for his higher education. Afterward, William gradually threads his way through North Carolina and Virginia seeking elusive professional fulfillment until finally settling in Elizabeth City, where he charms a notable young engaged lady, Emma Cobb Sawyer, into canceling her original wedding plans and marrying him. He creates a real estate empire in the town and surrounding area, and Emma demonstrates remarkable shrewdness in directing operations for nearly two decades after his death.

On my mother's side, David Thomas Fuller, my grandfather, loses his respected father from wounds and disease after the final gasp of the Civil War. Soon his mother charges the twelve-year-old boy with supporting the financially collapsed family. Embracing her entreaty as a sacred mission, young David astonishes everyone by building a vast agricultural realm in Franklin County, North Carolina. His resolute widow, Annie Elizabeth Mangum Fuller, enters politics after women finally gain the right to vote. Annie becomes one of the first women to hold elective office in the state and serves for decades without facing a single opponent. Her talented fifth child, Ida Powell Fuller, possessing a trained singing voice and stellar education, marries my father, William Edward Dunstan II, a deeply flawed man holding a postgraduate certificate from Harvard.

As Ida and Edward's firstborn, I enter boyhood long before parents herd their offspring from one activity to another and watch their every move. We children enjoy the vital freedom to roam and explore virtually unhindered. My remarkable friends, both boys and girls, relish great adventures, particularly those of rare dimensions. We examine the marrow of human existence and applaud the wonders of the earth. We prove that children can uncover pivotal clues about baffling murders and mysteries, investigate heated controversies, exhibit heroic courage, and create mischief galore. We come face to face with strange lights, inscrutable ghosts, and famous literary, educational, and political figures. We hold hands in the moonlight and steal kisses. We cannot imagine ever saying farewell or parting.

As a unique feature, much of the narrative rests upon newspaper accounts of local, state, national, and world events. Many people during this time frame pore over newspapers and avidly discuss the articles they encounter. For research, I consumed years scouring newspapers on microfilm, from the eighteenth century to the twentieth, and gradually amassed a trove of material describing family activities, prolonged wars, corpse-littered battlefields, economic crises, unusual murders, sensational scandals, inspiring achievements, surprising betrayals, steamy romances, and numerous bizarre tales. I quote newspaper passages to reveal not only family and personal developments but also attitudes of the day about slavery, segregation, conservation, birth control, abortion, adultery, political skullduggery, religious hypocrisy, and many other critical issues.

Written for general readers and students of history, my narrative focuses on conveying concrete pictures of real people and their thought-provoking lives. Generally, I avoid recently coined words or terms and favor the customary vocabulary employed during the period under discussion. To make quoted newspapers passages easier for readers to absorb, I correct most typographical errors without comment, spell out many numbers, and italicize titles of books and periodicals.

Acknowledgements

Numerous colleagues deserve my warmest gratitude for their enthusiasm and indispensable suggestions, especially Harry L. Watson, Atlanta Alumni Distinguished Professor of History at the University of North Carolina at Chapel Hill, and John M. Riddle, Alumni Distinguished Professor of History at North Carolina State University. Access to the superb libraries of the University of North Carolina at Chapel Hill aided significantly in my exhaustive research. Robert Anthony, Curator of the North Carolina Collection, and his able staff welcomed me for years of perusing microfilm and examining priceless books and maps. Several additional members of the extensive library community offered untiring academic or technical support, including Thomas J. Nixon, Beth L. Rowe, Philip M. McDaniel, Chad Haefele, Jennie Goforth, Kirill Tolpygo, Josiah Drewry, Angela Bardeen, Carolyn Shoemaker, Emily Spunaugle, Mitchell L. Whichard, and Joseph Mitchem. I gained crucial archival assistance from Sarah Downing of the Outer Banks History Center, Pat Hinton of Louisburg College, and Martha Fonville of Meredith College. My friends Katherine and Milton Futrell, guiding lights of the Southampton County Historical Society, Courtland, Virginia, enhanced my understanding of the Nat Turner revolt. Numerous relatives helped immeasurably by sharing information about family history and providing photocopies of noteworthy family documents. Many friends mentioned in the series encouraged me at every step of the writing process. My talented cousin Kyle Keeter, a professional artist, created three pen-and-ink drawings of houses crucial to the story, the Rebecca Vaughan House and Walnut Hill in Southampton County, Virginia, and the Gregory-Dunstan House in Elizabeth City, North Carolina.

1
Death and Devotion

Surely the sun hides its face in sorrow on Monday morning, August 22, 1831, as galloping riders reach the Nottoway River valley in Southampton County, Virginia, and cry out warnings of an ongoing bloodbath. The extraordinary slave leader and mystic Nat Turner, claiming possession of a command from the Holy Spirit and a divine sign from a recent solar eclipse, has organized an armed band of his fellows to massacre the planter class of the county and free his people from bondage. Although differing on details, all accounts agree that Nat Turner's follows burst from the dense forests and gloomy swamps of the lower part of the county after midnight. The insurgents blaze a serpentine path along Southampton roads and byways. Wielding weapons ranging from axes to firearms, the band embarks upon the worst slave rebellion in Southern history and cuts down more than fifty whites, mainly unarmed women and children. Many people flee to the sparsely populated county seat, Jerusalem, later renamed Courtland, by wagons and horseback, but not everyone has heard the ghastly news.

The hospitable widow Rebecca Vaughan, living off Barrow Road, remains unaware of Nat Turner's rampage. Rebecca's tranquil house stands roughly four miles southwest of the agitated county seat. From her entrance portico she sees great dust clouds churned by midday riders speeding down her long private drive from Barrow Road and apparently mistakes them for her son George and a party of foxhunters she plans to entertain on her plantation that afternoon. Rebecca's eighteen-year-old niece, Anne Elizabeth Vaughan, celebrated for her classic beauty, busies herself upstairs while awaiting the guests. When the ruthless band, now fifty or sixty strong, invades Rebecca's tree-shaded yard, she dashes into the house and pleads with them from a window to spare the lives of everyone on her property. Shots ring out.

Rebecca falls on her knees in prayer. Cursing, several of the men storm the house and interrupt the kneeling Rebecca's heavenward petition for a holy death. The floor runs with her blood.

Anne Elizabeth rushes downstairs and takes a fatal bullet. One of Rebecca's sons, fifteen-year-old Arthur, hears loud noises while occupied in the Vaughan distillery, valued for transforming the juice of pressed apples and peaches into potent brandy. Arthur comes running, probably expecting to find his older brother and the foxhunters, but a lethal shot extinguishes his young life in the yard. The overseer dies between the house and the distillery.

The murders toss Anne Elizabeth's body outside to bake under a withering August sun. The men have snatched Anne Elizabeth from the threshold of Holy Matrimony, according to family tradition and a brief, disjointed account of the Southampton catastrophe, Samuel Warner's *Authentic and Impartial Narrative of the Tragical Scene* . . . (New York: Printed for Warner and West, October 1831).

Anne Elizabeth had hastened to her Aunt Rebecca's house that morning to prepare for her wedding the next day to a young North Carolina gentleman. He approaches the plantation with lighthearted expectations only to find the house and land soaked in blood and littered with bullet-stabbed corpses. Samuel Warner fails to identify Anne Elizabeth by name but quotes a correspondent describing her as "an amiable young lady . . . to have been the day following united in marriage to a young gentleman of North Carolina," who arrives "to witness the mangled remains of her whom he was so shortly to espouse!"

Family history adds that Anne Elizabeth did not come alone to the home of Rebecca. She brought along her eight-year-old sister, Mary Louisa, from their own house, Walnut Hill, within easy riding or even walking distance. Someone conceals Mary Louisa in a small clothing chest at the first sign of trouble. Terrified, she survives in the chest while hearing the bloodcurdling massacre around her. Had she perished with her loved ones that day, I would not be writing these lines. Mary Louisa Vaughan was my great-grandmother.

Before catching Rebecca Vaughan by surprise, a group of the raiders assaulted the home of Captain John T. Barrow at the head of Barrow Road. A respected veteran of the War of 1812,

John had married Rebecca's daughter Mary. John has been forewarned of the urgent danger and rushes to escape, but his fair young wife refuses to leave home in her everyday clothes. Mary Vaughan Barrow consumes fatal minutes primping and then donning a more presentable outfit.

As the fierce band approaches, John stands his ground and calls to his beloved to flee for her life. Captain Barrow fights courageously in the deadly struggle and fends off the men with the butt of a firearm after exhausting his ammunition, but they finally overpower him and slit his throat. The remorseless intruders pay tribute to his unflinching resistance and seek to become equally fearless by drinking his blood. During their murderous rampage they treat his body alone with respect. They honor Captain Barrow by shrouding his corpse with a quilt and crowning the coverlet with a plug of tobacco. In the meantime Mary slips through the garden into the woods with the help of a loyal family slave.

The efficient killing band then races down Barrow Road into the eastern sun. They come upon and butcher George Vaughan, brother of Mary and son of Rebecca. George had been on his way to Mary's home with the intention of escorting her to the afternoon entertainment planned for the foxhunters.

Tolling church bells break an eerie hush over the melancholy landscape and call attention to the Southampton bloodbath. Distraught armed men of the county militia rush to the scene and suppress the massacre by scattering the rebels. The chilling slave uprising leaves the tiny planter class paralyzed with terror and erodes Virginia sentiment for gradual emancipation.

Nat Turner evades capture until October 30. After trial and conviction in court at the county seat, Turner and many of his confederates meet death by hanging. Mary Louisa Vaughan's nineteen-year-old brother, John, places the noose around his neck, attested by family records as well as Benjamin B. Winborne, in his *The Colonial and State Political History of Hertford County, N.C.* (Raleigh: Broughton and Edwards, 1906).

Winborne notes, on page189: "Nearly all [members] of [Mary Louisa's] . . . family were killed in the Nat Turner insurrection in 1831. Her sister [Anne Elizabeth] was also killed.

Her brother of 19 [John] was permitted to fasten the rope around Nat Turner's neck that swung him into eternity."

The complex and intertwined relationships among the county slaveholders means that Mary Louisa has lost at least a score of kinspeople by blood or marriage in the fateful onslaught. The family shields the psychologically wounded little girl from additional trauma by remaining tight-lipped year after year about her brush with death. The dismal peace following the revolt sees Mary Louisa enduring a deeply scarred childhood at Walnut Hill, north of the late Rebecca's house.

For unknown reasons Nat Turner had circled around Walnut Hill. Mary Louisa continues living on the estate with her surviving siblings and her bachelor uncle, Henry Briggs Vaughan. Her father, John Thomas Vaughan, and mother, Mary Foster Newsome Vaughan, had suffered untimely deaths by natural causes before the revolt. Uncle Henry quietly tells his neighbors what happened at Walnut Hill on August 22. When word reached him of the ongoing massacre, he assembled the slaves and gave them liberty to remain or join the rebels. None deserted.

Uncle Henry owns the local inn and spends much of his normal daily life directing operations there, while an overseer manages the plantation. Henry finds himself castigated publicly in the *Richmond Constitutional Whig* not only for providing mediocre services to the troops sent from Richmond in the wake of the revolt but also for presenting an outrageously steep bill. On September 3, 1831, the newspaper describes him as a "wealthy" Southampton notable who sometimes offered the troops "stinking fare" and then greedily "produced a bill exceeding $800!" One week later the *Baltimore Niles' Register* relates that an officer in Petersburg offered a sneering toast to the absent Henry Vaughan, labeling him a rapacious, insensitive man "who speculated on the bones of his kindred...."

Many other prominent citizens become targets of criticism as the shock waves of the revolt bequeath a legacy of recriminations in Southampton County. Somehow the Vaughans of Walnut Hill weather the melancholy storm. Behind their impressive house lies the family cemetery, marked with many fresh graves from the recent carnage, and neighbors soon whisper that restless ghosts roam the burial site to torment all trespassers.

Edmund and Mary Louisa. Some years later Mary Louisa marries my Great-grandfather Edmund Fleetwood Dunstan of Bertie County, North Carolina. The shadows of eternity veil the story of their first encounter and courtship, though clear voices from the past describe the privileged class of Antebellum Virginia and North Carolina enjoying family-friendship linkages transcending state boundaries. Perhaps the two meet at a seaside resort during summer vacation. Perhaps they attend the same elegant ball in coastal North Carolina or Virginia and dance the night away. Perhaps Edmund journeys from his home northward to Murfreesboro, a prosperous town in Hertford County, North Carolina, to receive Easter Communion in the Episcopal parish church and there kneels beside Mary Louisa in prayer.

She often visits relatives in Murfreesboro and certainly would have attended church on Easter. At the time few people in Southampton County or Bertie County still maintain ties to the once-established Church of England (Anglican Church) falling into ruin after the American Revolution and suffering considerable prejudice from shrill anti-English elements. In the late eighteenth century the beleaguered Anglican Church undergoes reorganization in the United States as the Episcopal Church, an autonomous body in full communion with the Archbishop of Canterbury (senior primate of the Church of England), sharing with the Church of England the essential doctrines and practices of the ancient faith. Mary Louisa and Edmund count themselves among the handful of remaining loyal Episcopalians and cherish the Eucharist and the sublime Book of Common Prayer.

Mary Louisa Vaughan, born 1823, and Edmund Fleetwood Dunstan, born 1814, exchange joyous wedding vows in 1840. Stressing the divine significance of the marital union, the Book of Common Prayer instructs a couple entering Holy Matrimony to promise lifelong fidelity "for better for worse, for richer for poorer, in sickness and in health. . . ." Family history suggests that Edmund and Mary Louisa flourish as a well-matched and happy couple. Edmund enjoys the life of a well-to-do country gentleman with the means to influence both his own destiny and local affairs.

The two initially live in Bertie County, on his ancestral plantation at Hyman's Ferry, near the confluence of the Roanoke and Cashie Rivers, about fifteen miles southeast of the small town of Windsor. Their sixth child, my Grandfather William Edward, born 1854, pens a brief narrative in the 1920s about his father and the Dunstan family. He describes his father and mother bidding farewell to Bertie County after the 1846 birth of their third child, Great-aunt Josephine, and settling on his land in Hertford County, at Fraziers Cross Roads, about twelve miles south of Murfreesboro, because ravenous mosquitoes crisscrossed their old river plantation and made life miserable for the entire household of family, slaves, and farm animals.

Once the home of Major John Frazier, who counted himself among the Loyalists to the Crown and served as a British officer during the American Revolution, Fraziers Cross Roads (later spelled Crossroads) stands on higher land than the old plantation site, enjoys a better climate, and possesses fewer mosquitoes. At this time the Dunstan-Vaughan family owns large stretches of land in three adjoining counties, two in North Carolina and one in Virginia, listed from south to north: Bertie, Hertford, and Southampton.

Meanwhile the Dunstan slaves undoubtedly resent their involuntary servitude. History shows time and again, as in Southampton County, that oppression generates the fruit of uprisings or attempted escapes. Edmund Fleetwood Dunstan's planter father, who bore the same first and last names as his son, advertised in the *Edenton State Gazette of North Carolina* on February 18, 1791, offering a reward for the return of two runaway male slaves named Page and Allen and one female slave named Peg, the last described as "a mulatto wench" and characterized as "remarkably lusty and homely shaped." At first glance, the modern reader might interpret the final five words to mean "remarkably lascivious and comfortably shaped," but the words probably mean "remarkably vigorous and plainly shaped."

Nevertheless, this blunt advertisement testifies to the naked fact that force defines the master-slave relationship. Regardless of age or gender, slaves experience the bitter thorn of yielding to the bravado and sexual desires of planters and their sons. No hint of this sort touches surviving documents passed down from Edmund and Mary Louisa, nor have I heard of their slaves ever attempting to escape. Edmund and Mary Louisa own a substantial number of field hands and household servants and provide them with medical care and old-age care. In his narrative, Grandfather mentions Mary Louisa's powerful planter uncle, Henry Vaughan, transporting ten or twelve more slaves to them as gifts from Southampton County.

Slaves dread being sent from one county to another, often entailing the breaking of cherished family and friendship ties. The pain of separation counts as one of the great horrors of the slave system. Slaves particularly fear the arrival of speculators. These men buy slaves and then sell them on the road for a profit. Children weep bitterly as speculators tear them from their sobbing mothers and hurry them off for sales to new owners. Most never will see their loved ones again or even know whether they still live or now lie in the embrace of the earth.

In 1855 the Edmund Fleetwood Dunstans take possession of a handsome house (demolished in the twentieth century) gracing the town of Murfreesboro. Exuberantly finished with a generously scaled double porch, as once described to me, the antebellum mansion exhibits ambitious exterior and interior ornamentation. Edmund and Mary Louisa have moved to Murfreesboro to educate their children in the private academies dotting this flourishing center of inland trade.

Endowed with impeccable manners, Mary Louisa strictly adheres to flawless etiquette and presides over gracious dinner parties and other festive social gatherings. In the meantime Edmund employs overseers on his various large tracts of land but personally rides back and forth daily on horseback to direct agricultural operations, with an eye toward reaping abundant harvests while preserving vital natural resources. This taxing routine injures his health and contributes to his death, from pneumonia, only two years after his change of addresses. He leaves behind six Dunstan children: Henry Vaughan, Adelaide Edmund, Josephine Jordan, Thomas Vaughan, Mary Augusta, and William Edward, the first three born in Bertie County and the younger ones in Hertford County.

Grandfather William Dunstan, nicknamed Willie, has celebrated only three birthdays. Later, he deeply regrets losing years of association with his respected father. Although later possessing no memory of Edmund, Grandfather treasures Mary Louisa as a pillar of strength. A communicant of Saint Barnabas' Episcopal Church, Murfreesboro, she often reads to him from the Book of Common Prayer. Moreover, Mary Louisa delights her children with riveting stories of Dunstan-Vaughan history and occasionally mentions her own miraculous survival hidden in a clothing chest during the Southampton County massacre but shies away from discussing her dreadful ordeal outside the family.

In Grandfather's handwritten autobiography, now lost, he begins with a warm portrayal of family life in Murfreesboro. I still recall his opening words from often reading the account as a boy: "My fondest childhood memories spring from cold winter nights, when Ma, Sister Adelaide, Sister Josephine, Sister Augusta, and I sat before a great roaring fire while singing those grand old Anglican hymns and reading from the Book of Common Prayer."

Accelerating discord between the North and the South dominates the 1850s. Edmund Fleetwood Dunstan dies almost four years before the cataclysmic Civil War, erupting in 1861, sees metal blasting into flesh and bone. The widowed Mary Louisa ardently supports the Confederacy. She and other members of the Southern ruling class—the planter elite—voice determination to retain their entrenched slave-based economy and protect their earthly bounties and cherished way of life.

Reflecting the flawed human condition in all times and places, most privileged Southerners not only describe the cruel institution of slavery as natural and moral but also cite the Bible to justify their strained arguments. They quote Southern clerics such as Irish native John England (1786-1842), Roman Catholic bishop of Charleston, remembered for insisting that both the Bible and Rome sanction domestic slavery. Leonidas Polk (1806-1864)— one of the largest slaveholders in the South—serves as Episcopal bishop of Louisiana until the Civil War breaks out and then dies in battle as a Confederate general.

Clearly, slavery forms the bedrock underlying the mosaiclike causes of the Civil War, though many Northerners underscore their desire to preserve a perpetual Union, the sole official goal of the Federal war effort, and many Southerners venerate secession as a matter of liberty and honor in the face of

Northern aggression. Mary Louisa vigorously endorses the drive for Southern victory and independence. Benjamin B. Winborne, on page 189, applauds her allegiance as "patriotic to the core" and states that "she made and unfurled the first Confederate flag in Hertford County and furnished one gallant son [actually two] to the cause...."

Mary Louisa helps sponsor a lavish ball to anyone bearing a purchased ticket, even blue-clad Union soldiers, to raise money for the Southern effort. The official correspondence of Brigadier General George W. Getty, commander of Union troops between the James River in Virginia and the Albemarle Sound in North Carolina, includes an unusual dispatch, dated October 30, 1863, that mentions a Confederate soldier crossing Union lines "to bring turkeys" and describes also the selling of tickets for "a grand ball at Vaughan's house" in Murfreesboro, to be held "on the 5th of November" (recorded in *The War of the Rebellion: A Compilation of the Official Records of the Union and Confederate Armies* [Washington: Government Printing Office, 1885-1898, ser. 1, vol. 29, pt. 2, p. 403]).

Apparently this dispatch does not refer to the house of Mary Louisa Vaughan Dunstan but to that of her prominent kinsman Colonel Uriah Vaughan. My late cousin Aurelia Dunstan Wallace, granddaughter of Henry Vaughan Dunstan and tireless compiler of family history, described to me several of Mary Louisa's preball stratagems. As a child, Aurelia often heard stories about Mary Louisa sending white-flag-waving Confederate soldiers to Union forces, all carrying turkeys for a feast. According to this account, my great-grandmother merely bluffs benevolence, for she instructs the gift-bearing Southerners to raise money for the Confederate cause by persuading the foe to purchase large numbers of tickets for admission to the grand ball.

Wartime Courtship of Dr. Henry and Mollie. Mary Louisa's remarkable first child, Henry Vaughan Dunstan, born 1842, grows tall, polite, and pleasant natured. Henry assumes the traditional persona of eldest son and wins applause at Murfreesboro as a pillar of strength and reliability. He learns to read Latin and Greek from boyhood tutors. Henry gains additional instruction at Wake Forest and the University of Virginia and completes his education in Richmond, at the Medical College of Virginia (as detailed in D. H. Hill's volume on North Carolina, in *Confederate Military History* [1899; extended and reprinted edition, Wilmington, N.C.: Broadfoot Publishing Company, 1987, vol. 5, pp. 473-474]).

Immediately after graduating from medical school at the age of twenty, in 1862, Dr. Henry volunteers for service to the Confederacy. Commissioned as a surgeon in June, he wears the distinctive gray uniform of a medical officer. A double row of gold braid adorns each sleeve, and gold embroidery graces his cap. The scarcity of paper often compels him to write home in the usual way and then turn the letter sideways to write across the lines, making even his graceful hand difficult to decipher.

Dr. Henry performs amputations under terrible conditions at a hospital near Richmond but requests a more hazardous assignment. He soon receives orders to report for field duty. Attached to what becomes the Eight Georgia Cavalry regiment— composed of men from North Carolina, Virginia, and Georgia—he spends long days and nights performing surgical duties during the ghastly military operations around Petersburg in 1864 and 1865. Meanwhile Dr. Henry writes home about the furious Battle of the Crater (July 30, 1864), marked by Union forces digging an underground tunnel and setting off a huge explosion to blow a hole in Confederate defenses, but countless Northern soldiers charge into the resulting "crater" in great confusion and find themselves ready targets for maiming and killing by the Southern defenders.

After every battle, the wounded on both sides often lie unattended for hours of wretched pain as they cry out for relief. Many suffer horrid, untreatable injuries of vital organs and will die in unspeakable agony. Sometimes when performing their duties in the field, Dr. Henry and his fellow surgeons must turn men and boys face up to discover if they are dead or alive. They carry primitive boxed surgical kits hardly changed since the eighteenth century. Their field kit includes instruments not only for removing arms and legs in fewer than five minutes but also for boring holes in skulls for relieving pressure on the brain.

The Confederates have exhausted their anesthetics by the end of the war, and Dr. Henry grimly hands each badly wounded or mangled soldier a shot of whisky to dull the pain of an operation or amputation. When the whisky eventually runs out, Dr. Henry and other surgeons offer each injured man a bullet to bite while able-bodied soldiers hold him down for the excruciating procedure. Unable to scream, soldiers leave deep tooth marks on bullets as testaments to the torture they endure as blood-smeared surgeons saw off their limbs. Bandages remain scarce, often compelling medical officers to take old ones from still warm corpses for reuse without even a quick rinsing. In the meantime emaciated and ragged gray-clad soldiers, many of them shoeless, stagger on battlefields before well-fed Union troops and face the impending oblivion of the Confederate States of America.

While President Jefferson Davis attends services at Saint Paul's Episcopal Church in Richmond on Sunday, April 2, 1865, someone hands him a fateful telegram from Robert E. Lee. The general insists that Richmond must be evacuated posthaste. President Davis quietly slips from the church. Starving, hollow-cheeked inhabitants now face the fiery fall of the capital of the Confederacy.

Before midnight, President Davis and the remnants of the Confederate government catch a train and desperately push southwest on a line of retreat to a more central location. Dr. Henry and his Georgia cavalry regiment dutifully act as an escort to the presidential party. The morning of May 10 sees Union cavalrymen take Jefferson Davis by surprise at his camp in Georgia. They taunt him mercilessly as a common criminal and deliver him by water to Fort Monroe, on the southern Virginia coast, where he spends some time chained as a prisoner but finally gains release two years later into a new world where four million former slaves have been transformed into citizens.

At the time of Jefferson Davis' capture, Dr. Henry finds himself seized along with other Confederate officers at Macon, Georgia. The severe victors tear the Confederate buttons from his tattered official frock coat and eventually release him to walk home barefoot across a bitter landscape ravaged by violence and destruction. Three months later he arrives at Murfreesboro in a state of near starvation but sighs with relief to see Mary Louisa's house still standing on her tree-shaded lawn. According to a family story handed down through several generations, marauding Union forces had decided to torch the house, but when their commander barges inside and sees a Masonic symbol on the parlor mantle, he instantly freezes and calls off his men. His Masonic loyalty proves stronger than the urge to destroy and plunder. We hear of other families proving less fortunate and fleeing to Mary Louisa's home for shelter after their dwellings succumb to the power of deliberately planted flames.

Dazed by the great loss of Southern life and property and the liquidation of their fortune with the Confederate defeat, the Dunstan family doggedly perseveres in Murfreesboro. Dr. Henry has been writing ardent courtship letters during his gruesome years of war service to Mary Eliza Miller, whom he calls Mollie, daughter of Frederick Christopher Miller and Mary Jordan Miller of Bertie County. He often contemplates his blood ties to Mary Eliza. As noted, he descends on the paternal side from his father, Edmund Fleetwood Dunstan, and his grandfather, Edmund Dunstan. Mary Eliza descends on the maternal side from her grandparents, Joseph Jordan (pronounced *Jerden*) and Nancy Ann Dunstan Jordan.

The late Nancy, daughter of Edmund Dunstan by his first wife, Elizabeth, had resided with her much older husband in the Jordan House (known also as the Charlton-Jordan House). The Jordan House rose during the early eighteenth century on the north bank of the Roanoke River in Bertie County. Resting on a high basement and generously shaded with lofty trees, the handsome Jordan House enjoys importance in the architectural heritage of North Carolina not only as an exceptional survival from the first period of durable building construction in the state and the oldest standing house in Bertie County but also as the possessor of resplendent eighteen-inch brick walls laid in Flemish-bond style. Other notable features include an English-bond foundation and splendidly designed interior end chimneys. The twentieth century will see the building listed on the National register of Historic Places as the Jordan House. A nearby ornamental iron fence surrounds the graves of Joseph (1756-1816) and Nancy (1787-1829), marked by a tall marble pillar crowned with a unique marble capital and decorative vase derived from ancient Roman architectural forms.

An air of mystery surrounds the early romance of Henry and Mary Eliza. Dr. Henry (grandson of Edmund Dunstan by his second wife, Martha Fleetwood) and Mary Eliza (great-granddaughter of Edmund by his first wife) count themselves as cousins, to be more precise, half first cousins once removed. They had fallen in love as teenagers. During the war she stays ensconced at her parents' beautiful home, Oak Lawn (later demolished), splendidly situated on prime acreage in Bertie County. Aurelia Dunstan Wallace gained copies of their wartime and later correspondence (from our late Windsor cousin Henry Cullen Dunstan) and shared this trove with me.

Dr. Henry addresses his beloved in letters as "My Dear Cousin" or "Dear Cousin Mollie" and apologizes for not writing as often as he desires, for their love remains a guarded secret, unknown to parents, friends, and acquaintances. In a letter to Mollie, dated January 9, 1863, he explains that he has not publicly acknowledged his devotion because "your father never knew anything about our love for each other," and the truth "might make him angry." He tries to comfort Mollie by professing his heartfelt commitment to her and predicting the speedy dawn of a brighter day "when we can greet each other in a free and independent Confederacy." In a letter written in the spring of the same year, dated May 27, Dr. Henry expresses relief that Mollie does not believe false rumors that he has established a romantic liaison with a Miss Alice. He promises never to "forsake old love for new faces" and vows always to cherish and honor Mollie.

He complains to her in a letter, dated June 10, written from a Confederate camp near Greenville, North Carolina, that "if I don't hear from you soon I shall have the 'Blues' dreadfully." His letters often take two or three months to arrive. He endures "the horrors of this unholy War," as he describes the conflict in a letter penned from Petersburg on June 10, 1864, while he expresses fear their long separation may lead her heart to another gentleman. On July 29 he reminds Mollie that her "letters are the only 'Oasis' to me through the desert of Military Life." Struggling with foreboding, on March 2, 1865, he thinks the Confederates "are preparing to evacuate Richmond and Petersburg," and implies the war will end badly for the old South inherited from Washington and Jefferson.

Robert E. Lee surrenders to Ulysses S. Grant at Appomattox Court House on April 9, 1865, essentially ending the war in Virginia. Slavery has died a violent death nearly thirty-four years after Nat Turner's momentous revolt. After the gaunt and ragged Dr, Henry trudges into Murfreesboro following his long walk from Georgia, the two cousins reunite, yet four years pass before he can afford to support a wife. On New Year's Day, 1869, he writes joyfully to her about their approaching marriage and reminds her that he had thought of little else "for the last ten years." Henry and his beloved Cousin Mollie finally reach the altar on March 5 and then honeymoon in Norfolk, Virginia.

Earlier, Dr. Henry had left Murfreesboro to practice medicine in his native country of Bertie, first at the village of Merry Hill and then at the county seat of Windsor. He becomes highly regarded and for many years serves as the only physician in the county. Virtually everyone calls him Doc. With few manufactured drugs available at that time, he carefully uses a mortal and pestle to grind appropriate materials into medicines and then stores them in handsome glass bottles graced with ornamental glass labels.

On numerous occasions he drives his buggy, pulled by a pair of robust horses, all day to reach and treat his rural patients, whether they can pay for services or not. Sometimes water rises dangerously beneath the buggy when Dr. Henry drives along the roads of the low and marshy county. He often stays with an ill person in the countryside for several days until the crisis passes and then wearily returns home, perhaps with a chicken or two or a bag of sweet potatoes as payment for his medical services.

Cash remains scarce, yet Henry and Mollie live in comfort. Her prosperous father, Frederick Christopher Miller, has given them two entire city blocks of land on Queen Street in Windsor as a wedding present. Henry and Mollie adorn the hilltop overlooking their expanse with a large wooden house, later sheathed in red brick, and they soon acquire not only prize sheep, whose grazing manicures the lawn, but also peacocks shimmering in colorful splendor.

Dr. Henry's mother, Mary Louisa Vaughan Dunstan, remains at Murfreesboro but eventually begins spending the bleakest stretch of winter with them in Windsor. Sometimes she becomes quite lonely at Murfreesboro, attested by a letter (courtesy of the late Aurelia Wallace Dunstan) that Mary Louisa pens to her son on August 16, 1882, criticizing him for coming to see her "three times only during the last seven years" and then scolds "that you were a son before you were a doctor or a husband or anything else."

Adelaide, Josephine, Thomas, and Augusta. Sister Adelaide, born 1844, wins praise for her gentle temperament and gracious manners. She remains at Murfreesboro with her mother until accepting a proposal of marriage. Tall and auburn-haired, Adelaide prepares to stand before the altar with Charles R. Hamlet of Blackstone, Virginia, roughly seventy-five miles northwest of Murfreesboro. They celebrate their marriage at Saint Thomas' Episcopal Church, Windsor, on September 8, 1876, according to the parish register, with the Reverend Edward Wootten serving as the officiating priest. Adelaide Dunstan Hamlet gives birth to loving and hospitable Eulalia, called Lalla, a family favorite. As an elderly lady in Blackstone, Lalla encounters a deranged soldier who viciously assaults and murders her.

Meanwhile Sister Josephine, born 1846, marries a daring Confederate veteran, John James Dyer of Suffolk, Virginia, who had been imprisoned in Norfolk by Union troops. Everyone address him as Colonel in the traditional manner of respect. Colonel Dyer had resided as a boy in Elizabeth City, North Carolina, where town officials named Dyer Street for his father, James B. Dyer. Dr. Henry writes to Mollie on July 9, 1863, describing John Dyer as "a particular friend of mine and a fair specimen of my other companions in arms." The *Elizabeth City Tar Heel*, on May 2, 1902, quotes an editorial from the *Newport News Daily Press* portraying "Colonel J. J. Dyer" as a "gallant and splendid Virginia gentleman" known for his wisdom and honor, "a gentleman by birth, instinct, culture, and predilection."

At the time of his marriage to Josephine, John purchases for their home a plantation of more than one thousand acres of rich earth, virgin timber, and lush wetland in the southeastern part of Southampton County. They immediately occupy an attractive frame plantation house near the settlement of Joynersville (later renamed Sunbeam). Their home, erected circa 1840, becomes known as the Dyer House or the Dyer Plantation House. Finished with stylish Greek revival elements, the Dyer House then possessed a handsome entrance sheltered by a central pedimented porch. Josephine, an accomplished pianist and amateur botanist, soon adds a rear wing with an impressive clerestory (high windowed wall rising above an adjoining roof). The clerestory brings outside light and fresh air inside for the benefit of her many potted plants. Passersby delight in hearing magnificent music drifting from the Dyer House as Josephine commands the keyboard.

John and Josephine produce two beloved children, Elizabeth Lee and Robert Oldner, called Ollie. Their daughter suffers an untimely death soon after marrying, but their son becomes a successful attorney in New York City. After John and Josephine are laid to rest in Suffolk, Virginia, residents of Sunbeam often report hearing a ghostly Josephine playing her cherished piano when they pass by the Dyer House late at night. Some say the sound of her playing echoes to this day.

Laura Holman Rawls, in her privately published *Old Houses in Southampton County*, penned in 1954, describes the Dyer House as "one of the three original homes built in Sunbeam." She adds: "Legend has it that gold was buried near this home, and many people have searched for it in vain. Recently [early 1950s] some of the neighborhood boys came with a metal detector to hunt for the treasure. By a shed near the house the machine went wild, as did the boys. Quickly they began to dig but instead of treasure they found a metal coffin. Upon opening the top, they found there the remains of man dressed in leather clothes. The body was in a remarkable state of preservation, but upon being exposed to air it immediately disintegrated. No one knew who he might have been." Sadly, the once beautiful old Dyer House has not been occupied in many years and has decayed severely from human neglect.

Hardesty's Historical and Geographical Encyclopedia, Virginia Edition (New York, Richmond, Chicago, and Toledo: H.

H. Hardesty and Company, 1885), page 437, includes an entry (here much shortened with misspellings corrected) for Josephine's beloved husband:

"JOHN JAMES DYER—was born in the city of Norfolk, Virginia, July 17, 1839, a son of James B. and Elizabeth (Oldner) Dyer [most published sources list Elizabeth City as his birthplace]. He married in Murfreesboro, North Carolina, February 20, 1868, Josephine J., daughter of [the late] Edmund Fleetwood and Mary Louisa (Vaughan) Dunstan. . . .

"In Elizabeth City, North Carolina, May 18, 1861, John James Dyer . . . [joined the Confederate army], serving in the three branches [infantry, cavalry, and heavy artillery]. . . . He acted as scout and spy part of the time. . . .

"He was residing in Philadelphia at the outbreak of the war but hastened South to support the movement . . . , in accord with his convictions . . . , and *stayed*. He was captured at Roanoke Island and held thirteen days and again captured near Norfolk City, in December 1862, and held as a spy, being kept in close confinement at Fort Norfolk up to March 1863. . . . His battles included . . . Roanoke Island [and other coastal engagements] . . . in North Carolina and, after transfer to the Army of Northern Virginia, [he saw action in] the fighting around the Petersburg and Richmond lines. His service was four years and two days, and he received parole at Albany, Georgia. . . ."

After their honeymoon, John James Dyer and Josephine Jordan Dunstan Dyer "settled in Southampton County," where he focused on his agricultural interests and dutifully served in various public offices. "Since 1869 he has held the positions of magistrate, overseer of the poor, supervisor, commissioner of the revenue, member of the [Virginia] House of Delegates, notary public, member of the Board of Visitors [of the] Medical College [of Virginia], and is now superintendent of the Southampton County schools. He . . . has served as judge of elections and [county] commissioner much of the time between 1869 and 1879. . . ."

Returning to Dunstan developments in North Carolina, Brother Thomas, born 1848, has grown tall and handsome. Tommy never marries and soon follows Dr. Henry to Windsor. Earlier, he had followed his older brother to war. Tommy began fighting clandestinely for the Confederacy in his mid-teens and relishes telling the family of his adventures dodging enemy bullets and escaping Union forces by wading through tangled swamps. While living in Windsor, he embarks upon agricultural enterprises in Bertie County but meets an untimely death at the age of twenty-six.

My late cousins Aurelia Dunstan Wallace and Cullen Dunstan (granddaughter and great-grandson of Dr. Henry Vaughan Dunstan) possessed extensive records concerning the Windsor Dunstans and shared many nuggets about Thomas and the others with me. Cullen once pointed out that the inside front cover of Tommy's surviving Book of Common Prayer bears this simple inscription: "To Thomas Vaughan Dunstan, from his loving Mother." After his death, Mary Louisa pens several poignant words on another page: "To H. V. Dunstan, keep this book for dear Tommy's sake, Mother." On the inside back cover she offers the mourning Dr. Henry additional advice: "Read this book in memory of dear Tommy. Use it for his sake, and may its teachings be a comfort to you."

Sister Augusta, born 1850, the youngest of three daughters, follows Brother Thomas in remaining single. Augusta answers to the nickname Gussie. Family history relates that everyone marvels at her unbridled frankness. Apparently she often denounces the institution of marriage with scathing words and always predicts a life of misery for any bridegroom, exemplified by, "You say Olivia has accepted John's proposal of matrimony? Well, that's the end of John's life!" Yet Gussie becomes a spellbinding teller of family stories, wins applause for masterfully playing the organ, exhibits both a caring heart and extraordinary intellectual gifts, and demonstrates superb artistic skills in embroidery and painting. She comes to Windsor to live with Henry and Mollie several years before her mother begins wintering there.

William's Boyhood in Murfreesboro. Mary Louisa's final child, my Grandfather William Edward Dunstan, born February 10, 1854, adores his much older brother Henry and crawls around the house following him. As a toddler, William, nicknamed Willie, moves with the family to Murfreesboro on the winding Meherrin River. Then tragedy strikes when the protective Edmund

Fleetwood Dunstan dies in November 1857, before little Willie reaches his fourth birthday. Seventy years later he writes his brief account of his father's life. Grandfather relates that Edmund's cousin and close friend Joseph Jordan, a wealthy Bertie bachelor residing in the handsome Jordan House on the Roanoke River, served as guardian to the fatherless Dunstan children. They call him Uncle Joe. Their appointed guardian flees west with his slaves to adjoining Halifax County during the horror and butchery of the Civil War, seeking greater distance from Union lines, and he vows to commit suicide if the South meets defeat but dies from natural causes about a year before the conflict ends.

Grandfather never receives a handsome bequest from Uncle Joe because an inept or dishonest executor mismanages his guardian's estate. Willie and his siblings lose a fortune also when Edmund's estate suffers from the incompetence or misconduct of the executor, Godwin Cotton Moore, who serves as the moderator of the Chowan Baptist Association for nearly four decades. The difficult times facing the family from the death of his father through the war and the hostile postwar peace denies Grandfather the private education enjoyed by his older siblings. Mary Louisa instructs him at home and sparks his zeal for literary masterpieces.

Bettie Freshwater Pool, in her *Literature in the Albemarle* (Baltimore: Baltimore City Printing and Binding Company, 1915), page 298, provides crucial insights about Grandfather's philosophy of life by quoting him: "I attribute whatever good that has come to me in life to my strict observance of the Fifth Commandment ['Honour thy father and thy mother: that thy days may be long upon the land which the Lord thy God giveth thee' (Exodus 20:12)], and the taking as my guide the First Psalm ['Blessed *is* the man that walketh not in the counsel of the ungodly, nor standeth in the way of sinners, nor sitteth in the seat of the scornful. . . .'], which I learned at my mother's knee." In terms of the Fifth Commandment, Grandfather employs the numbering system recognized not only by Jews but also by Anglicans, Orthodox Christians, and most Protestants. Roman Catholics and Lutherans list the same edict as the Fourth Commandment.

Much information about Grandfather's time in Murfreesboro survives through his marginal notes and comments in his personal copy of Benjamin B. Winborne's *Colonial and State Political History of Hertford County, N.C.* According to his marginalia, Grandfather spends many happy hours during his boyhood and young manhood socializing at the Wesleyan Female College (later closed) and the Chowan Baptist Female Institute (rechristened Chowan College in 1910 and Chowan University in 2006). He enjoys spending time also with various cousins such as Bettie Vaughan, third daughter of the affluent and gentile Colonel Uriah Vaughan (whose large antebellum home underwent twentieth-century restoration, completed in 1972, to house various offices, including the Murfreesboro Chamber of Commerce and the Murfreesboro Historical Association).

The much-applauded Bettie soon marries a man roughly thirty years her senior, the silver-tongued Judge David A. Barnes, who served as aide-de-camp to Governor Zebulon B. Vance during the Civil War. In 1874, David and Bettie begin erecting in Murfreesboro a stately Victorian home that will echo generation after generation with the footsteps of their descendants.

In the meantime Willie enjoys a close friendship with an older youth, the polished and scholarly Thomas R. Jernigan, born 1847, who later becomes a Democratic senator in Washington, consul to Japan, and consul-general to Shanghai, China. As a member of the old conservative ruling class, Grandfather remains bitterly opposed to Republicans, whose Reconstruction politics he regards as badly injurious to the South, and he seeks only Democrats as associates and compatriots. He applauds and cheers so enthusiastically with wild rebel yells at a speech given by Jesse J. Yeats of Murfreesboro, who will run successfully as a Democrat for Congress in 1875, that the orator takes special notice. Grandfather records that Jesse Yates became "a great friend of mine when I was young" and "referred to me as one of his boys and came around to see me."

Willie counts among his adult acquaintances and friends many notables of Murfreesboro such as William N. H. Smith, who was graduated from Yale Law School in 1836 and became chief justice of the North Carolina Supreme Court in 1878. Willie takes pride that his maternal cousin Martha A. Exum, from adjoining Northampton County, has married Matthew Whitaker Ransom, who served as a Confederate general and later, in Washington, as a

Democratic senator from North Carolina. Senator Ransom descends on his mother's side from the Anglican priest Alexander Whittaker, remembered for baptizing the American Indian princess Pocahontas and then solemnizing her marriage, in the spring of 1614, to the tobacco exporter John Rolfe of Jamestown, Virginia, the first permanent English colony in the New World. John and Pocahontas (baptized Rebecca) exchange their wedding vows in the chancel of the wooden church of Jamestown, erected 1608, a fascinating site yielding vital material remains to a team of twenty-first-century archaeologists.

Apparently Grandfather's own sweethearts from his youth never kindle a love equaling that of Brother Henry for Mollie. Yet one of his surviving childhood books, detailing the lives of notable military leaders fighting for the American Revolution and the young United States, contains several originally blank pages he has employed to list the names of ladies whose company he enjoys, including Miss Emma Warren, Miss Bellie Lee, and Miss Bessie Wright. On one page he writes the name Miss Emma Warren and underneath draws a prominent heart and gives her address as Portsmouth, Virginia, but then proceeds in the space below to inscribe the name of perhaps a competitor for his heart, Miss Mollie Jones.

This book, now without a cover, first belonged to older brother Thomas, whose signature appears on several pages, sometimes merely as Thomas Vaughan and at others as Thomas Vaughan Dunstan, but the volume eventually passes to Willie's library and much later to my library. Grandfather adorns several pages with his classic signature. On one blank page he writes his name as W. E. Dunstan, the name of his much-admired older brother as Dr. H. V. Dunstan, and finally his own name again as Master W. Dunstan.

These serene boyhood days often see Mary Louisa sending Willie to sit up all night watching over the bodies of deceased family friends. Boys of the time frequently provide this melancholy service. The body, after being prepared for burial, remains at home until the funeral, usually the third day after death. The attending boys often know the exact moment of departure because many families stop clocks on the minute the person dies, a superstitious gesture designed to prevent future misfortune. Willie sits up with Dr. R. H. Shields, a distinguished unmarried physician from the nearby county seat of Winton, who has died suddenly in the Murfreesboro office of his closest friend, Dr. William H. Hutchinson. A few nights later Grandfather sits up with Dr. Hutchinson, also an aristocratic bachelor physician, who apparently falls dead from grief at the loss of his devoted companion.

During this same period Grandfather loses a young cousin, Robert B. Miller, in a bizarre accident. Brother of Mollie and grandson of Nancy Dunstan Jordan, Robert drives his horse and buggy over curving rough roads to a tavern in Bertie County for an evening of socializing. The return trip sees him follow the popular practice of napping while the horse negotiates the familiar route. Robert wraps the reins around his leg and tells the horse to take him home. Somewhere along the way he tumbles from the vehicle and, failing to free himself from the reins, becomes tangled and mutilated in the spinning wheels. The horse arrives at Robert's house dragging the badly mangled corpse. The dead boy's mother had foreseen this tragedy several months earlier when she dreamed of glimpsing a bloody and lifeless body at the bottom of a distant well. The North Carolina historian Robert Watson Winston, who spent his boyhood in Bertie County and enjoyed ties to the Dunstan family by marriage, describes this gruesome event in his *It's a Far Cry* (New York: Henry Holt and Company, 1937), page 23, but sidesteps identifying the victim by name.

William Threads His Way to Elizabeth City. In 1868 fourteen-year-old Willie kisses his adoring mother goodbye and bravely catches a northbound train, his destination Poughkeepsie, New York, to enroll as a student at Eastman National Business College, usually called Eastman College, the most distinguished American institution specializing in the business arts at the time. Enrolling more than fifteen hundred American and international students, this innovative school occupies five buildings and sponsors a large brass band whose members play at civic functions around the country. Eastman students gain practical training in banking, investing, accounting, business management, bookkeeping, and many other endeavors that will serve them through life. American education at the time remains far from standardized, and the prescribed course of study, divided into three concise stages, provides an accelerated path to a Master of Accounting degree. Eastman graduates become business titans, senators, congressmen, governors, mayors, accountants, lawyers, and bankers. The institution (officially rechristened in 1873 as Eastman Business University but usually called Eastman University) eventually attracts Willie's younger contemporary James Buchanan Duke, whose tobacco money later transforms a small, struggling denominational school, Trinity College, into wealth-washed Duke University.

Young Willie's neighbors and friends in Murfreesboro marvel at the courage and determination he demonstrates in riding a train far into the North so soon after the Civil War to gain training in a field known later as business administration. Grandfather endures mortifying ridicule about his accent and heritage, but he never entertains second thoughts about his decision to journey above the Mason-Dixon Line for this specialized instruction, with Southern education so tattered and threadbare after the war.

Two years later, having completed the only formal education of his life, sixteen-year-old Will, as he has become known, possesses youthful dreams and a master's degree. He begins a long stint as an accountant-bookkeeper in Windsor and nearby towns. Along with Sister Augusta, he lives in the house of Dr. Henry and Mollie until he decides to seek his fortune away from Windsor, first at Harrellsville, then at Plymouth, both close enough for him to return home frequently for visits.

Soon he envisions a bright career in his mother's native Virginia and by 1882, the year of his twenty-eight birthday, he has acquired a promising position in Norfolk. When time permits, Will dabbles in real estate, identifying his address as Norfolk on an 1882 deed. Meanwhile one of his old sweethearts, Cora Riddick, who has married W. N. McAnge, persuades her husband to employ Grandfather to oversee his profitable enterprises in nearby Suffolk. Will's later glowing poetic references to Suffolk suggest these days brought him much contentment. Not long afterward he gambles on electrifying the real estate profession in Roanoke,

Virginia, but fails miserably. He enjoys one bright moment when a gentlewoman from North Carolina sends him a volume of poetry by Alfred, Lord Tennyson, bearing the simple inscription "To W.E.D., Christmas 1891."

In June 1892, at the age of thirty-eight, Will faces utter ruin and borrows money from one of his nephews to buy a train ticket to Elizabeth City, then thriving as the largest town in swampy northeastern North Carolina. Two years earlier, in 1890, according to the national census, the town claimed a vigorous population of 3,251. Elizabeth City lies within the Tidewater area of southeastern Virginia and northeastern North Carolina, the celebrated region of early English settlement. Will has formed close ties with at least one native of the town, his brother-in-law John Dyer. Elizabeth City residents speak with a strong Tidewater accent that curls into an unforgettable vocal tapestry and forms a well-known dialect of American English.

Perhaps, as his train steams southward, his mind sways with nagging thoughts about possibly facing his last chance of achieving professional success. Descendant of planter barons, penniless Will arrives in Elizabeth City wearing shabby clothes and carrying all his worldly goods in a small handbag. He must survive on his wits. Squaring his shoulders, Will immediately heads for a tailor's shop and opens a charge account solely on the basis of his magnetic charm. The tailors carefully measure him for new suits and shirts.

He boldly asks them to name the most eligible and prosperous lady in town. At once they begin creating a warm portrait of Miss Emma Cobb Sawyer as a rare damsel possessing her own horse and buggy but cautiously describe her also as almost young enough to be his daughter and, besides, she has accepted a proposal of marriage from a distinguished member of the Aydlett family. While being measured for new suits and shirts, Grandfather persists in his line of questioning to gain additional information about Miss Emma and plans to make her acquaintance at the first opportunity, engaged or not.

Children of Dr. Henry and Mollie. Meanwhile Will uses the postal system to communicate with his cherished relatives in Windsor. Many developments have unfolded there since the marriage of Dr. Henry and Mollie, in 1869. Their first child, Robert Miller Dunstan, born 1870, dies at the age of four. Sister Augusta pens an unusual sympathy letter to the grieving parents. She begins in traditional fashion by offering the comforting words that little Rob "had entwined himself around my heart" but then abruptly announces "what a privilege it is to die young and thus to avoid many" of the "hardships and disappointments that must meet us somewhere and often on the journey" ordained by "Him who makes and rules all things." My Great-aunt Gussie, one of the most fascinating Dunstans of her generation, remains an outspoken and fearless freethinker in a country known for censoring brave souls forming opinions outside the suffocating boundaries of established authority and tradition.

The couple's second child, Henry Vaughan Dunstan, Jr., born 1873, suffers severely from asthma and often struggles to catch his breath. At the age of twenty-one he earns a medical degree from the University of North Carolina and begins practicing medicine. Family history relates that he fails to strengthen his lungs by exercising with a contraption over his bed and ultimately resorts to using, probably by self-prescription, the highly addictive analgesic and sedative morphine. Such drugs remain medically approved and readily available. Dreadful heroin, for instance, attracts many buyers when marketed as a cough medicine from 1898 to 1913. Even Coca-Cola employs a shot of cocaine for euphoric effects, thus the name, until the company removes that particular ingredient in 1904. Henry becomes addicted to the drug helping him endure the asthmatic attacks and, as a result, relinquishes his medical practice. Later, he frees himself from addiction through determination and professional treatment but never resumes his chosen career. On July 10, 1896, the Windsor newspaper, the *Ledger*, alerts readers: "H. V. Dunstan, Jr. is an agent for A. Wrenn and Son's buggies. He can sell you [one or more] buggies, and good ones too, from $50 up." This venture proves short-lived. Unmarried, Henry Vaughan Dunstan, Jr., lives a long life yet often frets to family members about enduring severe bouts of melancholy over the wreckage of his life.

The couple's third child, Frederick Miller Dunstan, born 1877, grows to manhood in Windsor. His godfather, Francis

Donnel Winston, brother of the historian Robert Watson Winston, helps guide Fred's crucial development as a young man and still finds time to achieve recognition as lieutenant governor of the state, superior court judge, president of the North Carolina Bar Association, and trustee of the University of North Carolina (where his brother George Tayloe Winston had served ably as the fifth president before becoming president of the University of Texas and then president of North Carolina State College of Agriculture and Mechanic Arts, ultimately renamed North Carolina State University). Fred marries his local sweetheart, begins his professional life as a gentleman farmer, and later serves also as sheriff of Bertie County for more than a decade, though always wearing a suit and necktie rather than a uniform and seldom bearing a pistol but occasionally donning a steel vest when confronted with the possibility of shooting scrapes. He maintains a sulky race track and owns a high-spirited harness horse known as Lillian Miller. Fred possesses much of the old Dunstan-Miller acreage and other large tracts of land dotting the long stretch south from Windsor to Williamston.

Dr. Henry and Mollie lose two additional offspring after they bury little Rob. Their fourth child dies unnamed on the day of her 1879 birth, while their fifth, Mary Jordan Dunstan, born 1881, dies at the age of one.

The faithful pair enjoy more than two decades of marriage. Besides household servants and two stable hands, they employ three noteworthy individuals—a live-in housekeeper addressed as Miss Nan, a literate and beloved freedwoman nursemaid addressed as Aunt Celie, and a companion to their two surviving sons, Henry and Fred, who address the man as Bro (term of endearment for Brother) Bowen.

The year 1887 sees Dr. Henry and Mollie erect one of the thirteen original cottages at Nags Head, located on the Outer Banks, the vital long narrow chain of sand islands shielding the North Carolina mainland from the might of the Atlantic. The isolated fishing village of Nags Head serves as a fashionable retreat for a handful of privileged Carolinians and Virginians, who arrive by boat to enjoy idyllic seaside summers in hotels or their own cottages. Mollie has purchased an ocean-front lot for the Henry Vaughan Dunstan Cottage (later known also as the Dunstan-

Drane Cottage), and family history relates that the Dunstans shipped hand-hewn timber by boat from Oak Lawn, her father's estate, for the construction of the dwelling.

Mollie spends far more time at the beach than her husband, who usually remains busy treating patients at Windsor. She keeps him abreast of her activities with frequent letters. Perhaps while enjoying cooling breezes from the porch of their cottage, she communicates with him by a surviving but undated letter (brought to my attention by my late cousin Aurelia Dunstan Wallace). As customary, she entrusts the letter to one friend or another embarking for Windsor. Mollie has brought Aunt Celie and several household servants to the beach for the summer and relates that she and the boys "don't do anything much but eat and sleep and ride about" in their horse-drawn cart. She sends alarming news concerning the illnesses of fellow cottagers and adds grim tidings about their dying infants.

She shows a caring side in expressing concern about her husband going to visit patients in the blazing heat of summer: "I fear you have had a hard time riding in the sun, and I have thought of you very often; in fact, you have not been out of mind long at a time since I left you." She sends "our love to Mr. Bowen [Bro Bowen] and Miss Nan." Apparently she can be snippy at times. Dr. Henry had spilled much ink during the Civil War sending her letters dotted with apologies for one trivial thing or another provoking her ire. Now Mollie adds sarcastically, "This is the third letter I have written to you, and I haven't had one letter from you since I came. You have not seemed to care to hear from me, if I judge from your frequent letters. Goodbye, the boys are teasing me to go bathing [swimming]." Yet she then shifts to sign off warmly, "Yours with much love," followed by her initials.

Dr. Henry and Miss Nan and Miss Bessie. Dr. Henry always demonstrates utmost devotion to Mollie and mourns deeply when she dies in 1890. He sells their summer cottage to the Reverend Dr. Robert Brent Drane, rector of Saint Paul's Episcopal Church at Edenton, from 1876 to 1932, and founding rector of Saint Andrew's-by-the-Sea Episcopal Church at Nags Head. This beloved priest spends his summers at Nags Head tending to his vacationing flock and celebrating sacred rites in a hotel or private cottages until the construction of Saint Andrew's-by-the-Sea, consecrated in 1916, on the Feast of the Transfiguration (August 6). He ultimately conveys the Henry Vaughan Dunstan Cottage, said to have been haunted by a peaceful feminine presence, to daughter Marian Drane Graham, whose husband, Dr. Frank Porter Graham, unfailingly demonstrates a progressive and humane spirit in his long career as president of the University of North Carolina, United States senator, and delegate to the United Nations.

Back in Windsor, Mollie leaves behind two teenage boys and a bevy of relatives and companions living at the family home and taking their meals together at a large walnut dining table, including Mary Louisa and Augusta. The grieving widower ultimately finds comfort, according to whispers, in the arms of his live-in housekeeper, Miss Nan. This plausible but unverifiable account relates that Miss Nan leaves his employ sometime before giving birth to a baby boy and then rears the child in Windsor, but not under the Dunstan name, with financial support from the father.

In 1891, Dr. Henry sends a written proposal of marriage to a neighboring lady, defying social propriety by launching his offer before completing one full year of bereavement, and she promptly rejects his untimely suit. He soon makes passionate appeals for the hand of a young lady of Bertie County named Bessie Tayloe. Miss Bessie must have been pleased that the leading physician of Bertie County, who ministers to innumerable patients and possesses vast fruitful acres of age-old Dunstan agricultural land near Windsor, envisions her as his wife.

They celebrate their marriage on March 3, 1894. A new twelve-place set of translucent wedding china from Germany will grace their home. The bride and bridegroom honeymoon by taking the train to Saint Louis. Dr. Henry has celebrated fifty-one birthdays, Bessie twenty-eight. Their first child, Thomas Edmund Dunstan, born 1895, grows muscular and tall and earns a reputation as an ill-tempered bully. Their second, Robert Tayloe Dunstan, born 1901, possesses an agile mind but proves small and delicate.

As a toddler, Robert, nicknamed Rob, develops chest congestion of such magnitude that his father and other physicians deem the case hopeless. Rob's experienced and beloved nursemaid, Aunt Celie, born a slave but taught to read and write as a young girl, brushes aside talk of impending death. Adopting an old home remedy, she spreads hot tar on a cloth, applies the plaster to his chest, and bakes the congestion away. Little Robert recovers but remains frail and makes an easy target for the abuses and sneers of older brother Thomas Edmund, nicknamed Tom. A ready source of comfort, Aunt Celie sometimes gives Robert a brief vacation from Thomas Edmund by carrying him to worship services in her church. Rob relishes the uninhibited joy there.

In the meantime Dr. Henry's sons from his first marriage, Henry and Fred, loathe his new wife. History and literature abound with stories of children judging their stepmother inferior to their biological mother. Although the teenagers Henry and Fred regard Bessie as far less polished and accomplished than the late Mollie, they form close bonds with their much younger half-brothers, Thomas Edmund and Robert.

Later, forty-one-year-old Henry and fourteen-year-old Rob build a seaworthy houseboat and take cruises for as long as two weeks at a time on the Cashie River and the Albemarle Sound. Several years earlier, according to my late cousin Aurelia Dunstan Wallace, the younger Dunstan boys and their two half-brothers had even construct a small working trainlike vehicle running on a sturdy wooden trestle across a protective trench behind the house. The clattering vehicle gives them easy access to favorite retreats for playing and exploring and also keeps them high above the dreaded trench, supposedly the haunt of a ferocious boogeyman.

2

Will and Emma

Will has taken huge strides since arriving at Elizabeth City in June 1892, attracted by a written offer of employment. He enthusiastically embarks upon his fresh career as general manager and secretary-treasurer of the recently established local ice plant, built along the banks of the bustling, stunningly beautiful Pasquotank River. Artificial ice factories are novel enterprises in North Carolina. Will now presides over an intricate realm of ice-making machinery and refrigeration cycles. His employees, charged with complex tasks, begin by boiling water and then condensing the steam into pure distilled water. Next they employ great apparatuses to freeze the distilled water. Will's pilots transport enormous blocks of artificial ice on boats to points east, including the Outer Banks, and his drivers deliver countless blocks of artificial ice on enclosed, horse-drawn ice wagons to addresses in Elizabeth City. The drivers wield ice picks to break the huge blocks of delivered ice into smaller blocks for storage in kitchen iceboxes that keep food and beverages cool.

In 1895, Will initiates a major expansion program. That year the enterprise begins selling coal also and adopts the name Crystal Ice and Coal Company. By 1912, Will has increased the daily capacity of the ice operation from twenty tons (40,000 pounds) to seventy tons (140,000 pounds) and has overseen the erection of a much larger brick plant to replace the older wooden one. Customers conduct business with the company by visiting the complex of buildings in person, at 202-204 North Water Street, or asking the telephone operator to connect them with number 16. The local telephone company has offered service since 1902, initially with fewer than one hundred subscribers, including Crystal Ice and Coal Company.

Not long after Will settles in his new executive position he receives a warm letter, dated December 9, 1892, from Mary Louisa, then wintering in Windsor. He has spent a substantial part of his first paychecks buying presents for her and other members of the family. She thanks him for the "box of good things" reaching her earlier and also for "the nice shoes" and other gifts that have just arrived. She adds that Dr. Henry expresses much delight over Will's gift of a necktie. The previous night had seen Dr. Henry adorn his high stiff collar with the silk beauty and then, with his two sons, Henry and Frederick, host a formal dinner party for friends. Mary Louisa and Will share a secret about Dr. Henry's new necktie.

She confides, "No one could tell that it had been worn; he thinks that you bought it for him." She adds that Henry's "nice new suit of clothes" reminded guests of a suit you once owned (described as "black checked with small blue stripes"), and the ensemble prompted a young gentleman to ask "if you had sent him your valise." Continuing, she discloses that fifteen-year-old Fred has gained temporary employment weighing cotton to earn money for Christmas. She trusts her son in Elizabeth City will have "everything good to eat" during the holidays and closes by relating that "Gussie is well and sends love." She signs the letter "Your fond Mother," after giving Will a gentle nudge to write soon. Will carefully files the letter with his other correspondence for preservation and reference.

Miss Emma and Her Family. Grandfather has already turned to wooing Miss Emma Cobb Sawyer, whose name he first heard in the tailor's shop upon arriving in Elizabeth City. Of impeccable Tidewater bearing, Miss Emma enjoys a privileged background. Her mother, Virginia Herrington Sawyer, descends on the paternal side from the Herringtons, a prominent landowning family. Herrington acreage stretches from the southern outskirts of Elizabeth City into Pasquotank County. Later, Elizabeth City State University and many other developments dotting the town occupy land the family once possessed. Euclid Heights, the first suburb of Elizabeth City south of Charles Creek, emerged on building lots carved from this ancestral terrain. Herrington Road, named for the family, pushes through tracts once blossoming as a rich Herrington landscape.

Miss Emma's father, John Lloyd Sawyer, has won laurels as a leading merchant of Elizabeth City and Pasquotank County. His two brothers, Charles and Leroy, have become distinguished physicians, the former in Elizabeth City and the latter in Great Bridge, Virginia.

The John Lloyd Sawyer family lives for years in a comfortable house off Herrington Road. Architectural historians count this building, the Charles-Herrington House, among the oldest standing dwellings in Elizabeth City. Skilled artisans built this transitional Georgian-Federal house in the early nineteenth century for the Charles family, whose name graces turtle-populated Charles Creek and, later, tree-shaded Charles Creek Park on the edge of the serene Pasquotank River. A nearby lot, ultimately numbered 1110 Herrington Road, serves as a private cemetery for the Charles and Herrington families and contains handsome gravestones reflecting funerary art of the mid and late nineteenth century. Miss Emma's maternal grandfather, Willet Herrington, had acquired the Charles-Herrington House around the middle of the century, and he bequeathed the dwelling to daughter Virginia, wife of John Lloyd Sawyer.

The Sawyer family resides here until the early 1890s, when John Lloyd Sawyer builds a generous Queen Anne style house at 200 West Main Street. About a decade later the noted physician Dr. Isaiah (Ike) Fearing, a major figure in the famous Nell Cropsey tragedy (discussed at length in volume 5), erects his spacious Colonial Revival style dwelling across the street from the Sawyers.

Miss Emma's parents arrange for her to attend college in distant Staunton, Virginia, a recognized center of education for young ladies. Prospective students chose from Episcopal, Lutheran, Methodist, and Presbyterian colleges. Because Emma and her parents count themselves among the most loyal Methodists in Elizabeth City, she attends the Wesleyan Female Institute. Here she wins numerous gold medals for both academic excellence and extracurricular attainments.

After successfully completing her program of study and returning home from Virginia, she accepts a marriage proposal from a prominent relative of Edwin Ferebee Aydlett, a wealthy and powerful attorney. Mr. Aydlett will gain a moment of national fame in the early twentieth century by pleading for the vilified young defendant in the notorious Nell Cropsey murder case, the most publicized trial in Elizabeth City history. The fifth volume of this series unravels much of the mystery surrounding the disappearance and death of Nell Cropsey, including the strong possibility of a despicable cover-up.

Will as Suitor and Local Notable. Grandfather scandalously oversteps the bounds of ancient and ironclad social codes by arranging to be presented to Miss Emma and then dazzling her with his seasoned charm. In my boyhood, an elderly lady once described Will as "a regular Lord Chesterfield," referring to Philip Dormer Stanhope, fourth earl of Chesterfield, distinguished eighteenth-century English statesman, diplomat, author, and conversationalist, admired not only for his courtly manners but also for his witty, exquisitely tailored remarks and observations. Lord Chesterfield demonstrates his superb wit in a letter to A. C. Stanhope, dated October 12, 1765: "In matters of religion and matrimony I never give any advice; because I will not have anybody's torments in this world or the next laid to my charge."

Will lavishes Miss Emma with gifts, including a surviving leather-bound volume of poetical quotations, presented at Christmas 1893 and inscribed "To Miss Emma, From W.E.D." Compiled by Henry George Bohn, *A Dictionary of Quotations from English and American Poets* (New York: Thomas Y. Crowell, 1883) extends a whopping 761 pages and covers categories from Abdication to Zeal. The compiler quotes innumerable authors from Longfellow to Shakespeare, from Keats to Tennyson. One of Will's favorites, Alfred, Lord Tennyson, has recently died (1892) after gracing Queen Victoria's reign as Poet Laureate for more than forty years and composing numerous familiar phrases, including, on page 311: "Tis better to have loved and lost / Than never to have loved at all."

On the same occasion Will hands Miss Emma a companion volume of Tennyson's poetry. Just twenty-four days later, on January 18, 1894, Will gives Miss Emma another book of poetry and encloses a flower-adorned printed card: "The sender thinks always of thee," signed "Will E. Dunstan."

Apparently Will easily kindles Miss Emma's heart, but she compels him to make one major and distressing concession before agreeing to marriage—any children from the match will be christened as Methodists, not Episcopalians. After celebrating their wedding on the thirtieth day of April, 1895, Will and Emma take "the evening train for a bridal tour," as reported three days later in one of the local newspapers, the *Economist-Falcon*. He has celebrated forty-one birthdays, she twenty-three. Initially, the happy newlyweds live in a roomy, newly purchased house on North Road Street.

Will thrives professionally and serves not only as general manager and secretary-treasure of Crystal Ice and Coal Company but also as secretary-treasurer of Elizabeth City Brick Company, manufacturer of brick sold locally and shipped to contractors by water and rail. At the turn of the twentieth century his name features prominently in newspaper advertisements for the ice and brick companies, particularly in the *Elizabeth City Tar Heel*. Additionally, he sponsors a promising railroad venture to give "the city both western and southern connections so essential to the progress and development of eastern North Carolina," as reported by another local newspaper, the *North Carolinian*, on July 3, 1902. Moreover, he buys and sells numerous pieces of real estate as a promising avenue of investment.

William E. Dunstan House. Grandfather desires a larger dwelling and purchases from Allen Krebbs Kramer—vice president of the flourishing Kramer Lumber Company and subsequent founder of a local motion picture theatre—his stately house on West Church Street. The *North Carolinian* reports on May 15, 1902, that "Mr. Kramer conveys his residence . . . to Mr. W. E. Dunstan." My grandparents occupy this showplace the remainder of their lives.

Erected circa 1895, the spacious new Dunstan house represents one of the most ambitious local architectural undertakings of the period. The splendid and elaborate Queen Anne style mansion graces the southwest corner of Church and

Persse Streets. Initially, the home stands alone at the end of West Church Street and overlooks vast stretches of woods and wildflower fields delightfully splashed by the setting sun into golden silhouettes.

The William E. Dunstan House possesses an array of beautifully turned ornaments, a multitude of porches dominating the second story, a wraparound porch on the first, a two-story bay window on each side, a long double-tier porch along the rear of the west side, a number of magnificently detailed pediments, a robust roof enlivened with slate-shingled gables, and an octagonal corner tower pierced with encircling arched windows and surmounted by a conical roof. Two impressive molded doors highlight the front entrance and contain delicately ornamented glass windows. After passing through the double doors, Dunstan guests gain entrance to the interior through a handsome marble-floored vestibule, complete with a second pair of superb doors fitted with fine glass windows. The vestibule leads into the spacious entrance hall providing access to the front parlor (for formally entertaining guests), library, dining room, back parlor (family sitting room), and other living spaces.

Behind the house Grandmother creates a large circular rock garden built of imported stones and adorned with a wide variety of stylish flowers stirring compliments from visitors. Dependencies eventually include a substantial pigeon house, equaling the size of a small cottage, while land across the back alley supports a long array of interconnected storage rooms, barns, stables, and a carriage house, the last providing shelter for buggies and other horse-drawn vehicles.

Furnishing a home of this size requires vast stores of furniture, art, and literary works. Mary Louisa begins sending treasures from Murfreesboro at the time of the wedding. She generously supports the age-old custom of launching weddings with ceremonial gestures and substantial gifts such as family heirlooms. Will and Emma must have been delighted to receive a fine china tea service, complete with dainty sterling silver spoons engraved with the initials MLD (inherited by my cousin John Dunstan, who generously showed me his collection of family heirlooms and documents as I wrote this series).

Mary Louisa ships to Elizabeth City also a magnificent mahogany American Empire sofa, circa 1815-1830, graced with superb roll over arms and legs. The ornamentation above the center of the curvilinear rail topping the upholstered back of the sofa features elaborate cresting forming a carved floral arrangement. The sofa arrives with a splendid set of four matching mahogany chairs. According to family tradition, the ensemble sprang from the hand of a master cabinetmaker of Southampton County, Virginia, and originally graced Walnut Hill, girlhood home of Mary Louisa. Apparently her bachelor uncle, Henry Briggs Vaughan, sent the handsome pieces to Mary Louisa and husband Edmund about the time of their wedding in 1840.

Fleetwood, Lloyd, Mary Virginia, and Adelaide. Between 1896 and 1917, Emma gives birth to seven children. She cherishes all her offspring but does not relish the nurturing role of holding or rocking them, whereas Will showers them with affection. As adults, after their parents have died, the Dunstan children always refer to Emma, whom they called Mother, with much respect and devotion but to Will, whom they called Papa, with virtual adoration.

Will and Emma decide to name their firstborn Edmund Fleetwood Dunstan II (years later he drops the II and presents himself simply as Edmund Fleetwood Dunstan). Born in the wee hours of Thursday, June 25, 1896, Fleetwood carries the name of his paternal grandfather, who had died in antebellum Murfreesboro thirty-nine years earlier.

Childhood attire of the day reflects parental status and wealth. As a privileged boy, Fleetwood often wears elegant white or colored sailor suits, with fashionable large nautical collars, fine buttons, short pants gathered at the knee, dark stockings, and black high-top shoes laced in the front. Fleetwood dons other stylish examples of boyhood clothing. A photograph of him from the studio of J. H. Faber in Norfolk portrays a serene-faced boy, about three years of age, holding a handsome riding crop and wearing a dark velvet suit with knee-length trousers, a large collar of ruffled lace, a generous bow at the neck, and a pair of dark stockings and high-laced shoes.

Another photograph, this one from Zoeller's Studio in Elizabeth City, shows a solemn, four-year-old boy in apparel reflecting the Little Lord Fauntleroy style. In this photographic portrait, dated September 25, 1900, Fleetwood wears a ruffled shirt with wide lacy cuffs and collar, tiny open velvet jacket, matching velvet knickerbockers edged with ribbons, silk stockings, and ornate buckled shoes. By his twelfth birthday he has adopted the knickered suit, complete with knee socks, white shirt, and four-in-hand tie. He continues to wear knee-length trousers until graduating to adult-style suits in his mid teens.

My grandparents find much to admire in Uncle Fleetwood. Mindful of harmony, he matures into a polished, courteous, brilliant, handsome, and charming boy who makes lasting friendships with young and old alike. He begins his formal education at a nearby private academy, the Isaac Tillett School, founded by a former officer in the Confederate Army and sheltered in a building (converted in the 1910s into a residence and later given the street address 410) several doors west of the headmaster's handsome antebellum Greek Revival dwelling at 300 (later renumbered 400) West Church Street.

In 1908 twelve-year-old Fleetwood writes to William Jennings Bryan, well-known not only as the Democratic candidate for president (Republican William Howard Taft will soundly defeat him) but also as an electrifying orator enlisting God to in a righteous political battle of good versus evil on behalf of humble and downtrodden American citizens. Fleetwood receives a reply, written on August 14, thanking him for his "pleasant letter" of support and reminding him that "boys of your age will be managing our government" in the future and "should inform themselves."

My grandparents' second child, John Lloyd Dunstan, named for Emma's father, comes into the world on Monday morning, December 10, 1900, but dies a mere month after his first birthday. Grandfather expresses intense grief over this loss and commissions a small upright monument with two cherubs in high relief to grace the little one's grave. Will notes the untimely death in the family Bible and adds that he has instructed the mason to inscribe five words on the monument: "Too sweet for this world."

Slightly more than nine months later, on Friday afternoon, October 31, 1902, Emma gives birth to Mary Virginia Dunstan. Will and Emma name the baby for both of her grandmothers. Only sixteen days elapse before Grandfather sorrowfully pens a tomb inscription for Mary Virginia: "To a better home with Brother Lloyd." The two infants share the small cemetery monument originally acquired for Lloyd. Their gravestone bears one additional inscription: "Just across on the evergreen shore," words borrowed for Uncle Lloyd and Aunt Mary Virginia from an old English hymn.

On Saturday evening, October 10, 1903, eleven months after the death of her second child, Emma gives birth to Adelaide Josephine Augusta Dunstan, named for Will's three sisters. Aunt Adelaide, who proves ebullient and warmhearted, enjoys human companionship and easily makes friends with rich and poor alike. She dons the fashionable apparel favored by young ladies of the day. One photograph shows her as a six-year-old girl wearing a large bow on her head and a fine embroidered linen dress featuring an elaborate square lace yoke framing the neck, long sleeves with delicate cuffs, a full knee-length skirt over unadorned pantalets reaching the ankles, and several hidden petticoats to make the skirt flare. Her shoes take the form of flat-heeled slippers.

On May 21, 1910, six-year-old Adelaide pens a short note to inform her father, "I am in school now. I am writing to you." Some time later she writes to Emma, seeking suggestions about selecting Christmas presents for various members of the family and then deftly asks what would you like "Santa Claus to bring you" this year?

In 1915 eleven-year-old Adelaide jumps headfirst into the ukulele craze sweeping the country. Her siblings tease her for decades about how she kept pleading, "But all the other girls have ukuleles," until her parents finally purchase one of the tiny four-stringed instruments, of Portuguese origin, which becomes a sensation in Hawaii before demand reaches a peak in the United States. Made famous by Hawaiian music, the instrument temporarily enjoys a wildly devoted following. After the mania finally ends, Aunt Adelaide's ukulele begins gathering dust on a closet shelf along with other discarded items.

Edward and Forrest. Several years earlier, on November 16, 1908, five-year-old Adelaide asks an older person to help her with a keepsake, for Fleetwood has given her a feather from an accidentally or deliberately killed bird. She preserves the gift in a tiny envelope used for church offerings and instructs her helper to write: "The feather out of the wing of the bird brother killed." Apparently Adelaide does not realize that the stork now prepares to bring her another brother.

Will and Emma's fifth child, William Edward Dunstan, Jr., my father, enters the world on Saturday afternoon, November, 28, 1908. Photographs show baby Edward, nicknamed Eddie, wearing fashionable white dresses abounding in lace and embroidery, then de rigueur for males of tender years, and later graduating to boyhood apparel such as white two-piece sailor suits with long navy blue ties, knee-length trousers, white stockings, and high-laced white shoes.

He proves to be a bright but difficult child. He adopts a belligerent mode of speech that remains with him through life. Edward complains incessantly about the menus Emma prepares for the family cook. Two of his brothers once told me that he ruined countless meals by his thundering barrage of criticisms. Although he finds fault with much around him, Edward demonstrates great fondness for horses. Will discovers that carrying the boy in his buggy has a soothing effect on his mercurial disposition and often invites his son to accompany him when he harnesses a horse and drives away on business. His parents notice also that Edward becomes less ill-tempered when engaged in a pastime he enjoys such as drawing. He possesses modest artistic talent, reflected by his surviving childhood drawing of a diving eagle threatening a terrapin trapped at the edge of a mountain cliff.

He becomes a familiar figure on the streets of Elizabeth City. The town lacked paved streets at the time of his birth. The two-year period after the initial street paving, in 1910, sees the enactment of a city ordinance setting the speed limit for motorcars at eight miles per hour and another banning snowball throwing. No doubt, Edward and most other children ignore the snowball rule whenever rare winter flakes blanket the city.

Edward gains another brother early Monday morning, April 27, 1914, with the birth of Forrest Vaughan Dunstan, whose middle name honors the family of Mary Louisa. His first name, meaning *of the forest*, had become popular thanks to the military feats of hard-charging Nathan Bedford Forrest, remembered not only for a checkered past but also for his innovative strategy as a lieutenant general commanding a famous cavalry division in the Confederate Army. The name, associated with trees and nature, matches the boy. When older, he spends much time exploring forests, developing a great affection for beautiful trees. He shares older brother Edward's love of saddling and riding horses. The handsome little dynamo, Uncle Forrest, provides a consistent source of joy for the family. He shows inexhaustible energy, charms everyone with witty remarks, and acquires a galaxy of loyal friends.

Two years earlier, 1912, proved memorable for Fleetwood, Adelaide, and Edward. They traveled by horse and buggy to join a throng gathering at the fairgrounds to witness the first attempted aeroplane fight made over Elizabeth City, as reported by a local newspaper, the *Advance*, on October 25: "A crowd . . . assembled around the big winged machine [a Curtis biplane], waiting for it to rise. At about quarter past four [everyone heard] the riflelike rattle of the airship's motor . . . , and hats flew and feet scampered as the crowd . . . felt the breeze from the big propeller. After another wait, as the motor got under way, the machine was released and shot away over the unlevel ground, skipping along like a big bird trying to rise in flight. About two-thirds of the way across the grounds it left the earth and soared upward slowly. Just before reaching the trees that skirted the park, the machine rose [abruptly] . . . but . . . suddenly dipped and came to the ground sharply. . . ."

The Curtis biplane succeeds the following afternoon: "Rising from the ground at about four-thirty, J. B. McCalley, who holds the Pennsylvania altitude record of 10,500 feet, circled over Elizabeth City at an estimated height of about 6,000 feet, going out over the town as far as the graded school building; turned back sailing over the fairgrounds and out over the bay; then back again over Elizabeth City; finally sweeping gracefully to the ground in front of the grandstand . . . amid the plaudits of the admiring multitudes. Many of these had never seen an aeroplane flight before. 'Man,' said one old darky who watched the flight with rapt attention, 'If I ever gits dat high, I'll go straight on to heben.'" This offensively written comment and *quotation* reflects the deplorable fact that the Dunstan children grow to adulthood in a tragically flawed society, where innumerable hidebound whites gain merriment by ridiculing persons of color, a form of humor then pervading newspapers, magazines, and conversations.

The *Advance* continues the account of the aeroplane flight by describing "Mr. McCalley . . . traveling at the rate of about 65 miles per hour. He was in the air 20 minutes . . . and made one of his celebrated 'dips,' dropping almost perpendicularly from the great altitude of 6,000 to 500 feet. Seeing him going to apparently certain destruction, many of the spectators who had a few minutes before been hooting at him as a fake and imposer were almost hysterical in their concern for his safety. Skimming through the air at a great altitude, swooping suddenly to earth like an immense hawk, the machine filled one watching it with wonder and awe. And there was a thrill of admiration too for the daring aviator, who with steady hand and iron nerve faced the untried perils of the most fickle of elements." Yet one spectator, little Edward, becomes terrified as the biplane plummets more than five thousand feet and retains a lifelong aversion to airplanes and flight.

Fleetwood's Commencement. On May 28, 1914, one month after Forrest's birth, seventeen-year-old Fleetwood gains his high school diploma during graduation exercises at Elizabeth City High School. As a student, Uncle Fleetwood has demonstrated passionate interest in the study of science, mirroring his cousins in Windsor, but he once created a potentially destructive accident during his high school years by absentmindedly throwing some unused powdered charcoal and sulfur from a home chemistry experiment onto a pile of raked leaves. Grandfather remains unaware of this discarded charcoal and sulfur and begins burning the pile, resulting in a frightening but quickly doused inferno causing no real injury to person or property. Fleetwood rarely generates such mishaps and achieves an enviable record in high school. He earns the trust and respect of his teachers and fellow students. He serves as the business manager of the school newspaper, the *Tatler*, named for the early eighteenth-century English triweekly launched by the essayist Richard Steele, and also as one of the four members on the debating team.

Over the years Fleetwood publishes numerous poems in the school newspaper. Clearly, he regards formulated thought as the essence of poetry and sometimes sacrifices rhyme to preserve the underlying idea. The March *Tatler* of 1914 carries his final poetic effort in high school. Apparently the rushed editor, having no title at hand, simply gives the poem a whimsical one.

SHOULDN'T THERE BE A HEADING?

While on a visit to Hades,
   I attended a public debate
Held in the Shakespearian Theatre
   And conducted by Calhoun, the late.

Cicero and Vergil, the Romans,
   Walked in and took their seat.
Then came their one opponent;
   The geometrician, Euclid the Greek.

Each side was to prove
   That more time was spent
On their works, by a mortal,
   Than they themselves had lent.

Cicero, the distinguished orator,
   Arose and made his speech,
Followed by the famous Euclid,
   Whose eloquence he failed to reach.

Euclid was likewise superior
   To Vergil's poetic debate;
And as he concluded his argument
   His opponents left it to fate.

> Then the decision of the judges
> Was it "Latin eloquence and poetry"?
> No, but in favor of Euclid,
> The founder of geometry.

The June *Tatler*, the commencement issue, carries the jocular Last Will and Testament of the Senior Class. The anonymous writer has Fleetwood bequeathing to a specified freshman his "prepared treatise on 'Debates: Here and Hereafter,' believing it will be of some benefit to said party." The Prophecy of the Class of Nineteen Fourteen asks the reader to imagine the student prophet, Ethel Mann, flying in a modern "airship" of 1920 to many lands, including a rugged South American country, where "a huge bridge was being constructed over the mountains" under the oversight of "Fleetwood Dunstan, whose ingenious mind was working on devices for facilitating this work."

Fleetwood always wears a suit and tie to school. His oval photograph in this issue of the newspaper shows him with a stiff high collar. An anonymous author or editorial committee describes him with warm sentence fragments flanking his photograph: "Fleetwood Dunstan. Inveterate user of Romeo route [past the home of a certain fair damsel] to (tennis) courts on afternoons. Student, speaker, friend, and good in all [endeavors]; one of the most enviable records in the whole class. Upright, sincere, frank has been his record among us—nothing less than the best does he deserve. Has always had the power to do good work without making a fuss about it. Has own views on most subjects, some well worth hearing. Ambition to outclass Edison in the realm of electricity. He has the best wishes of his class."

The sponsoring advertisers for this issue include the Elizabeth City Buggy Company, still proudly manufacturing "fine buggies and phaetons [various four-wheeled horse-drawn carriages]," and the Alkrama, "Elizabeth City's Moving Picture Show and Theatre." With high school graduation behind him, Uncle Fleetwood turns his thoughts toward college.

Tears for Mary Louisa and Four of Her Children. Meanwhile many developments have affected the Dunstan family in Elizabeth City since the birth of Uncle Fleetwood in 1896. Mary Louisa dies suddenly in Windsor on Christmas Day, 1901, in the house of Dr. Henry Vaughan Dunstan. Her upright gravestone stands near the entrance to Saint Thomas' Episcopal Church. The sloping top of the monument bears the inscription "THE LORD KNOWETH THEM THAT ARE HIS," and its face carries the name "MARY LOUISA," described as the widow, or the "RELICT OF EDMUND F. DUNSTAN."

These sad tidings weigh heavily on Grandfather. Later, he clips and files in the family Bible an undated newspaper article applauding a gracious Southern lady of an older generation. Grandfather writes in the margin, "This was my mother or like her." The unnamed author paints a riveting picture: "She never surrendered, she was never reconstructed. She believed as firmly to the day of her death in the justice and righteous of the Southern cause as she did while there was still a hope of its success. . . . She was a lady of the ancient Southern regime, well-born, well-bred, well-educated, with the delicacy of refinement, the spiritual heroism and the high sense of obligation that belong to nobility of character." This portrait seems quite generous by twenty-first century standards and demonstrates that scholarly opinion on controversial subjects can shift radically from generation to generation, even from decade to decade, teaching astute observers the lesson of caution.

Clearly, my great-grandmother, born 1823, viewed secession as a matter of honor. Mary Louisa failed to dissect slavery and discover a deadly malignancy, yet the student of history should examine her and her children not only in the light of their era but also in the context of her life as a survivor of the Nat Turner massacre. She and her children come down to us in letters and other documents as genuine and principled human beings laboring under the dark flaws of their era, just as people today mirror the many dismal flaws of our era. Echoing the sentiment of their friends and neighbors, Grandfather and all his siblings honor the memory of the Confederacy and salute the fallen soldiers who wore the gray. He frequently clips newspaper articles paying tribute to them. One article saved in the family Bible portrays Confederate soldiers dying in battle as "the noblest patriots that

God ever gave the world," heroes who "received the crown of blissful immortality."

The year 1908 sees Grandfather attend the funeral of one Confederate veteran dear to his heart, his older brother Dr. Henry Vaughan Dunstan. The Bertie County Board of Commissioners has recently accepted Dr. Henry's report as Superintendent of Health, an event described in the *Windsor Ledger* on May 28, but the beloved physician dies on June 30, stirring the heartfelt sorrow of the town and county. Profound expressions of sympathy and glowing newspaper obituaries comfort the Dunstans in Elizabeth City and Windsor. Meanwhile Dr. Henry's account books show that certain of his patients have run up a combined total of more than ten thousand dollars of unpaid bills, an impressive sum in 1908, and these parasites never come forward with money for the financial succor of his widow and children. Will corresponds frequently with his now widowed sister-in-law, Bessie Tayloe Dunstan, and offers unfailing moral and financial support to her and her two sons, Thomas Edmund and Robert.

Following the death of Dr. Henry, Grandfather loses his beloved sisters one by one, Augusta in 1909, Adelaide in 1915, and Josephine in 1925. Augusta's obituary, published in the *Windsor Ledger* on February 25, 1909, describes "Miss Gussie Dunstan" as a "very popular . . . cultured and intelligent . . . leader in social and educational endeavors. Her remains were interred [beside those of Mary Louisa] in the Episcopal churchyard. . . ."

3

Will as Husband, Father, Poet, Business Trailblazer, and Civic Leader

As a boy, I often heard my aunt and uncles say that Will and Emma stumbled into only one known argument during their thirty-three-year marriage. The cause of the conflict seems unusually trivial. Will particularly savors mincemeat pie, whose latticed pastry crust cradles a delectable filling of finely chopped (minced) tart apples mixed with raisins and aromatic spices such as nutmeg, cloves, and cinnamon. On one occasion he buys a mincemeat pie at a bakery. When he arrives at home with his favorite desert in hand, Emma bristles and accuses him of not appreciating the meals served at her table.

Apparently my grandparents enjoy a comfortable and pleasant marriage but share few common interests. Emma relishes antique furniture and spends years collecting choice pieces. She maintains lifelong bonds with her closest friends, but does not enjoy large social gatherings, whereas Will adores dinner parties and any possible opportunity to mingle with others. He remains an avid reader and amasses the largest private library in the northeastern part of the state, known as the Albemarle. He reserves an entire room of the Dunstan house for his library and freely lends books to friends and students.

Literary and Commercial Achievements. Will frequently writes articles on current events and composes poems for local and regional newspapers, usually under his own name but sometimes under the thinly disguised penname Nat S. Dun. In the meantime Bettie Freshwater Pool seasons her *Literature in the Albemarle*, pages 297-300, with several of Grandfather's poems. In the first selection, "My Violet," he fondly recalls days in Suffolk, Virginia, with references to Lake Kilby, popular site situated not far from the heart of town and attracting throngs for pleasure boating and relaxation. People in his day treasure the vital lake not only for providing water for Suffolk but also for enhancing the outskirts of the Great Dismal Swamp and possessing encircling juniper trees beautifully draped in long swaying Spanish moss (southeastern Virginia marks the northern range limit for the lacy plant taking its moisture and nutrients from the air and rain).

Grandfather's poetic reference to Melnotte possibly suggests Claude Melnotte, a character in a five-act romantic melodrama, *The Lady of Lyons*, written in 1838 by English author Edward Bulwer-Lytton, 1st Baron Lytton. Claude Melnotte, son of a French peasant gardener but disguised as a foreign prince, persuades a fair damsel to marry him. She discovers the truth. Melnotte suffers remorse over his deceit and chooses another *star*, or destiny, by enlisting in the French army. He eventually returns as a gallant officer and hero and rescues his beloved from a wealthy trickster. She expresses her love for Melnotte and envisions remaining beside him through all the joys and sorrows of life.

Perhaps, on the other hand, Grandfather refers to Violet Melnotte, the stage name of an English actress who performed regularly in the late nineteenth century in comic opera and then created a thriving new theatrical district in London by erecting what soon became known, by royal permission, as the Duke of York's Theater, today said to be haunted by her ghost. Thus Violet Melnotte chose theatrical *stars*. Although familiar to the public as Violet Melnotte, the actress' real name was Emma Solomon, and Will's possible reference to her might be a subtle allusion to his cherished wife Emma.

Finally, the name Melnotte could be a typographical error made by the typesetter. Perhaps Grandfather actually penned the name Melotte, referring to the well-known British astronomer Philibert Jacques Melotte, whose observation of the *stars* led to important discoveries, including, in 1908, one of the moons of Jupiter.

My Violet

Your little namesakes all are gone,
   Not one sweet flow'r is left to wear,
To smile my lonely heart upon,
   And charm away each cloud of care.
There must be something in a name—
Violet sets my heart aflame.

In this South Land in early May—
   The month of all we hold most dear—
Are buds and blossoms, rich and gay,
   And song-bird's notes to charm the ear;
The fields are deck'd in gorgeous hue,
But all will pale at sight of you.

For bygone days I'm pining still—
   For picnic days on Kilby's Lake,
For drives beyond the old grist mill,
   For plates of cream, with angel cake.
Those happy days are gone for aye—
Their mem'ry sweet as flow'rs of May.

The sky is full of stars tonight.
   Must I choose one—as did Melnotte—
Where love will be immortal, bright,
   To be our home—sweet blissful spot?
I'll find a star, and name it yet,
For my heart's queen, my Violet.

    As noted, Will has pursued the business of real estate in Elizabeth City since the late nineteenth century. After beginning on a modest scale, he soon becomes one of the most successful businessmen in Elizabeth City. On August 28, 1914, the *Advance* publishes his notice, as the owner, to sell or rent a thriving farm in Camden County, "half of which is good open land and half in woods, mostly original growth," and on November 13, the newspaper carries his advertisement to sell or rent John Andrew Kramer's elaborately gabled and lavishly decorated house on Pennsylvania Avenue (later known as the Kramer-McMullan House and, after the renaming of Pennsylvania Avenue, designated 709 North Poindexter Street). Mr. Kramer, local lumber baron, has become prominently identified with the business and financial communities of the city.

Grandfather resigns his position as general manager and secretary-treasurer of Crystal Ice and Coal Company in the early days of 1915, as reported in the *Advance* on February 9, after more than two decades of service, to devote full attention to William E. Dunstan Real Estate. He opens an office on the second floor of the impressive Hinton Building (later more commonly known as the Carolina Building and later still, in 1967, succumbing to fire) on East Main Street.

Will attracts attention with a splashy new advertisement in the *Advance*, published on February 19, 1915: "HALLO THERE!! Are you looking for me? Well, I am not selling Ice or Coal now, but homes. . . . If you are not in a hurry for a house, I have a lot [measured parcel of land] for you to put it on when you are ready. Lots of 'em—See? Oh! Perhaps it's a farm you have in mind. Yes, I have an assortment. Come in and take your pick—and come quick—and turn the trick. We buy, sell or trade, and never afraid. W. E. Dunstan, Room 203 Hinton Bldg."

His advertisements show that his holdings include a large number of farms and residences. Meanwhile he remains a guiding force at Crystal Ice and Coal Company. On June 25 the *Advance* announces that he continues on the company board of directors and describes the members of the board as "substantial citizens and well-known in the city."

The period from August 1 to August 18, 1916, sees him run four identical large advertisements in the *Advance* for the sale of an "elegant farm" located between Elizabeth City and Norfolk. "The land is well drained—the main boundary being a river." Rich loamy soil yields an abundance of "cotton, corn, peanuts, potatoes," and other crops. The lovely farm includes "a large modern dwelling (9 rooms), barn, stables, shelters, carriage house, smokehouse, dairy, fowl house," as well as a "neat [family] schoolhouse on large lawn. There are two tenant houses on the farm.... Beautiful shade and ornamental trees" frame the "grand home" and spacious grounds.

About this time, Grandfather clips and saves an article about his business success but fails to record the specific newspaper or date (probably published between 1915 and 1917). The anonymous writer notes that William E. Dunstan "has been a well-known figure in the social and commercial life of Elizabeth City for a number of years.... Having large property holding[s] in the city and county, Mr. Dunstan finds his time fully occupied in handling his individual business. In other words, he acts as his own rental and sales agent. His motto is, 'Never a squeal after a [Dunstan] deal,' and he" maintains an extensive catalogue of "homes and small farms, both for sale and for rent. Mr. Dunstan is a man of pleasing personality, and by his affable manner and unfailing courtesy, as well as his fair and square [honest] business dealings, [he] has won a host of friends for himself. Well connected socially . . . , he has, in his idle moments, turned his attention to the muses and is the author of several attractive poems and sketches, some of which appear in a volume entitled *Literature in the Albemarle*, recently published [1915]. Mr. Dunstan is a man of broad and liberal ideas, progressive in all the word implies, and can always be relied upon to lend his aid to anything leading to the betterment of the community."

On May 31, 1917, readers of the *Advance* discover a playful front-page story about a "demure maiden and bashful male," natives of "a remote hamlet in northern Virginia," becoming "victims of 'love microbes' . . . under the direction of Cupid himself.... Very soon there was a wedding. ..." An uncle of one of the newlyweds suggests they begin marriage on the right foot by living in Elizabeth City. Their train arrives, and the generous uncle promises "to build and furnish for them a modern home. 'First, we will go in and confer with my friend W. E. Dunstan, who is well informed on real estate values. He . . . came here about 25 years ago, liked our city, and has made good in business as a citizen, who is now giving his time to buying and selling real estate and looking after the several scores of houses he owns in Elizabeth City.' Sure enough Mr. Dunstan sold them a nice residence site on which they at once proceeded to build" a magnificent home of "symmetrical . . . appearance and commodious . . . interior arrangements. . . ."

During this period Will clips and saves, again without noting the newspaper or date, a long article from his own pen: "Our Real Estate Progress," coupling the rapid "growth of our city" during the previous quarter century to the substantial rise in "the price of real estate." Probably writing after the national census of 1920 shows the population of Elizabeth City has climbed to 8,925, a huge leap from the 3,251 in 1890, Grandfather amusingly tiptoes around the old seer who seriously underestimated the local urban expansion and saw future's "door slammed in his face . . . ."

His article abounds with astronomical, cultural, and historical references. He describes "former [local] lowlands . . . now . . . [rivaling] Mars . . . with [lengthy drainage] canals," referring to nineteenth-century astronomical observations (based on optical illusions) of long straight lines on the Martian landscape, with the American astronomer Percival Lowell (1855-1916) even championing the idea that intelligent beings had built an intricate network of canals on the red planet.

Grandfather then points to the old "haunts of Brother Fox and Brother Rabbit" giving way to "some of the finest homes in our proud city today." He applauds new "elegantly paved and swept" avenues and magnificently designed houses forming "immense piles of brick and mortar, steel and slate, plate glass and marble, where once stood old gables and stables and cook tables."

Grandfather praises the waterfront and harbor as "equal to any in Old Dixie Land" for its beauty and commercial vigor, with the primitive "little schooners" of yore replaced on the Pasquotank River by a steady stream of "palatial steamers" and "millionaire's yachts" and ware-laden barges. Even "the athletic frog . . . wont to leap the broad Pasquotank" enjoys the alternative today of "cross[ing] . . . on the [early twentieth-century, single-draw] cantilever bridge [the river's first vehicular span], if . . . business bent or . . . would a wooing go. . . . Would you wonder then that values in realty . . . are soaring in whatever direction the weather vane . . . points?" Level heads welcome our new prosperity: "No ill winds . . . turn the arrow . . . for Miss Betsey [nickname for Elizabeth City], the bright . . . star . . . [on] the Narrows [of the

Pasquotank]. . . ." Grandfather's athletic frog refers to a familiar old poem beginning, "Way down yonder on the Pasquotank, / Where the bullfrogs jump from bank to bank. . . ."

Earlier, Will had envisioned owning one hundred houses and lots. By 1919 he has achieved that goal through continuous home construction and real estate purchases. He rents many of the houses and farms, particularly the more modest ones, as a source of income and sells others via his real estate office. Not satisfied, he and Emma double their holdings to two hundred houses and lots. Elizabeth City possesses too few streets at the time to accommodate the aggressive Dunstan building program. Accordingly, Grandfather begins opening streets for development and naming them. These include Dunstan Lane, Fleetwood Street, Spruce Street, and Magnolia Street. Years earlier, as noted, town officials had named Dyer Street for the father of his brother-in-law John James Dyer of Southampton County, Virginia. Elizabeth City possesses streets named for Grandmother's family also, including Herrington Road and Cobb Street.

People in all neighborhoods of Elizabeth City see Will driving his horse and buggy every Monday to collect rent from tenants. He never owns or drives an automobile. Once I asked a personal friend of mature years, the late Mary Horner Chambers, to tell me anything she remembered about Grandfather. She described him as the sole adult in town who always stopped his buggy to chat with children and to inquire about the health and well being of their parents. She added that children greatly respected him for regarding them as kindred spirits and treating them with dignity.

Another gracious friend of the same generation, the late Anne Wilcox Sanderlin, who spent her childhood residing just two or three blocks from the Dunstans, told me of a neighboring boy once giving her valuable information about acquiring soybeans for her pea shooter. "Just steal them from Mr. Will Dunstan's barn on the alley behind his house. He has far more than his horses can eat." Anne takes a handful and discovers that many other children come to the same spot to replenish their supply of the small round beans that made ideal ammunition for the shooters. Apparently glad to contribute to simple pleasures of childhood, Will neither censors the little thieves nor complains to their parents.

Birth of Garland and Whispers of New Romantic Arrangements. On Monday afternoon, July 3, 1916, Emma gives birth to her seventh and final child, Garland Herrington Dunstan, whose middle name honors the family of his maternal grandmother, Virginia Herrington Sawyer, and whose first name means *crowned in victory*. Only two years separate Uncle Garland and Uncle Forrest, and the two brothers soon become fast allies and friends. They possess warm personalities and captivating charm. In time, Grandfather names two of his larger farms for the boys, calling one Forestvale and the other Garlandale. Later, he honors his older sons by dubbing two other farms Fleetwood and Weddew, the latter a play on Edward's initials W.E.D.

The birth of Garland possibly leads to discreet but monumental changes in the Dunstan household. I once heard a colorful story from a reliable relative that forty-four-year-old Emma decided at the birth of Garland to move into a separate bedroom to avoid the possibility of another pregnancy. At this time wives wanting no additional children often abandoned the bedroom shared with their husbands as a method of birth control. Such husbands frequently regard the new sleeping arrangement as license to break their wedding vows and seek intimacy outside the home. The account reported to me has sixty-two-year-old Will seeking romantic comfort elsewhere and even producing a daughter not carrying the Dunstan name but closely resembling Adelaide. I cannot verify any aspect of this story. Several years after hearing the report I questioned an older well-informed family friend about the matter. True to his upbringing, he deftly shied away from the discussion. Yet perhaps a clue exists.

As noted, Will employs the large family Bible as a filing cabinet, inserting more than sixty separate items between the leaves. These include letters, telegrams, postal cards, newspaper and magazine articles, inspirational pictures, programs for special events, poems, songs, family genealogical diagrams, and drawings and other art work created by the Dunstan children. As a young boy, I often pored over this provocative assortment with fascination but became baffled by the inclusion of three unusual photographs of a woman named Mary. These images seem completely out of character with the other items in the Bible.

Mary has signed the back of the photographs with her first and last names and listed her street address, in Norfolk, Virginia. The national census of 1920 shows eleven people residing at the same Norfolk address, perhaps a boarding house. Mary sports a pompadour-style coiffure, with her hair swept into a loose full roll around her flawless oval face. At first glace she appears modestly attired in the feminine style of the 1910s, for Mary has donned a white dress with a high collar and a dainty broach at the throat. Yet closer examination shows that her shockingly sheer dress clearly reveals her undergarments! Adding to her boldness, Mary poses provocatively for the camera. Her hands playfully touch the back of her neck in one photograph, and her tilted head reclines upon her cradling hands in another.

The photographs appear strikingly seductive for the time. Even today most people would describe them as boldly inviting. I can only imagine how they found their way into the family Bible. A woman by the same first and uncommon last name once lived in Elizabeth City, on Bell Street, where Grandfather owned several unpretentious houses rented to tenants. The city directory for 1912-1913 includes her name and address. Could this be the same Mary? For the sake of discretion, does she move to Norfolk? Does Grandfather catch the train for Norfolk to enjoy romantic liaisons with her? He possesses real estate in the vicinity and frequently travels to Norfolk on business, easily managed with three northbound trains leaving Elizabeth City daily for Norfolk and three southbound train leaving Norfolk for Elizabeth City. Instead, does he form romantic bonds with another woman, someone who lives and remains in Elizabeth City?

The truth about whispers of long ago often proves impossible to recover. Whether or not Grandfather ever strayed, to me he will always be a larger-than-life figure whose virtues far exceeded his defects. He died long before my birth, but I often heard people speak of him in the most glowing terms during my childhood and have always regretted knowing him only through sensing his spiritual presence and guidance.

Fleetwood in Peace and War. The fall of 1914 sees Uncle Fleetwood diligently preparing to enroll as a freshman at Trinity College (later showered with gold and renamed Duke University), a small but sound institution offering a liberal arts education in the tobacco capital of Durham. When his parents embrace him with warm farewells at the new train station, located on a street later renamed Hughes Boulevard, no doubt they fight back tears knowing they have lost forever the comfort of his daily presence. Grandfather hands Fleetwood a long newspaper article, explaining via a marginal note that his son might profit by reading and absorbing the message.

The unknown author criticizes the majority of writers, for they exceed their expertise and "pose as authorities on subjects" far beyond their understanding or involvement. The author next rebukes longtime "bachelors like St. Paul [who] dogmatically lay down the laws which should govern marital relations." The author has been greatly irritated recently by another example: Someone "thrust under our nose a 'Treatise on the Pleasures of Old Age,' contributed . . . by a callow youth beneath whose ambrosial locks are stored the luxurious fancy of twenty-four summers and the wisdom ripened by as many winters." The aforementioned youthful writer dares "teach a lesson he has not learned." Contrast this "boyish presumption" and "rash excursion into unknown lands" with the judgment of someone in the twilight of life. "Age understands Youth because the veteran of Today was the boy of distant Yesterdays and has not . . . forgotten . . . how he felt when the days were all too short for the pleasures that filled them and the nights too long that postponed the coming of a joyous Tomorrow." The author recommends never crossing the boundaries of experience and knowledge with a free-wheeling pen, exemplified by the young man writing about old age. "The territories of senectitude [old age] must ever be terra incognita et proscripta [unknown and forbidden] to all but those who dwell therein." In his polished *De senectute* (*On Old Age*), even the great "Cicero makes only an impressionist's picture," for he remains "too juvenile by a score of years to appreciate or reproduce the atmosphere of Life's Twilight."

Uncle Fleetwood had become an avid photographer long before reaching Trinity. During the period of his professional career he maintains a well-equipped darkroom and excels in taking and developing photographs of distinction. He documents his entire college career with photographs and arranges them in a protective album with his usual precision and artistry.

As a freshman, Fleetwood pledges Sigma Chi Fraternity at the close of the fall rushing season. The local chapter of the social fraternity takes pride in attracting men of high scholastic ambitions and noteworthy campus leadership. Uncle Fleetwood finds time to sandwich his studies between his many other activities. He achieves a superior academic and extracurricular record. He writes a newsy letter to Will on April 21, 1916, and adds two messages to Emma on the back of the envelope, first about feasting on a cake just received from her kitchen and second about treasuring an invitation to dine the following night at the home of the dean of the college.

Yet storm clouds loom ever closer as Fleetwood advances from year to year. The blood-drenched Great War (known also as the World War and later as the First World War), raging since 1914, casts agitated shadows across the globe. Some Americans itch to join the conflict, thanks in part to fierce anti-German propaganda, while others fervently pray for the maintenance of neutrality. April 1917 sees the United States enter the clash on the side of the Allies (most notably the United Kingdom, France, Russia, and Italy) against the Central Powers (most notably Germany, Austria-Hungry, and the Ottoman Empire). Citizens of North Carolina shift attention from local concerns to the ruthless war effort.

Taking a leave of absence from Trinity College, Uncle Fleetwood accepts a commission as a first lieutenant in the Army and embarks on a program of military training, initially at Charleston, South Carolina, then at Camp Greene in Charlotte, North Carolina. He sees the nation falling into the grip of fear mongers.

Back in Elizabeth City, the *Advance* strikes terror with lurid reports not only of German assaults on the United States but also of German spies lurking around every corner. On April 18 the newspaper conjures up dark images of coastal residents in Massachusetts hearing "heavy firing" from a German "submarine or [a] raider [fast ship made for naval warfare]" but concedes the following day that the dreadful roar "may have been thunder." The following year the war ripples into the coastal waters of North Carolina, with everyone exchanging accounts of German submarines (called U-boats) sinking both a lightship (a vessel equipped with a strong light and moored at a spot dangerous to navigation) and a British tanker.

On May 24, 1917, the *Advance* quotes and applauds an editorial from the 1880 *Elizabeth City Economist*, whose editor, Colonel R. B. Creecy, had allowed himself to say with chilling bluntness: "Constituted as we [humans] are [toward belligerence and violence], war is a necessity and, in the ordering of God's providence, is sometimes, perhaps often, a blessing. War reduces redundant [excess] population. Standing armies give remunerative employment to agricultural and manufacturing labor. It [war] is a great field for the production of giants among men. . . ."

In 1917 a spirit of near frenzy consumes the public as innocent German-born men with "foreign accents" pass through northeastern North Carolina and find themselves arrested as spies, though time proves each innocent of any disloyalty or wrongdoing. One of the men has served four years in the United States Navy! Yet, on June 4, the newspaper warns everyone to continue ferreting out suspected German spies, for "the next one may turn out to be REAL."

On May 26, 1917, the *Advance* publishes an article from the United Press (an agency reporting and transmitting stories to newspapers) that even raises questions about the substantial German ancestry of King George V (reigned 1910-1936): "References to his German blood are commonplace [in the United Kingdom], but this is regarded as his misfortune rather than his fault, and there is none to say that he has not played up to his part as an Englishman. . . ." With anti-German feeling running high, King George soon issues a royal proclamation, on July 17, changing the dynastic name of his family from the House of Saxe-Coburg-Gotha (German) to the House of Windsor (English).

Meanwhile, on August 31, the *Advance* splashes the front page with a long letter from Fleetwood to Will, describing his life at Camp Greene. Fleetwood ends by saying he has gained a first-rate post "in the finance department. . . . Our work will really begin when the [first conscripted] troops arrive. . . . The military discipline and courtesy appeal to me. . . . Even though I can't return to Trinity this fall, I am still in school [learning new skills and acquiring valuable knowledge]."

To Arms! About this time Will clips an untitled poem for Fleetwood from a local newspaper but records neither the name of the publication nor the date (clearly 1917). The introduction begins with the headline "Inherits Uncle's Gift at Rhyme" and continues: "The following patriotic poem was written by sixteen-year-old Robert Tayloe Dunstan of Windsor, who, by the way, is a nephew of Elizabeth City's own W. E. Dunstan" and first cousin of Fleetwood, Adelaide, Edward, Forrest, and Garland. In his boyhood innocence Rob sees the Great War as a romantic and untried adventure but later will become a devout pacifist:

> To Arms! Ye sons of Freedom
> Our Country now defend!
> A noble step she has taken
> We'll stand by her like Men.
>
> To Arms! Let us die fighting
> To hold for all we're worth
> The standards of Old Glory,
> The greatest flag on earth.
> To Arms! 'Tis now our duty
> And do it, we'll do our best,
> To crush the hand tyrannic
> That has the weak oppressed.
>
> To Arms! We as a nation
> Of free and prosperous men
> Can't see our brothers suffer
> And help to them not send!

To Arms! 'Tis not we're fighting
For power, lands or fame,
But justice, peace, protection
Against despotic shame.

To Arms! The fiendish savage
Autocracy, by name,
Crushed, and then Democracy
Shall stand, indeed, supreme.

    In August 1918, sixteen months after the United States enters the hideous war, Fleetwood receives an urgent summons to return home. Emma has lost her beloved mother, Virginia Herrington Sawyer, known to friends and family as Ginny, who has outlived husband John Lloyd Sawyer by twelve years. Fleetwood remembers Ginny expressing pride over John's brilliant career, including serving on the board of directors of the Citizens Bank of Elizabeth City, opening in 1899 on the southeast corner of Poindexter and Fearing Streets. The handsome Chateauesque-style commercial brick structure (later transformed into a retail store) originally possessed a prominent tower and conical roof over the front turret.
    Fleetwood remembers Ginny showing him numerous clipped articles about his grandfather. John's name frequently graced local newspapers. The *Elizabeth City Tar Heel* announced on September 13, 1901, that "Mr. Jno. L. Sawyer has returned with his family from [their beach cottage] at Nags Head, where they have spent the heated [summer] season." The *Elizabeth City Economist* adds on September 22 that "Mr. J. L. Sawyer left on Thursday for [business in] Philadelphia" and traveled part of the way with his son "Mr. Walter W. Sawyer," who "goes [to Baltimore] to enter his third year in the study of medicine at the University of Maryland." The *Elizabeth City North Carolinian* reports on July 10, 1902, that "Mr. John L. Sawyer [and his family] left Tuesday for Nags Head, where they will spend the summer." The same newspaper informs readers the following year, on May 2, that "Mr. Cliff Sawyer left Saturday for Baltimore, Maryland, to

be present at the graduation exercise of the Medical School, in which his brother, Mr. Walter Sawyer, is a student."

In 1905 the lumber manufacturers Kramer Brothers and Company crow in a company catalogue: "We furnished . . . lumber and mill work used in [twenty-three local buildings, including] the . . . residence of J. L. Sawyer" on West Main Street.

The Kramer family must have been astonished when my great-grandfather took his last breath so soon thereafter, on Friday, January 24, 1906, as gales and heavy rains raged in Elizabeth City. Three days later the *Daily Economist* publishes a front-page article about John's funeral (earlier issues of the *Economist* and the *Tar Heel* carrying his obituary do not survive in any known library or archival collection): "The remains were laid away in Hollywood Cemetery, where, despite the stormy weather, a large number of those who knew him in life assembled and paid him a last sad tribute. As a mark of respect the dry goods stores of the city closed between the hours of three and four."

The newspaper adds, on January 29, that his secluded family has been much comforted by "the kind attention shown Mr. Sawyer during his illness and for the sympathy expressed to his family in the sad hour of death. . . ." They have been consoled also by "the estimation in which he was held by the townsmen, demonstrated by the act of closing the business places during the burial hour. Such acts of loving kindness and expressions of esteem" lightened "the dark clouds" accompanying "the eternal breaking of earthly family ties in death."

After Ginny's sudden death, on Saturday, August 17, 1918, Will composes surviving first drafts of the warm notes he and Emma will pen to friends who have sent flowers or offered other expressions of sympathy. The family must have reflected about the life and accomplishments of Ginny and how she had almost met tragedy nineteen years earlier at the Sawyer family beach cottage. Husband John had purchased the James Gatlin Cottage, erected 1868, one of the original thirteen summer dwellings at Nags Head. The Sawyers enjoy many carefree summers at the enchanting beach, but mid-August 1899 sees Ginny and her four sons witnessing a shrieking hurricane crashing into the Outer Banks without warning. No system exists then to alert beach cottagers of an approaching tempest. The furious battering breaks apart at least seven ships trapped in the churning surf and snuffs out many human and animal lives on shore. The local historian Edward R. Outlaw, Jr., peppers his *Old Nags Head* (Norfolk, Va.: Liskey Lithograph, 1952, p. 29) with a riveting picture of this storm: "Tremendous waves of the sea beat against the beach . . . until the ocean swept across the sandy strand from sea to [Roanoke] Sound. . . . Cottagers looked through their windows to see on all sides nothing but raging sea," with only the tops of sand dunes remaining above the destructive waters. "Some cottagers on the beach made their way to the hotel on the Sound side by using lifelines to which each person was tied. They struggled through water about four feet deep. I moved Mrs. John L. Sawyer and her family in their [horse-drawn] cart and returned to the beach" to continue rescuing many threatened souls.

As a boy, I often heard spellbinding stories of Great-grandmother Ginny tying her four sons, ranging in age from eleven to eighteen, to the cart with ropes to prevent them from being swept into the maelstrom, their vehicle serving as a crude boat or raft for the short but perilous journey to the refuge of a nearby lofty sand dune rather then to the more distant hotel, with the high wheels rarely jolting against the sand beneath the seething, debris-laden water.

Several days after Ginny's funeral, the stylishly-dressed Dunstans gather at a photographic studio for a family portrait before Fleetwood departs by train for a new assignment in the Great War. Everyone seems serene and composed, but only young Edward, my father, smiles. The older members of the family must have labored with somber thoughts of Fleetwood possibly encountering unspeakable dangers. His face relaxed but grave, Fleetwood wears his crisp Army uniform as he stands behind his seated parents. Will they ever see their son again? The Dunstans grow increasingly alarmed in the following weeks about the welfare of Fleetwood, with the staggering casualties and horrors of this cataclysm seeming to circle ever closer to him.

Emma repeatedly expresses anxiety about her firstborn but soon receives a much-welcomed letter, dated Sunday, September 29, 1918, from the vacating physician Dr. Sydney P. Hilliard of Rocky Mount, North Carolina, then a guest at the Emerson Hotel in Baltimore, Maryland. "My dear Mrs. Dunstan," Dr. Hilliard begins, "Have just met and had a pleasant conversation with your son Lieutenant Dunstan. By mere accident I saw him in the lobby of the Emerson and, even before talking, knew he was one of our North Carolina Boys. His pleasing personality appealed to me. Mrs. Hilliard soon joined us, and we enjoyed so much being with him. He spoke of his early departure for France, and I want to tell you that our progress will follow and attend him. I find that he is enthusiastic and happy. I threw him a few bouquets [compliments] because of his fine appearance and high attainments. Do not be uneasy about him—he is coming back to you and before very long. I feel that the war will soon be over and doubt if those who go [abroad] now will have to go to the front at all.

"Mrs. Hilliard and I, now getting along in years . . . , carry ever with us the precious memory of our only child, a son, who some years ago went to meet 'the golden dawning of the grander day' and just when in the full flush of young manhood [Dr. Hilliard quotes from an oration the notable agnostic lawyer and lecturer Robert G. Ingersoll delivered in 1879 at the grave of his beloved brother Ebon C. Ingersoll: 'on his forehead fell the golden dawning of the grander day.']. He [our son] was the very sunlight of our existence and while the alighting sorrow has to some extent 'veiled in the folds of time,' it ever abides. And so, we are glad for those whose loved ones now are with them. No, do not be uneasy about Fleetwood—he is coming back."

Indeed, the war ends six weeks later, on November 11, in victory for the remaining Allies (the ruthless Bolsheviks have seized Russia from a new provisional government, forged a one-party dictatorship, withdrawn from the war, and murdered dethroned Czar Nicholas II and his family). The war has not only shattered vast territories and claimed millions of lives but also witnessed the fall of great ruling houses, collapse of powerful empires, growth of new ideologies and political movements, and development of countless fearsome weapons.

Fleetwood returns untouched and completes his studies at Trinity. May 24, 1919, finds him taking a brief break from studying for final examinations to compose a letter to Will. Fleetwood hopes "to find something good" in his quest for a career and looks forward to commencement. "If the war had not broken up my college life, perhaps I would feel a touch of sadness at the finals, as some say they do. But I have not been able to enter into college life again, and I shall be glad to get out into the world once more." Fleetwood struggles with the mournful clouds encircling Trinity, for twenty-one of his fellow students have forfeited their lives in the Great War. The college yearbook, the *Chanticleer* (renamed *Victory* for the year 1919), lists his nickname as Fleet and applauds him as "'Fleet' of brain."

Summer Paradise. Uncle Fleetwood soon enjoys a pleasant interlude with the family at the William E. Dustan Cottage. The cottage graces Nags Head, a community on the extraordinary Outer Banks, the cherished string of thin sandy islands off the North Carolina mainland, extending roughly 175 miles from the Virginia border to below Cape Lookout. The Nags Head of those days remains an isolated resort village on a barrier island possessing a small number of year-round inhabitants earning their livelihood mainly by fishing, but they share the land with a few privileged summer dwellers attracted by the spiritual and regenerative properties of fresh air and seawater.

The William E. Dunstan Cottage, rising in the early twentieth century on the sound side facing Roanoke Island and the mainland (but moved to the oceanfront before 1940 for the calming effects of the mighty Atlantic), offers the family a summer paradise through its simplicity of design and harmony with the natural setting. Early designers partly sidestep the dangerous forces of wind and water by constructing such cottages on timber pilings and giving them sweeping rooflines. At first, the Dunstan Cottage and several others exhibit unpainted clapboards as siding and slowly weather to the appealing color of driftwood. When moved to the oceanfront, the Dunstan Cottage sees carpenters adding unpainted wooden shingles for siding. The wooden shingles gracing most early cottages weather to a rich brown that pairs beautifully with the sand stretching north and south along the ocean as far as the eye can see. Broad shady porches serve as favorite gathering places and offer families not only pleasing vistas of sea and dunes but also cooling, salt-scented breezes.

Cottages often spend much of the daytime visiting one another on the inviting porches. Guests and family members relax on corner hammocks, rocking chairs, swings, and protruding benches built into the arms of porches. Propped wooden shutters, hinged at the top, protect interiors from sun and storms but catch the slightest heat-expelling breezes. Cottage designs invariably include a separate wing for one or two servants, usually a single housekeeper-cook-nursemaid.

Families and their household servants spend entire summers at the beach in the comfort of their starkly beautiful and resilient cottages. The Dunstans and neighboring cottagers arrange for the transportation by boat of everything required for the summer, including bedding, carts, horses, milk cows, and egg-laying chickens, but they depend on the natives, called Bankers, for supplies of fish, meat, and fresh vegetables.

Earlier, Fleetwood always accompanied the animals and a housekeeper-cook-nursemaid to Nags Head several days before the rest of the family made the annual trip. In this role he supervises the opening and airing of the cottage and the introduction of the jumpy animals to the seaside environment. After his first year of college, this obligation falls on the next oldest son, seven-year-old Edward, who complains bitterly about the loneliness and unpleasantness of the task, though he enjoys riding a Dunstan high-wheeled, horse-drawn cart up and down the beach. Horse carts had become a popular fixture at Nags Head in the nineteenth century.

With the Outer Banks possessing no bridge to the mainland, the other Dunstans pack large trunks of clothes and other items for their seasonal pilgrimage and depart on one of the steamers operating between Elizabeth City and Nags Head. For decades the large and comfortable *Trenton* makes the forty-five mile run six days a week. Other vessels offer fewer trips. One of these, the spacious steamer *Annie L. Vansciver*, transporting both passengers and freight, runs to Nags Head on Sundays and attracts passengers with a popular group of musicians, persons of color, who entertain everyone aboard by playing bones (flat clappers), bass fiddle, and kazoo. A handsome large mural depicting the *Annie L Vansciver* (painted by local artist and teacher Melvin

Meekins in 1971) adorns an interior wall of the Colonial Restaurant in Elizabeth City.

In the early 1920s, Fleetwood captures the slow pace of Dunstan beach life on the sound side with his treasured camera. He stands at a distance from the sand-nestled William E. Dunstan Cottage to snap one of the photographs, the resulting sepia image showing the generous wraparound porch and simple, clean lines of the architecture. At this time cottagers take pride in their casually elegant dress at the beach. Fleetwood preserves a record of Dunstan beach attire in several additional photographs. He hands the camera to Edward or a guest for a shot showing Fleetwood grouped with four other family members on the porch. A young sailor-suited and grinning Forrest peeps out at the camera from behind a rocking chair. Three older Dunstans sit side by side on rocking chairs while seemingly ignoring the camera to enjoy the natural beauty before them.

A smile of contentment on his face, Will wears a fashionable boater, or stiff straw hat with a shallow flat crown and straight circular brim, as well as a white shirt with bow tie and cufflinks, dark trousers and stockings, and dark leather shoes. Fleetwood sports a white sailor cap, white shirt rolled to the elbows, four-in-hand tie of striking light and dark pattern, and white duck trousers, all complemented by dark belt, dark stockings, and dark oxfords. Emma confronts the heat and humidity of summer by keeping her hair brushed up in the front and sides but obeys her strict lifelong standard of modesty by wearing a dark silk dress extending to her ankles. Sitting on a cushioned swing facing the camera, Adelaide has her black hair arranged in graceful waves. She wears a delicate sweater vest, frilly white blouse, long pleated skirt matching her vest, dark silk stockings, and stylish white sports shoes (blocked from view in this photograph but clearly visible in another). The Dunstan gentlemen still wear pocket watches, though the wristwatch has gained popularity from wartime use by soldiers, who appreciated a timepiece they could observe with their hands full.

Fleetwood employs the porch also as a convenient photographic setting to capture a seemingly unposed image of teenage Edward, leaning far back in a rocker while reading a private letter. Edward seems surprised and slightly annoyed as he glances from the letter to the camera. He has parted his short black hair on the side and donned a collarless white sports shirt with thin vertical stripes and decorative buttons, worn with a dark leather belt and crisp white trousers.

The relaxed elegance of the photographs masks the absolute primitives of Nags Head at this time. In the early 1920s, the Outer Banks remain virtually untouched by the technological developments of the preceding decades and possess no running water, indoor toilets, telephones, or electricity. Several families dig wells to supply water for themselves and their horses, chickens, and other animals. At the William E. Dunstan Cottage someone must vigorously push up and down on the handle of a simple mechanical pump to raise water from below the sandy terrain. Oil lamps suffice for light after dark. Nags Head lacks regular roads, and cottagers reach their destinations by trudging through difficult, yielding sand or by traveling on their horse-drawn wooden carts. Infrequent chilly spells leave them either shivering or huddling for heat around the kitchen stove, though the Dunstan cottage possesses a rare fireplace. Cottagers lessen the constant threat of drowning by swimming in groups. Because Nags Head then claims no resident physician, cottagers face grave dangers from accidents, sudden physical afflictions, or outbreaks of disease.

As a boy, I often heard a gripping story about Uncle Garland, then a toddler, tumbling from the cottage porch at Nags Head and biting off his tongue. One of the Dunstans rushes to summon a vacationing physician, who sews the tongue back after family members firmly grasp terrified little Garland and hold him down on the kitchen table for the torturous procedure. He heals without permanent damage, but the Dunstans never forget the lesson of tempting fate by spending their summers at an isolated resort. Moreover, they add a protective railing system along the edges of their front and back porches.

Robert (Rob) Dunstan Enters Trinity College. This period sees Grandfather writing frequently to Bessie and Rob, Dr. Henry's widow and son in Windsor. Their comfortable life declined after Dr. Henry's death, with the bulk of his estate going to his older sons by Mollie. Thus Aunt Gussie leaves a trust fund, administered by Will, to cover part of Rob's higher education. Even so, young Rob struggles financially as a student at Trinity. He enters college in the fall of 1917, just three months after his cousin Fleetwood has volunteered for services in the Great War. Here Rob excels in creating sublime literary monuments.

On February 2, 1918, Rob writes his Uncle Will about college life and adds a poignant plea for funds. Although Rob serves as a waiter for half his board, he has exhausted the money Will sent last fall and has "several bills due now that I want to settle, so I'm going to ask you to send me a little more, please sir, when it is convenient for you. . . ." Sixteen days later an elated Bessie writes Will that his "letter and check were gladly received." In the meantime Grandfather also lends or gives college money to several young men outside the family.

Although his generosity to others becomes a well-known magnet to those with various needs or causes, Will does not tolerate deadbeats. On April 22, 1927, he pens a curt note to a delinquent tenant and (according to the copy made for his files) concludes with a warning: "Your way of paying rent is not satisfactory and unless you settle up by Saturday night or Monday evening, I must have the house—and I hope you will not force me to evict you." Meanwhile he continues to buy and sell houses, farms, and lots. His surviving rough draft of an agreement to sell a house on Culpepper Street, in 1922, indicates he has accepted thirty-five dollars as the down payment, or part of the total amount due, six hundred dollars.

4

Edward and His Circle

This period sees many changes for Edward, my father, who lives in a beautiful mansion adorned with an extensive library, exquisite antiques, valuable family heirlooms, and lovely gardens. His careful upbringing suggests an echo of lace-edged antebellum grandeur. Although his parents' efforts often prove fruitless, they encourage him to honor the family name by seeking sound pastimes, exploring the world nobly, and espousing the guiding principle of self-discipline. Ample documentation shows his privileged class enjoying a comfortable existence burnished by devotion to duty and gracious living. Yet the radiance of the favored few casts a short, ragged beam on the rest of society.

Early Years. Edward's hometown shares with countless other conservative settlements across North Carolina both a charming and harsh side. In his day and long afterward, polite individuals of all complexions refer informally to persons of color as colored people and formally as Negroes. Politeness aside, arbitrary concepts separate people in Elizabeth City according to color, for the ruling class regards white citizens as far superior to colored citizens, and this lethal thinking pervades newspapers, schools, churches, and every aspect of life. Edward's boyhood sees newspapers regularly unfurling prejudiced attitudes. An article published in the *Advance* on August 18, 1919, for instance, describes the United States as "a white man's country, by impregnable right of its conquest and occupation by the most masterful of breeds [Europeans]...."

In 1914, as Edward approaches his sixth birthday, he hears frightened whispers of a colored man and woman firing bullets at several white men. The *Advance* spotlights this unusual story on August 4. "The shooting occurred shortly after the passage of the southbound night train," when four white men walked along the railroad tracks. "Seeing a man and woman ahead coming toward them and supposing them white people, the group . . . stood to one side to let them pass, when suddenly a pistol spat fire and a bullet struck at the feet of the group. At an exclamation of surprise and caution from the white men, a Negro's voice shouted, 'Don't you like it?' and the pistol was fired again. This time the bullet struck" one of the four white men, "plowing around the front of a rib and going through his arm. . . ." When the attacked men pounced on the Negro man, the woman threatened one of the white men with the gun, but he "threw her to one side. She got to her feet and fired blindly," mortally wounding an uninvolved man standing near the train depot. The attackers fled, but the police apprehended and arrested the hiding couple. The shooting quickly arouses "a pitch of intense excitement," and the chief of police declares that if the crowd had succeeded in holding "the Negro man at the depot, he would undoubtedly have been lynched on the spot."

According to the newspaper, police officials ask the captured man "what the white men had done to him. The Negro said, 'Nothing,' and would give no further explanation of his act." This senseless shooting of 1914 strangely prefigures an extraordinary ambush killing from the same railroad tracks on January 1, 1943 (described at length in volume 2).

On September 21, 1914, Edward begins the first grade with great enthusiasm. Although more than two months shy of his sixth birthday, Edward demands to begin school as a five-year-old boy and, as usual, gets his way. Will probably tells him that the Elizabeth City public school system, organized seven years earlier, grew from a preparatory school established in 1878 by a revered educator from Pennsylvania, Samuel Lloyd Sheep. Professor Sheep sacrifices financially by closing his private school and helping to establish the new public school system. He becomes superintendent of public schools the same year, 1907, and remains in office until the year Edward reaches the first grade, 1914, but serves again as superintendent from 1918 until 1927 and dies in 1928.

Edward and his classmates address their beloved young teacher as "Miss Susie" (Miss Susie Stevens later marries Herbert Wright Morrisette and continues teaching ably as Mrs. Susie

Morrisette, though still called Miss Susie, until retiring in 1957). Edward counts himself among the 487 students studying in the old Harney Street Primary School accommodating first, second, and third graders. The *Advance* announces on September 25, 1914, that the primary, elementary, and high schools have a total enrollment of "1,071, which is equal to . . . last year. This statement is made without reference to the Negro schools, only one of which has opened."

The following month Edward hears townspeople talking about pollution and contamination in the water supply. On October 27, 1914, the publisher-editor of the *Advance*, Herbert Peele, stuns readers with a bizarre editorial headline: "Are We Drinking Sewage?" After reminding everyone that "salt from the [Albemarle] Sound finds its way to Knobbs Creek," source of local drinking water, Mr. Peele suggests that untreated "sewage from the Pasquotank [River] . . . find[s] its way there also, and few of us want to drink sewage even if it is cooked" by a process of boiling our drinking water on cookstoves. Five years pass before the newspaper can announce, on December 2, 1919, that the Elizabeth City Water Company will install a "new and modern filter plant" to reduce salt and bacteria from city water.

Edward observes his sixth birthday on November 28, 1914, and then celebrates several days later with a grand party. The *Advance* describes the merrymaking on Tuesday, December 15: "Little Edward Dunstan was host Thursday afternoon at the home of his parents, Mr. and Mrs. W. E. Dunstan, on [West] Church Street to a large number of his young friends at a party to celebrate his sixth birthday anniversary. Various games were played for the amusement of the little folks, and delicious refreshments were served." The forty-one listed guests include Braxton Dawson, Elizabeth Etheridge, Marjorie Fearing, Joseph Kramer, Virginia LeRoy, Lister Markham, Mary Meekins, Zack Owens, Margaret Sawyer, Wesley Sheep, Mary Louise Spence, and Vivian Turner. "Miss Adelaide Dunstan, sister of the host, assisted in entertaining."

Two days later Adelaide mourns the tragic loss of one of her friends, a boy named Aydlett, whose younger sister had attended Edward's birthday party. On Tuesday, December 15, the

Advance describes the heartbreaking death of twelve-year-old Aydlett, son of prominent parents residing on East Church Street. He awoke Saturday morning as "a vigorous, whole-souled [enthusiastic], healthy boy," but by "evening his young form lay still in death. The accident took place Saturday afternoon" when another boy, Leslie, one of Aydlett's dearest friends, visited him, and the two chums decided to enjoy a leisurely tub bath together. Meanwhile the family cook's son, described as "a Negro boy," came to the house to see his mother. He passed by the bathroom door and "heard labored breathing inside. He told his mother [the cook] of what he had heard, and she went at once to the room where she found both boys unconscious and she thought both dead."

Three summoned physicians revived Leslie but not Aydlett, who "had fallen forward, and his face was submerged in the water. Leslie's feet rested against Aydlett's back, and . . . this may have prevented [him from] . . . slipping down into the water. The cook says that when she entered the room the gas was burning both at the heater and at the hot water tank. It is supposed that asphyxiation was due to the fact that oxygen in the small room was depleted and became supercharged with carbon dioxide. . . ." The revived "Leslie . . . says that he heard the colored boy come to the house but was unable to speak or move. He was in the midst of his bath he says when lethargy overcame him. The tragedy has cast a gloom over the entire community. . . .

"The funeral was attended by a large crowd, and the body was laid to rest in the Episcopal cemetery. A number of the dead boy's playmates acted as pallbearers." News of Aydlett's death ripples far from Elizabeth City and sparks an unusual sequel (covered in volume 5) to the notable Nell Cropsey tragedy.

Childhood Pleasures, Successes, and Tribulations. Emma seldom wakes Edward from his morning slumber on Saturdays or during his summer vacations. He sleeps as late as he pleases, enjoys a hearty breakfast, and heads outside during fair weather to ride horseback, play baseball, lie in the grass, study clouds, draw pictures, read books, daydream, or seek other amusements in an era of robust childhood freedom.

Edward has succeeded quite well under the excellence guidance of Miss Susie, and he progresses, in September 1915, to the second grade. The *Advance* announces on October 29 that he has made the honor roll "for the first month" of the new school term. The coming years see his name in the newspaper frequently as an honor student. During the same period Edward gains public recognition also for his writing skills, as exemplified by the following clipped and undated newspaper announcement: "The prize for the best letter [entered] in the *Advance* 'Best Advertiser' contest goes to W. E. Dunstan, Jr., by decree of a capable judge . . . who did not know the names of the contestants and . . . could hardly be prejudiced in the matter in any respect. The *Advance* congratulates young Dunstan and is mailing him [a] check [for five dollars] today."

December 1915 finds seven-year-old Edward dispatching a letter to Santa Claus. He asks for a bicycle and toolbox and then adds a request to "bring my little brother [nineteen-month-old Forrest] some toys and an orange [and] an apple. . . ." He ensures that Santa will know where to deliver this bounty by writing "From Elizabeth City" at the bottom of the page. About the same time he pens a choppy letter to an unnamed friend: "I am now reading a new book. It has [Jack and the Bean Stalk and other] tales . . . and I like it. . . . Forrest has gone to bed early, and we [twelve-year-old Adelaide and I] can study. You know how Adelaide used to worry you. It is very cold today but I have a heavy overcoat and don't mind. . . . A mouse ran down the back of my overcoat last night!"

During this period Edward wins an additional honor, no doubt with some modest help from home. A clipped and undated *Advance* article reports his achievement: "Prize winners have been announced for the five best answers to the question, 'Why eight of the most prominent business men of Elizabeth City and Edenton have within the last four months paid [a combined total of] $17,700 in cash for New Series Studebaker cars.' [The date seems to be 1916, when New Series Studebakers begin gracing American byways.] The prize winners are: First prize, $10.00—William E. Dunstan, Jr. Second prize, $7.50—Roscoe Foreman, Jr. Third prize, $5.00—Edna Morrisette. . . . The prize winners should call at the Studebaker Show Room [opposite the Southern Hotel] for their awards. These prizes were offered by J. H. McMullan, Studebaker dealer. . . ." Each contestant has listed five answers to the posed question. Edward crafted the following responses: "1st—Their good sense prompted them to get the best car on the market for the price. 2nd—They knew the very name of Studebaker was a guarantee of both quality and service. 3rd—Also that it [the Studebaker] shows up and holds up; and is not lacking in any feature for comfort or pride. 4th—Each of them [the businessmen] coupled his judgment with other good judges who selected this car to swap their cash for. 5th—And because of the plain fact that J. H. McMullan, Jr., had chosen the Studebaker to handle (exclusively) over the other 'best cars' he could have obtained the agency for." Edward's last answer, perhaps suggested by buggy-driving Will, must have pleased the prize donor. Mr. McMullan assures the public that the three judges remained "ignorant of the author and made the award on a basis of merit."

Such noteworthy successes hardly mask the fact that Edward has been a difficult and demanding child. He often prefers the company of the Dunstan horses, pigeons, and other animals to people. Grandfather yields when little Edward's insists on possessing his own horse, christened Sir Galahad.

Edward must have experienced shock and sadness to hear a report in the *Advance*, on May 12, 1916, about an unfortunate horse in the nearby village of Shawboro. Known for being "much afraid of automobiles," the horse had been tied to a roadside hitching post. The animal became unnerved when "two automobiles bore down on him from opposite directions. The horse stood trembling while the machines passed him . . . and a moment later dropped [dead from] . . . fright." Ten months later, on March 17, the newspaper tells the story of a local horse becoming terrified by a passing automobile and then "rearing and plunging and backing" until "the buggy, its occupants, and the horse" fall from a bridge into the water, though the driver of the motor vehicle quickly rescues all involved.

If Edward reads the newspaper on October 11, 1916, he probably sees a large display advertisement promoting the "wonders of modern Gas Lighting," described as "satisfying . . . cheerful . . . beautiful," though the vast majority of people in his circle illuminate their homes with electric lamps rather than antiquated gas fixtures. Moreover, gas lighting fixtures can pose a grave danger to humans and pets. Some people have mistakenly viewed them as essentially similar to oil lamps or candles and thus blown them out rather than shutting them off, to deadly effect!

Edward retains lifelong memories of two widely discussed events of November. The first occurs on Friday, November 10, and starts with a colorful parade led by Colonel William Frederick Cody, known as Buffalo Bill, who has captured the national spotlight for his exploits, partly legendary and partly fabricated, as a rider for the Pony Express, scout, soldier, Indian fighter, bison hunter, and later organizer of popular shows with cowboy themes. Newspaper readers learn that the parade will begin at ten o'clock in the morning, with Buffalo Bill in the saddle, and this great cavalcade will be followed by two rip-roaring Wild West shows. School has been canceled for the day. Edward and his friends reach a fever pitch of excitement over the extravaganza.

The *Advance* (just converted from a biweekly to a daily and rechristened the *Daily Advance* but affectionately known locally by its original shorter title) suggests on Thursday that activities at the railroad depot early Friday morning will attract a huge young throng: "The unloading of the show trains is one thing no normal boy can withstand." Boys will push and shove to see brightly "decorated Indians, cowboys, cowgirls, scouts, and old plainsmen, with a lively coloring of Russian Cossack, Arab, Japanese, and Mexican soldiers. . . ."

The afternoon and night shows will feature "Buffalo Bill himself, the famous scout and Indian fighter whose fame extends around the world." The following day the newspaper describes the "gallant Buffalo Bill" as "the ideal of the small boy" and on Saturday quotes the celebrated man's assessment of Elizabeth City: "'I have visited no place [of similar population] on my 180-day trip which looks so thoroughly progressive and prosperous. . . . [Yet] I'll be glad when my campaign is over,' laughed Colonel Cody. I have enjoyed the trip but I need a rest badly, and I shall be glad to get home once more.'" Buffalo Bill desperately needs a rest, for he dies surrounded by his family just two months later, on January 10, 1917, at the age of seventy.

Edward's second unforgettable memory from November 1916 springs from a fatal tragedy. On Wednesday, November 15, as reported that afternoon in the *Daily Advance*, an eighteen-year-old youth named Frank, a neighbor of the Dunstans, comes face to face with the Grim Reaper. According to the newspaper, Frank "was electrocuted this morning . . . while operating an electric milk shaker at the Standard Pharmacy [then flourishing on East Fearing Street but later closed]. . . ." In the meantime "another employee was shocked into unconsciousness a few seconds later when he rushed to the main switch and turned off the current from the entire building [by pulling a lever]. . . .

"For 20 seconds or more [a vastly amplified charge] . . . of electricity had hurtled through . . . [Frank's] body. Crossed [street] wires [dangling overhead just doors away greatly magnified the voltage entering the pharmacy] and . . . produce[d] the circumstances that cut short the life of a boy of brightest promise while he was engaged in the routine of his usual duties. He had taken an order for a milkshake" from a careless employee of the electric company, who had been informed of the crossed wires but decided to enjoy breakfast at the elegant fountain of the pharmacy before cutting off the electricity. Frank "turned on the current to mix the drink without mishap." He then "turned to his machine to switch off the current, [and] the customer who had ordered the drink heard a snap, a startled expression, and then saw Frank . . . crash to the floor where he lay entangled in the wiring of the dismantled machine, sparks flashing from his head and clothing and the pungent odor of burning hair filling the room [the newspaper has sanitized the physical horror]. . . ." The dreadful news flashes across the city, reaching the ears of Edward, and he shuns milkshakes from that day forward.

Two days later the newspaper laments the death of Frank, "whose untimely end on Wednesday cast a pall of sadness and a sense of tragedy and loss over the city. . . . The body . . . was laid to rest at noon today in Hollywood Cemetery after a simple but beautiful funeral service at the First Methodist Church," where "a sorrowful band of relatives and friends . . . gathered to witness the last sad rites over . . . one who but a few days ago [enjoyed] . . . the . . . vigor of perfect health. The casket was borne into the church by . . . [six] members of the boy's Sunday school class. . . . The other [five] members of the class acted as honorary pallbearers and followed the casket carrying the floral offerings. . . . Mrs. Wesley [Annie] Foreman rendered softly 'Beautiful Isle of Somewhere' [lyrics by Jessie B. Pounds (1861-1921)]. . . . After the invocation, the choir sang 'Asleep in Jesus' [lyrics by Margaret Mackay (1802-1887)]. Though hardly eighteen years old, Frank [had prospered in life as] . . . a boy of unusually attractive personality." His late father was "a well-known tailor in the city. He is survived by his mother . . ., three brothers . . ., three sisters . . ., and his [beloved, gentle] twin sister, Miss Elizabeth. . . ."

Another sad story arousing the horror of eleven-year-old Edward and his circle occurs on December 28, 1919, when relatives of a young lady of Pasquotank County find her "dead in her bed," according to a front-page article in the *Daily Advance* five days later. "There was no disturbance of the bed clothing. . . . The evidence was that she died in her sleep." The Pasquotank County Coroner, Dr. Isaiah (Ike) Fearing, gave her family "permission to proceed with the funeral without an autopsy. Later, Dr. Fearing changed his mind and ordered the body held for an inquest. His orders came after the funeral service had been held and the body was being moved to the grave. An [official] automobile dispatched from Elizabeth City Monday morning [December 29] headed the funeral cortege off and turned it back. Coroner Fearing found no trace of any drug or chemical that could have caused her death. Dr. Fearing removed her stomach, which he is holding for a chemical analysis. The . . . [delayed burial] was held Tuesday morning." Dr. Fearing had somersaulted into the national spotlight during the sensational Nell Cropsey murder case (discussed at length in volume 5) that generated lurid front-page headlines across the country from 1901 to 1903.

About this time young Edward, on thunder-hoofed horseback, occasionally crosses swords with a haughty member of the Board of Alderman, a neighbor, who demands absolute silence and obedience from children. On January 9, 1920, the rambunctious *Independent*, fierce competitor of the staid *Advance*, berates the "grouchy alderman" for having "filled the books with ordinances prohibiting children doing pretty much everything . . . play-loving children like to do." The man's narrow policies leave him "utterly unfitted to hold an office other than that of public executioner." These saucy sentiments must have given Edward a delicious taste of revenge.

Edward in High School and College. The year 1921 sees twelve-year-old Edward reach his freshman year of high school—the eighth grade—and he persuades buggy enthusiast Will to buy him a motorcar for launching a piston-powered future. Edward's plenty contrasts with the want of many undernourished and indigent school children whose impoverished parents possess bare cupboards and give their perpetually hungry offspring "tobacco and snuff" to curb their appetites, thus greatly undermining their growth and academic achievement, as reported by the *Advance* on December 12.

As noted, Edward causes no end of misery for his mother by bitterly criticizing most family meals, generally scrumptious affairs, while praising the fare served at the nearby home of Walter Cohoon, son of a notable attorney and apparently his one close friend. The *Spotlight*, the school annual, lists the few extracurricular activities he pursues during high school. Edward secures membership in the Literary Society, Athletic Association, and Glee Club.

Fortunately, he never joins (or fails to secure an invitation to join) the notorious Grand and Exalted Supreme Order of the F.F.F., brazenly occupying two full pages of the 1924 *Spotlight*. The meaning of the abbreviation F.F.F. pertains to the seduction of damsels and ranges from "Find 'em" to "Forget 'em," but the coarseness of the second F. does not belong in this book. With cigarettes dangling from their smirking lips, members of the club pose in the *Spotlight* sporting fine suits and neckties while reclining or lounging on the running board, fender, hood, roof, and front seat of a four-door sedan parked beside Elizabeth City High School. They brag of dedicating their lives to debauchery, including heavy gambling and imbibing immense quantities of moonshine whisky in Prohibition America, but the boys focus most attention on the seduction of desirable young ladies. In the annual they identify their favorite song as "The Little Brown Jug in the Woods" and rhapsodize about thinly veiled erotic activities. They add a tongue-in-cheek statement of moral purpose: "Our aim in life is to make the 'F.F.F.' a name to be remembered and revered by our descendants as one of the most moral and respected clubs in the State of North Carolina." Their unbridled bravado probably represents at least a degree of youthful exaggeration (additional information about these youthful seducers and their scandalous school club appears in volume 4).

No prude by any standard, Edward enjoys numerous social activities. One of my high school teachers, Mary Ludford Owens (1908-2013), once told me that Edward attended many dance parties on the porch of her house on Road Street. These pleasant evening affairs saw her roll out a large windup phonograph for music and serve lemonade and cookies for refreshments. Meanwhile Edward acquires his own musical skills, first on the violin, but he ceases to demonstrate artistry with the bow before reaching adulthood. Additionally, he plays an alto horn in the Elizabeth City Boys' Band, whose members sport magnificent gold-trimmed white uniforms and attract applause with their spirited tunes.

Edward gains his diploma from Elizabeth City High School in June 1925. The Class Prophecy, written by an anonymous student and recorded in the *Spotlight*, looks ahead to various radio programs available twenty-five years in the future. The prophet detects a familiar voice on one station: "Mr. Edward Dunstan, the famous veterinarian, delivered a short talk on 'The Care of Dumb Animals.' Mr. Dunstan told of his experiences with horses, which began at an early age, and of his faithful steed, Sir Galahad."

The oval photograph of handsome Edward in the yearbook shows him with his customary schoolboy suit and tie. An unnamed writer or editorial committee reveals his telling nickname, *Hunkie*, but discretely omits the fact that males of his generation usually call him *Stud*. The writer or writers then describe his unique characteristics: "There is only one thing definite we know about Edward—he likes to have his car full of pretty girls, otherwise he's hard to understand. He is Walter's chief sparring partner, and considering that they are such very good friends they have an unusual number of fights. Edward doesn't like to study, but had rather ride [fast on] horseback.

Indeed, he says the threes things he likes best are a horse, a nice car, and a pretty woman."

By the time he completes high school, sixteen-year-old Edward has become so consumed by a torrid love affair with a fourteen-year-old girl named Virgilia that Will and Emma pack his bags and send him to Guilford College for a summer of cooling down with college preparatory courses. He transfers in the fall to Fleetwood's alma mater, already renamed Duke University in gratitude for avalanches of money pouring onto campus from the deep pockets of the tobacco-rich Duke family. Few college students possess an automobile at the time, but Edward has successfully badgered Will for a second one. Thus he now owns a pair of the beauties, a sedan for inclement weather or ordinary driving and a roadster (an open motorcar seating two and having a folding fabric top) for sunny days and steamy romantic evenings. Grandfather follows the longstanding Dunstan practice of pacifying Edward by bowing to his endless demands.

The brothers of the local chapter of Sigma Chi welcome Edward and initiate him into their social fraternity. They boast in the March 1926 issue of the *Duke Sig* that they have attracted to their house "the brother of Fleetwood Dunstan," then establishing a distinguished record as a banker in New York City. The same publication carries a full-page photograph of Fleetwood, along with those of three other prominent alumni.

Edward enjoys his carefree days at Duke. His cosmetic and tantalizing charm attracts many naive young ladies of Durham. They dream of a princelike boy holding their hands and stealing gentle kisses in the shadows. Edward has different dreams. An avid reader with an astonishing memory, he regales them by liberally sprinkling his seductive remarks with quotations from the Bible and other literary masterpieces before escorting them to the nearest unoccupied bedroom.

Marriages and Births. While Edward pursues his collegiate education at Duke, the Dunstans in Elizabeth City not only celebrate several pieces of happy news but also suffer a number of grievous losses. The spring of 1925 sees Adelaide complete her college education at Greensboro College, a respected small school for ladies, where her cousin from Windsor, Rob

Dunstan, soon will begin a long teaching career in romance languages after earning his Ph.D. at the University of Wisconsin. Popular Adelaide inherits all the high spirits and hospitality of her Dunstan kin. She becomes a popular figure at Greensboro College and serves as society marshal her sophomore year, class treasurer her junior year, and class historian her senior year. The 1925 college yearbook, the *Echo*, publishes her class history, including warm sentiments about the magic and glory of school days: "Well do we remember the hours we spent together wandering near the little brook, which winds onward to the sea, and eventide when we strolled among the pines . . ., trusting our secrets to one another and looking forward to . . . [meditative] days . . . strolling with our memories. The winds of fortune will carry us far away and scatter us over the earth, but . . . we shall . . . be bound [together eternally by] . . . indissoluble ties of love . . . to our Alma Mater. . . ."

Not long after graduation, Adelaide meets tall, well-read Bascom Marvin Harrison, sixteen years her senior, who has pursued a career in the Army rather than follow his father into the Methodist clergy. Aunt Adelaide wins Marvin's love with her generous heart and fun-loving nature. In 1927 they celebrate their marriage with joyous dignity and then make their home in Raleigh, later in Fayetteville.

In the meantime Fleetwood writes many letters home telling of his professional progress and personal life. After completing college in 1919, he begins his banking career in Baltimore, at the historic Mercantile Trust and Deposit Company. Fleetwood meets an enthralling but fiery young lady of the city named Ada Anita Buckley. Anita kindles his heart with her undiplomatically candid but fascinating comments and her alluring brown-eyed, blond-haired beauty. She promptly mesmerizes and marries him before his customary reason directs his sail into calmer waters. The year 1921 sees Fleetwood and Anita move to New York City, where he joins the bond department of Bankers Trust Company. On December 27, 1926, Anita gives birth to their only child, Edmund Fleetwood Dunstan, Jr., known by the nickname Ted.

Three days later Will writes to Fleetwood: "The old year has about departed, but the world still stands fast. . . . We all enjoyed Christmas . . . and the usual amount of Santa Claus—followed by good news from you. . . . Thinking over the arrival at your home of Edmund F. Dunstan (III), it came into my mind to send you the picture of his grandsire and namesake, E.F.D. the first [Will remains unaware that his son intends to christen the newborn as Edmund Fleetwood, Jr., rather then Edmund Fleetwood Dunstan III]. My mother [Mary Louisa Vaughan Dunstan] kept this picture through all the ups and downs of her long life and gave it to me a few years before she died . . . . I am perfectly sure [you] will prize it and preserve it safely." Will adds that all the Dunstans in Elizabeth City are trying "to step into the new year with firm hand and high head—looking up to Him who giveth every good and perfect gift [from the Epistle for the Fourth Sunday after Easter in the Book of Common Prayer, Saint James 1:17: 'Every good gift and every perfect gift is from above, and cometh down from the Father of lights. . . .']."

Loss of Dr. Charles Sawyer. In 1927, the year Congress authorizes construction of the Wright Brothers National Memorial in eastern Dare County to commemorate the flight achievements of Wilbur and Orville Wright, Emma loses her revered uncle Dr. Charles W. Sawyer. Unmarried, he has served Elizabeth City for many years as a physician and surgeon, with an office on East Fearing Street near the Citizens Bank, where his late brother John Lloyd Sawyer once sat on the board of directors. Dr. Sawyer becomes known as a pathfinder during his early days as a physician. He remains ahead of his time over the years and equips his medical suite with one of the earliest telephones in Elizabeth City. The few patients possessing these instruments in 1902 reach him by asking the operator to connect them with number 159, as noted that year, on July 15, by the *Elizabeth City Tar Heel*. Some years later (according to my late cousin Charles LeRoy Miller), a masked bandit creeps silently up the flight of stairs to his office and robs him. Emma's uncle enjoys mechanical skills and rigs up a hidden electrical switch under one of the steps to sound a bell in his office and warn of any intruder. No robber again invades his building. Dr. Sawyer's patients acquire medicinal drugs directly from him and avoid the greater expense of relying upon a pharmacy. He prepares drugs and stores them in large wicker-covered bottles and then transfers appropriate medicines into small bottles for the individuals under his medical care.

Additionally, Dr. Sawyer demonstrates entrepreneurial skills. In the early twentieth century he establishes on the sound side at Nags Head a flourishing resort hotel-boardinghouse providing lodging and meals for one price, the Albemarle Cottage, erected on supporting piers over the Roanoke Sound. Guests often fish directly from the spacious wraparound porches of the comfortable twenty-four-room hotel. Dr. Sawyer frequently sails from Elizabeth City not only to review the efficiency of his hotel staff but also to enjoy a short vacation. The *Daily Advance* reports on July 18, 1917, for instance, that "Dr. Chas. Sawyer arrived [at Nags Head] today to spend a few days at the Albemarle Cottage."

On the dry sand behind the Albemarle, Dr. Sawyer constructs the Pavilion, a large wooden building with numerous open, breeze-catching windows. The Pavilion immediately becomes the center for evening dancing and social life at Nags Head. Colorful hanging lanterns cast soft illumination, while orchestras and bands provide dance music, though a boy on the staff cranks a Victrola (trademark for a particular windup phonograph) whenever musicians prove unavailable.

Dancers ignore summer heat and arrive in prerequisite finery, with ladies in long dresses and gentlemen in suits and neckties. The local historian Edward R. Outlaw, Jr., in his *Old Nags Head*, pages 54-55, describes throngs crowding the airy Pavilion to enjoy both dancing and "bootleg liquor" during the disastrous Prohibition era seeing millions of Americans becoming lawbreakers overnight. Local officials value this influx of money and ignore the rash implementation, in 1920, of the Eighteenth Amendment, prohibiting the manufacture and sale of alcoholic beverages. Countless ordinary people deeply resent Prohibition, while members of the educated urban elite virtually ignore this so-called "noble experiment" resulting from a shrill antidrinking crusade mounted by conservatives.

The *Daily Advance* carries Dr. Charles W. Sawyer's front-page obituary on Monday, December 19, 1927, and reports that the seventy-year-old physician died in his medical office of a heart attack the previous evening. On December 23 the popular rival newspaper, the *Independent*, features a long article about his generous bequests. "In his will, made in 1923, Dr. C. W. Sawyer of this city . . . set aside a trust fund of $4,000 . . . for the education of four boys and girls [of modest means]." After listing his openhanded bequests "to numerous kin," the unnamed writer adds that Dr. Sawyer "bequeathed $1.00 each" to Prosser and Cliff Sawyer. Everyone knows the meaning of these meager gifts. He has acted to protect his estate from the possibility of a lawsuit by acknowledging the existence of two disappointing nephews, younger brothers of Emma, with token bequests signifying his displeasure with the path of their lives.

  The newspaper then provides the reading public with additional information about Dr. Sawyer. "Not less than $500 he wills to be spent on a monument to his memory, and he left his watch and chain and other jewelry to [the attorney] J. B. [Boush] Leigh of this city. . . . To [a widow living on the ground floor of his office building] . . . he bequeathed a legacy of $12 a month to be paid to her as long as she lives. His property consists of numerous pieces of real estate and . . . [many] stocks and bonds." His handsome upright monument in Hollywood Cemetery bears the simple epithet "He Lived for Others."

  Lamentation for Will. The Dunstans suffer a crushing financial blow about this time over a recently enacted sanitary privy measure stipulating that city dwellings must have running water and indoor toilets. Many local addresses still maintain a privy, known also as an outhouse, a small structure covering a pit toilet. The State Board of Health mails Will a typed list of more than one hundred of his houses requiring connection to water and sewer lines. He reels with dismay over the monumental task and expense of installing numerous items such as pipes, drains, sinks, basins, and flush toilets to fulfill his legal obligations. He proceeds as economically as possible by enclosing a small space on the back porch of each house for a cramped bathroom. Tenants can enter one of these new facilities only from the porch after exiting the house. As the taxing project advances, Grandfather's health gradually declines. The family expresses grave anxiety when he showed signs of faltering physically, yet seventy-four-year-old

Will keeps personal problems to himself and refrains from burdening others with complaints.

Will enjoys a sumptuous dinner on Saturday, May 19, 1928. Perhaps the meal sees the Dunstan family discuss a strange newspaper article about a foot-powered aircraft recently unveiled in Florida. The Saturday issue of the *Daily Advance* highlights the failure-inviting machine under the riveting headline "Flyer to Take Air in Plane that Flaps Wings like Bird."

Will leaves the table in high spirits but suffers a severe attack about nine o'clock, and he lingers until half past six the following morning. Emma immediately relays the devastating news to Fleetwood, who must have blinked back tears while hurriedly typing a personal tribute to Will:

"My father died today. No one ever had a more wonderful father. His influence on my life has been immeasurably good. Anything in me that may be mean, selfish, unkind or even inconsiderate is there in spite of him. Such things were not part of his make-up. He had that cheerful philosophy of life which ever looked on the bright side of things. As he was human, of course, he must have had his dark moments, but no one ever knew when they were. He pushed them aside. His disposition was to be happy . . . always. Unconsciously, I think, he was a teacher; and in his own way he impressed those about him to look for the light.

"I never knew of him doing anyone an unkindness. In fact he loved all people and thoroughly enjoyed doing for them. He never asked anything for himself. He was the most unselfish man I ever knew. No doubt few men have . . . had such self-mastery in submerging personal preferences when others were concerned. His love for people and companionship was more than usual.

"He was proud too. Proud of his name and his heritage. He walked erect with a high head and ready smile—and carried on.

"He was a man in every sense of the word. Physically he was a model, strong and courageous. His mind was active and forceful. A profound believer in the Bible and a respecter of . . . things good for the soul, he could not be called narrow. His was the broadest outlook on life.

"As a boy, I did not look around for an athlete of the moment or some prominent statesman as a hero. I had mine at home: William Edward Dunstan, Feb. 9 (1854)-May 20 (1928)."

On Monday, May 21, the *Daily Advance* publishes a front-page obituary under a long eulogistic headline: "Wm. E. Dunstan Dies Suddenly at End of Day—Well-Known Businessman and One of Community's Best Citizens Will be Buried this Afternoon—Began Work Early, [Active Professionally] from Time He was 16 until Death Came at Age of 74. . . ." The unnamed writer, surely publisher-editor Herbert Peele, continues the lengthy warm obituary, quoted below in part: "William Edward Dunstan, Sr., aged 74, died at his home here Sunday morning at 6:30 o'clock, following an attack of acute indigestion. Mr. Dunstan was about his business on Saturday, coming in from the day's work in his usual bright frame of mind about six o'clock. About nine o'clock he was seized with the attack of acute indigestion from which he could not rally. . . .

"He began work at the age of 16 [having already earned a Master of Accounting degree from Eastman College, Poughkeepsie, New York] and was very active and industrious in business throughout his life. . . . Mr. Dunstan has been quite successful in the real estate business in Elizabeth City. In 1895 Mr. Dunstan was married to Miss Emma Sawyer, a daughter of John L. Sawyer of this city.

"Mr. Dunstan was a fine . . . citizen. He loved Elizabeth City, always showing keen interest in every forward step and in every movement for good. . . . In spite of his unusually active life, Mr. Dunstan found time for some writing and often sent in communications to the *Daily Advance* on questions of public interest. He showed a keen interest in business enterprises . . . of significant importance to the city, to which he was so much devoted. . . ."

Later in the week the *Independent*, known for quirky candor, issues a front-page obituary under the striking headline "Broke at Forty, Made Fortune by Plugging." The commentary begins: "William E. Dunstan borrowed $10 for railroad fare from a nephew in Washington, D.C., 36 years ago and came to Elizabeth City with all his worldly goods in a very ordinary little handbag.

His clothes were a bit shabby and he bought a new suit of clothes upon arrival here, on a charge account.

"Wm. E. Dunstan died at his home in Elizabeth City Sunday morning, May 20, leaving an estate worth more than $100,000. Before coming to Elizabeth City in 1892 he had failed in the real estate business in Roanoke, Va. He was then a man of 36 or 38 years. He never told his age. But in middle age he was down and almost out. He came to Elizabeth City to take a job as book-keeper and manager of the Crystal Ice & Coal Co., which was a very small and unsatisfactory local enterprise in those days. He was manager of the ice plant until 1914 [should read early 1915]," and he built the company into a substantial operation.

"By industry and thrift and by a fortunate marriage to a remarkable woman, who was Miss Emma L. [should read C.] Sawyer, a daughter of the late John L. Sawyer, Wm. E. Dunstan prospered. He invested his savings in . . . [real estate]. He said that his ambition was to own 100 houses and lots and have an income from the rentals. He realized his ambition nearly 10 years ago and then said to a friend: 'I thought I would be satisfied when I owned a hundred houses: I own my hundred houses now and yet I keep right on buying more houses.' At the time of his death Mr. and Mrs. Dunstan owned nearly 200 separate pieces of property in Elizabeth City.

"Wm. E. Dunstan was a familiar figure on the streets of Elizabeth City, riding around in his horse-drawn buggy every Monday collecting rents. He never bothered about owning or driving an automobile; he lived simply and leisurely and lived long. He might have lived longer, but he ate too heartily last Saturday and became ill with acute indigestion Saturday night. He died early Sunday morning.

"Wm. E. Dunstan was a good husband, a good father, a good neighbor, a good citizen; patriotic, religious-minded, upright and conservative [about investing and saving]. Down and all but out at 40, he was content to come back by patience, industry, and thrift; conserving his income, investing cautiously, building slowly but steadily, he became wealthy, as wealth goes in a small town.

"He is survived by Mrs. Dunstan and a family of five children: they are E. Fleetwood Dunstan, manager of the bond department of Bankers Trust Co., of New York City; Mrs. B. M. [Marvin] Harrison, of Raleigh; Edward Dunstan, Jr., a student at Duke University; and For[r]est and Garland Dunstan of this city. Wm. Edward Dunstan was a native of Murfreesboro, Hertford County, N.C."

The same issue of the *Independent* carries an article describing Grandfather's funeral at home and burial in Hollywood Cemetery: "William Edward Dunstan, long an active figure in the business, social and religious life of the city, who died suddenly Sunday morning, were conducted Monday afternoon at the residence on West Church Street," where "special music by a quartet" drifted over "exceptionally numerous and beautiful" floral arrangements. Burial follows in the linden-shaded Dunstan plot, marked by a handsome granite monument, in Hollywood Cemetery. Grandfather begins his eternal slumber beside his beloved little ones, John Lloyd and Mary Virginia, who had departed this life more than twenty-five years earlier.

The newspaper catches the eye also with the headline "A Whimsical Will Made by W. E. Dunstan" and then provides readers with more information about Grandfather. "One of the simplest and most unusual wills ever recorded in this county was that of Wm. E. Dunstan, deceased, probated in the office of Clerk of the Court of Pasquotank County, Wednesday, May 23rd. Here is the will [dated April 29, 1925]: 'I am feeling about as well as usual today, but I may be gone in a few days. My old friends are going fast. [The senior] Noah Burfoot [prominent wholesale grocer] died suddenly last night—about my age I think. I am not scared, for I believe I am prepared. But before it happens I want to record in my own handwriting that, what estate I leave, real and personal, I wish to devise and bequeath to my wife, Emma Sawyer Dunstan, having full confidence in her judgment of managing same for her own welfare and that of our children; doing also as much good for the world as her income will afford. And may the God of Peace and Love guide and direct her.'

"The will was in the handwriting of the testator [person leaving a will] and on a single sheet of his business stationery. It was found by his son Fleetwood Dunstan among some private papers in a trunk after the death of the deceased. . . . There were no witnesses to the document, but in North Carolina law no witness is necessary to a will confined to the handwriting of the testator: it is only necessary to prove the handwriting by competent witnesses, which was easily done in this case."

Grandfather leaves behind numerous newspaper clippings of articles and poems from his own pen, albeit never recording the specific publication or the date. One short newspaper notice urges readers: "If you failed to read Mr. W. E. Dunstan's poem yesterday, gat a copy of the paper and do so."

As Edward Advances from Duke to Harvard to Wall Street, Fleetwood Counsels Emma. Grandfather's death presses the Dunstans into numb grief. Whenever the children reunite for the rest of their lives they spend happy moments retelling precious memories of Papa. They reminisce about his cheerful disposition, polished mind, and Chesterfieldian manner. Even troubled Edward realizes that Will's departure means the loss of unqualified love. Edward must have marshaled bright boyhood memories of Will carrying him on long buggy rides and offering him years of lofty counsel, falling oftentimes on deaf ears.

Edward returns to Duke after the funeral and earns his diploma on schedule, in the spring of 1929. As noted, he had pledged the social fraternity Sigma Chi as a freshman He played alto and French horns in the university band for four years, served as an associate editor and the sports editor of the student newspaper (the *Chronicle*), and gained membership in the commercial fraternity Psi Kappa Alpha.

For several years after leaving Duke at the age of twenty, Edward pursues the lofty goal of making a worthy name for himself and achieving professional success. He has dreamed of enrolling in one of the top postgraduate business schools in the United States and focuses his attention on a group of prestigious northeastern colleges soon termed the Ivy League. Edward applies to two leading programs, the Harvard Graduate School of Business Administration and the Wharton School at the University of Pennsylvania, and gains acceptance letters from each. He wrestles with his decision and finally chooses the former.

With a feeling of exhilaration, he enrolls as a postgraduate student at Harvard University and attends his first class on

Monday, September 23, 1929, the beginning of the academic year. Edward counts himself among the three students from Duke attending the postgraduate business program at Harvard. As a boy, I heard that he suffered much unhappiness living in the Sigma Chi Fraternity House, with the undergraduate brothers offering a cold shoulder to the slightly older and uninvited man possessing a fresh degree from an upstart Southern university. Edward spends much of his time alone in his room away from the hostile brothers, who take delight in teasing him about his Tidewater accent and his tendency to exaggerate his accomplishments.

He gains temporary relief whenever Fleetwood and Anita drive up from New York to attend Harvard football games. He cuts his program short, to one year rather than two, and settles on a Certificate in Business Administration. His decision stems partly from his wrenching unhappiness but chiefly from the cascading economic decline plaguing the country within days of his enrollment at Harvard. After the New York Stock Exchange crashes in October 1929, the Great Depression pushes industry and banking into a tailspin. Business owners slash the salaries of workers. Countless businesses and individuals face bankruptcy, while every town and city sees companies and banks closing and citizens facing destitution.

Meanwhile Fleetwood pens many letters to Emma, assuring her his banking position remains secure, for Bankers Trust Company, though facing lean times, will stand firm in the economic storm. Her worry about Fleetwood intensifies on December 20, 1930, the so-called "Black Friday in Elizabeth City," when frightened customers find posted on the locked doors of the Savings Bank & Trust Company a notice stating that many heavy withdrawals have forced the bank to close for the protection of patrons and depositors.

Fleetwood tries to sooth Emma's concerns about his career in a letter dated October 29, 1931. "I am a senior officer of one the world's best banks—my salary remains the same, although I think everybody will get a cut by the first of the year. . . ." He then pleasantly switches to thank his mother for three antique chairs, one now reupholstered in "henna silk," the other in "gold silk. . . . You have certainly helped us to have a nice home with all your gifts. I like them better than anything we have."

Fleetwood, Anita, and Ted frequently head to Elizabeth City, either by catching a southbound train or by motoring in their handsome Packard sedan, for a visit with Emma and young Forrest and Garland. Photographs showing Fleetwood with Forrest and Garland seem to capture the kindled joy whenever the three brothers reunite at the family home. In contrast to the strong photographic and documentary presence of Fleetwood and his family, no family album contains a photograph of Edward taken at the Dunstan dwelling after his high school graduation. No known letter to his mother survives.

Edward virtually ignores Emma but maintains communication with Fleetwood. With Fleetwood's help, Edward gains a position, in 1930, at a municipal bond house on Wall Street. Late the following year Fleetwood and Edward motor far from the city into the countryside. Fleetwood preserves a record of the excursion with his camera. The brothers stand near Fleetwood's Packard on an unpaved scenic road, beautifully flanked by white birch sentinels. Each man wears a handsome derby, double-breasted wool overcoat, silk scarf, tailored suite and necktie, and leather shoes. The aura of success and prosperity can hardly mask the simple truth that Edward has arrived in New York at the worst possible time to establish substantial roots in the fields of banking or finance.

On November 9, 1932, Fleetwood pens thanks to Emma for sending word that the *Daily Advance* has featured a glowing article about him, and he promises to mail her an upcoming favorable piece about him scheduled for publication in the *American Business World.* He lists the various stocks he has purchased on her behalf, including shares of Pennsylvania Railroad Company and American Telephone and Telegraph, but cautions his mother against increasing her portfolio further at the present time because "business conditions are too unsettled." Fleetwood then turns to family matters. "I am ashamed to say that I haven't written to Forrest [then a sophomore at Duke] this fall. . . . I have nothing to report on Edward. We see him only once in a while. I believe he has had another salary cut along with everyone else in his organization." Fleetwood expresses concern about a previously wealthy friend who has been stripped of "almost all he had" by the ravages of the Depression and then closes with an expression of "love to you and Garland."

Fleetwood conveys a rare tone of urgency when writing to Emma on February 25, 1933. "The banking situation all over the country seems to be getting worse. The purpose of this note, therefore, is to caution you again against having very much money on deposit with the First & Citizens [National Bank]. I certainly would not keep over $100 with them—$50 should be enough. Keep your cash in the safe deposit box. . . . If you have too much on deposit with the bank, I suggest that you take it out Monday. Today, the state of Maryland has closed every bank in the state until Wednesday. No one knows on what basis the banks with open then. . . . During these [difficult] times it is best to have the cash or United States Government bonds. . . ."

Fleetwood then expresses much concern over news that Forrest has become stricken with an odd debilitating illness in college. "He is too fine a boy to have any serious trouble. I am especially fond of him and want only good to come to him. Perhaps worry over examinations pulled him down, and he will be OK again quickly. In the meantime, we send him our hopes for speedy recovery and our love. All of us, including Edward, keep well. I trust you and Garland are in good health."

Meanwhile Forrest bravely faces his strange, taxing illness, made even more exhausting when coupled with the rigors of college studies, but regains his full stamina after spending the following summer in the invigorating mountain air of Lake Junaluska, near Asheville. In the spring of 1935 he will leave Durham with his fresh diploma and yearbook, the *Chanticleer*, bedeviled that year with numerous illustrations showing smoke rising from pipes, cigars, and cigarettes held by privileged people, gripping images applauding the "Romance of Tobacco" and cheering the source of Duke's great wealth, "Tobaccoland," bankrolling splashy new campus spires and arches.

W. O. Saunders Sprinkles the Independent *with Sensational Stories.* In January 1933, a month before Fleetwood warns Emma of the dire banking vulnerability extending from Elizabeth City to the last corner of the nation, the *Independent* runs several articles of considerable local interest. The reading public looks forward to the engaging editorials and articles in this weekly, published by the fearless W. O. Saunders, who employs his stinging, witty pen not only to advocate regional development but also to expose corrupt politicians, dishonest merchants, unprincipled citizens, hypocritical moralists, and two-faced churchgoers. His remarks often enrage the die-hard members of the ruling class, who prefer the views expressed in the straitlaced, conservative *Daily Advance*, but most people—whether openly or secretly—eagerly await the *Independent*. W.O. Saunders attracts national attention with his unique editorials but suffers prosecution for liable more than fifty times and endures repeated threats on his life and limb.

January 20, 1933, sees him publish a photograph of a new attorney and a brief accompanying commentary on the front page: "Most recent addition to the overcrowded local bar is Frank Meekins, nephew of Judge I. M. Meekins of this city. . . . Frank is young, single and nice-looking, which should interest the local girls."

Frank's uncle, Isaac Melson Meekins, had served as a member of the State Republican Executive Committee, from 1900 to 1918, and later President Calvin Coolidge appoints him Federal Court judge of the Eastern District of North Carolina. As one of the leading Republicans of the region, Judge Meekins acts as host to William Howard Taft (president of the United States from 1909 to 1913), whose travels take him through Elizabeth City after he leaves office. Decades later, on February 14, 1945, the *Daily Advance* recalls when "Mr. Taft was the houseguest of the Meekins at their home here."

The judge and his family live in a lavish Neo-Classical Revival house, complete with a monumental columned porch and suburb stained glass windows, at 212 (later renumbered 310) West Main Street. His esteemed wife, Lena Allen Meekins, spends many hours overseeing the necessary silver polishing, furniture dusting, carpet beating, and lawn manicuring in preparation for their exalted visitor. She plans an elaborate dinner to satisfy President Taft's well-known hearty appetite. When the ample-figured former president arrives, the Meekins family entertains him with lighthearted conversation and sumptuous fare. Perhaps Lena, a gifted musician, plays the piano or organ for him and also lifts her magnificent voice in song. In due course the former president retires to the guest room for the evening and departs early the next morning with warm words of thanks for the kind hospitality.

Lena then enters the guest room and discovers to her mortification that, despite all her minute preparations for the visit, she has neglected to provide the presidential bed with sheets or pillowcases. Her esteemed guest has slept upon unshielded ticking, the tightly woven and rough cotton material then generally used for pillow and mattress coverings. For decades people in Elizabeth City erupt in gales of laughter over the story that President Taft had slept, or at least spent the night, upon a naked mattress and pillow.

Besides calling attention to the arrival in the city of young attorney Frank Meekins, the same issue of the 1933 *Independent* carries two grim stories bringing home the horrible toll of the Depression. First, the preeminent hotel of Elizabeth City, the Virginia Dare, has plunged "hopelessly in debt" with obligations of around $236,000. Recently, the directors of the Virginia Dare assembled with stockholders and revealed to them the distressing financial burden, and they handed each of them "five-cent cigars, which some regarded as the first dividend on their stock. Those [stockholders] who don't smoke and those who were absent didn't even get a cigar."

Second, the newspaper reminds readers that two banks in Elizabeth City had closed in 1929, each falling "in the hands of a liquidation agent," leaving only the First & Citizens National Bank in operation. Local residents have witnessed an "amazing shrinkage of bank deposits," exceeding $3,300,000, from January 1, 1929, to January 1, 1933. The sole surviving bank, the First & Citizens National, has lost more than $1,250,000 in deposits. Thus this "region has grown poorer at a rate of more than a million dollars a year for the past three years. . . . And the plight of Elizabeth City is but the plight of America and the world. Unless there is a stabilization of [American] business and an upward turn, our every dollar will have been exhausted by Jan. 1, 1935. We would have no bank deposits and no bank; and every thrifty citizen who tried to hold out [protect] something would be the prey of mobs driven to desperation by hunger, cold and panic." The alarming article ends with a glimmer of hope, reminding readers that the darkest days of history always end with "a new deal for mankind and a new and better era."

In the meantime Edward has left his position as a municipal bond specialist on Wall Street to accept an attractive offer from Bradstreet's, a notable establishment providing commercial credit ratings. Subscribing to the *Independent* and receiving his copies by mail, Edward becomes ruffled by the above article and responds in late January with a long letter to the publisher-editor. His remarks differ radically from the letter Fleetwood will send Emma a month later, urging her to transfer most of her money from her bank account to her safe deposit box immediately.

Edward's piece, when published on February 3, 1933, attracts considerable attention not only for attacking the *Independent* with the comment "that the 'pen is more destructive than the sword,' to paraphrase an old saying [by the seventeenth-century English pamphleteer John Taylor]" but also for suggesting that the spawning of "fear is causing more hardship today than economic conditions warrant. . . ."

Edward identifies several reasons for the downward spiral in banking assets throughout the country, including the "withdrawal of bank deposits. . . ." He quotes several paragraphs from Lord Thomas Babington Macaulay's essay "Southey's Colloquies on Society," published in the *Edinburgh Review*, January 1830, with the celebrated English writer and Whig political leader asking: "'On what principle is it that, when we see nothing but improvement behind us, we are to expect nothing but deterioration before us?'" Edward shares with readers the assessment of an unnamed banker in his New York circle that "few small town banks make as good a showing as the First [& Citizens] National of Elizabeth City," and thus depositors should express "no fear in keeping . . . [their] cash funds there." Edward closes by directly addressing the editor: "So, Mr. Saunders, I firmly believe your article too pessimistic. Wise planning today will be repaid handsomely in the years ahead."

February 7 sees the president of the bank, William G. Gaither, dashing off a grateful letter addressed to W. E. Dunstan, 415 Riverside Drive, New York City, offering complements on "keeping close contact with things back home." He adds, "I congratulate you on the able and interesting way in which you have handled your subject [in the *Independent*] and assure you that I appreciate your taking the time and trouble to bring out the other side...." Several weeks later Mr. Gaither hears of Edward being caught in the same financial inferno he has pooh-poohed as a temporary hardship.

5

Edward Retreats from Wall Street and Wrestles with the *Independent*

Franklin D. Roosevelt takes the oath of office as president on March 4, 1933, and launches his promised New Deal for the American people. The monumental wreckage of the Great Depression has reduced countless once-prosperous workers and businessmen to selling apples or shining shoes on street corners. Endowed with buoyant charm, President Roosevelt soothes the crisis of confidence in the shattered banking and business system by preaching his "firm belief that the only thing we have to fear is fear itself—nameless, unreasoning, unjustified terror which paralyzes needed efforts to convert retreat into advance." His New Deal leaves the essential capitalistic structure of the United States intact but nimbly focuses on protecting workers, farmers, consumers, small-scale business owners, and the jobless, not merely large corporations.

Meanwhile the worldwide economic downturn costs Edward his position with Bradstreet's (compelled by dire financial circumstances into a merger with its arch competitor under the combined name Dun and Bradstreet's). He returns to Elizabeth City and makes his home with Emma and young brother Garland, a proud senior in high school. Garland and his fellow seniors will graduate after completing the eleventh grade, then the final year of school. Edward and his mother have never been close, but she generously employs him to manage her extensive real estate holdings.

Juicy Morsels in the Independent. After three years of sampling the multifaceted reading fare in the *New York Times* and the *Wall Street Journal*, Edward has difficulty readjusting to a steady diet of the *Independent* and the *Daily Advance*. The hell-raising *Independent* has been regaling readers with its characteristic juicy morsels gathered by Keith Saunders, the young junior editor and son of the senior editor, and reported in his column "Heard and Seen on Main Street." Keith Saunders' colorful remarks attract numerous subscribers and divert troubled minds from the calamities of the Great Depression. On January 27, 1933, he asks, "Did you hear about the high school boy who got tight and used the sidewalk in front of the New Southern Hotel for a urinarium [reservoir from which urine drains from a stable for fertilizing fields]? He was given a 10-day jail sentence, which was suspended upon condition of good behavior for a year."

On February 24, Keith alerts readers that "a well-known young man who has been married less than two years" has become "infatuated with a sweet young thing of about sixteen summers. . . . This fellow usually consorts with the girl on the . . . mezzanine and balcony [of the Carolina Theatre]. Some of the boys in the girl's 'crowd' are making life miserable for the young married man by telling him they are going to expose him. He'll probably boil with anger when he reads this."

Keith adds another tidbit in the same column: "Two high school boys, sons of . . . prominent families, went up on the roof of the school building on the night of a recent basketball game and peeked into the girls' dressing room thru the skylight. The skylight, of course, was of opaque glass, but the boys had removed one of the panes. They were caught, however, and narrowly escaped being expelled from school. And one of them had to plead hard to keep from being made to turn in his basketball uniform, I am told." On March 3 the newspaper adds: "The two young men, scions of leading families, who were caught peeping . . . were by no means the only boys who have been guilty of this rather ordinary practice. I understand that this has been going on for two or three years, and that a good many of the high school boys have participated."

Keith splashes the same issue of the *Independent* with another surprise: "Down at the Aydlett Products Co., on Poindexter Street, works a boy who has rather long blonde hair and who looks very much like a girl. Some Camden [village just east of Elizabeth City and serving as the county seat of Camden County] boys came to town the other night, dressed this boy up in a girl's clothes, and took him over to Camden with them. They had previously told some of their friends that they knew a 'hot' girl in town and that they were going to take this girl to ride that night. Stopping at a filling station at the crossroads [of Camden], they introduced the 'girl' to several of the boys. One young man, the son of a Camden county official, called one of the boys aside and begged him to let him take the 'girl' for a short ride. The request was granted and the young man stayed off with the 'girl' for quite a while. After he returned to the filing station, a garage mechanic got into the car. This fellow had always boasted of his power over the opposite sex. He thought himself quite a Romeo. Taking the 'girl's' hand, he lost no time in drawing 'her' to him and kissing 'her' passionately. He hugged and kissed the 'girl' quite a few times until the boys who had carried 'her' over to Camden said they had to bring 'her' back to town. It was not until two days later, when some of the boys told them of the joke that had been played upon them, that the two self-satisfied Romeos knew they had been 'necking' a boy."

One of the most widely discussed articles in the *Independent* appears in 1933 under the striking headline "When a White Woman is Below a Black Man." In the year 1933 Southerners of all complexions customarily speak of Caucasians as white people and of Negroes as colored people, though the *Independent* occasionally refers to Negroes as black people. Many Elizabeth Citians of the time regard the term black as insulting but regard the terms colored (informal) and Negro (formal) as polite. The bold newspaper article, dated February 24, reports that the "Recorder's courtroom on the third floor of the Carolina Building was filled to overflowing and the corridor outside the courtroom, as well as the sidewalk in front of the building, were thronged with persons, mainly Negroes, who [were] morbidly curious to see a white woman who had consorted with one of their kind. . . ."

According to the newspaper, the chief of police had gone to a vacant house on Harney Street "to investigate a black-and-white prostitution case." The chief apprehended "a colored man" leaving by the back door of the house and discovered "a white woman" inside, "with her coat and shoes off and her dress torn around the breast. He placed the white woman and colored man under arrest, charging them with prostitution." He recalled that the same woman "was found stark naked roaming around in a colored residential section of the city abut two years ago" and afterward "banished from the county for a year as a result. On that first occasion, the officers had quite a time getting the woman into the patrol car because of her weight and fighting disposition. She proved almost equally retractable this week. Several Negro men of the neighborhood had to be deputized to assist in getting her to police headquarters, and even then she managed to implant a few hard kicks on different parts of the chief's anatomy."

The judge, finding the charged pair guilty, rules that the woman bears greater criminality "in a prostitution case involving a white woman and a colored man" and then imposes his sentence, with "the woman to serve 18 months in the county jail, and the man to serve 12 months." The judge also delivers "a sort of oration," deploring the presence of such "moral putridity" in Elizabeth City. The newspaper adds that fortune has shined on the man because this region "is not inclined toward mob violence. Had a colored man been caught consorting with a white woman in some sections of the country, the result might have been horrible." Everyone knows the writer alludes to lynching.

The *Independent* often reports on the activities of bootleggers in Prohibition-era Elizabeth City and vicinity. On March 24, Keith Saunders employees his column to quote a crewmember of a yacht docked in the harbor for the past four months: "Elizabeth City is about the wettest little town I ever visited. . . . Look up the population figure and take about twenty-five per cent of that number" to calculate the number of bootleggers flourishing in the city.

W. O. Saunders realizes people savor articles about illegal activities, human frailties, sexual episodes, colorful events, and thought-provoking opinions. He showers them with an abundance of the material they crave. On June 2 the paper relates that self-styled "young communists" at Amherst College recently "burned a small American flag to 'show their internationalism,'" with three of them suffering injuries when other students broke up their meeting.

Seven days later Keith turns to a local matter. "They tell me a certain blonde lady-killer in the Southeast section of the city is having a hard time getting his father's car at night now. The father, they say, took the keys from the boy to keep him from courting a young lady about five years his senior," apparently regarding her as "a dangerous woman. From what I know of her, I hardly think she would corrupt the morals of this young man. Indeed, judging from reports, a young lady needs age and experience to resist this sheik's love-making."

Keith regales readers, on June 30, with a tale of martial infidelity. "The other night, a certain married lady . . . drove alone in her husband's car to a dark spot near the intersection of Road and Burgess Streets. She stopped alongside a parked car, in which sat a man who is married and who has a family. The man, her lover, then started his car and followed her as she drove [to a specified location]. . . . What then transpired is best left to the imagination."

On July 7 the newspaper comments on "new styles of bathing suits" seen at Kitty Hawk and Nags Head, reporting that females no longer "conceal anything more than their sex organs." Keith's column of August 25 elicits interest with a question: "And did you hear about the girl who had a date at nine o'clock the other night and went to ride with some other fellows earlier in the evening? When she reached her home, her date was sitting on the front porch waiting for her. Imagine the thoughts and feelings of all concerned when her panties dropped to her feet as she stepped out the car."

Keith ends his column of the 25th with an enigmatic sentence: "I now close the book." He completes this piece sometime before the publication date. Three days later the starchy rival newspaper, the *Daily Advance*, stuns readers by pointing out the meaning of the mysterious words—W.O. Saunders has received a letter written by Keith from New York City, grimly "announcing that he had decided to take his life. . . . Members of the family positively identified the handwriting as that of Keith and said that while his death had not been confirmed, it was feared that the threat would be carried out."

W. O Saunders bares his churning emotions in a lengthy editorial, dated September 1, 1933, informing readers of experiencing a "crushing blow . . . at the local post office when I opened a letter . . . from my son Keith, conveying the information that by the time I received his letter he would be a suicide."

Mr. Saunders then crosses paths in the post office with Judge Isaac M. Meekins, who invites the horrified father to his chambers. There the two men pore over the detailed account of Keith's "sorrows and his motives" and the "explicit directions for the disposition of his estate. Judge Meekins . . . [offers] hope that the boy, after having gotten his troubles off his chest, may have reconsidered. . . ." A recent severe storm downing telephone and telegraph lines between Elizabeth City and Norfolk makes normal electronic communications impossible, but "Judge Meekins . . . [motors] to Norfolk and attempt[s] to establish communication with New York from that source."

The judge returns to Elizabeth City with a telegram from Keith received at the Western Union office in Norfolk: "'Home tomorrow on Old Dominion [Steamship] Line. Will explain everything.'" His father reveals in the editorial that Keith, endowed with a sensitive nature, has become troubled by the "selfishness, sordidness, and hypocrisy" of humanity. Of far more importance, he has become distraught over an unrequited love with a "beautiful and highly intelligent girl" living in New York, "the daughter of an internationally famous man with cultural connection in London, Paris, Berlin, and Rome." Keith traveled to New York to bid her farewell before taking his life, but she locked him in a room until he relented. W. O. Saunders confesses, "I do not know what passed between him and the girl in that trying hour, but . . . the boy recovered and came home in exuberant spirits. . . ."

Keith speaks to readers through his column in the same issue of the newspaper. "Well, let's open the book again. Readers were probably puzzled when I ended my column last week with the words, 'I now close the book.' No other person knew it at the time, but I intended committing suicide and thought that would be the last appearance of my column. But here I am again, to the great disappointment of many," though "most of my acquaintances seemed very glad to see me alive and well. I deeply appreciate the kind words that so many have had for me. I realize now, more than ever, that it's great to be alive. . . . So here I am again. Hereafter, however, I probably will be a little more considerate of others."

On February 9, 1934, the *Independent* runs a large photograph of a seemingly naked woman standing on her hands, with her legs spread aloft in a provocative manner. A short description accompanies the illustration: "The Carolina Theatre stages a midnight show Thursday, Feb. 15, featuring 'Nudity in Gold.' They say the beauties won't have on a durn [variation of darn] thing but a coat of gold paint. There will be a [burlesque] fan dance too, just as the [risqué] sensation was staged at the [1933-1934] Chicago World's Fair. In fact, it is billed as a Chicago World's Fair outfit." Keith's column of February 16 estimates that "600 to 800 persons attended" on a bitterly cold night, "despite the fact that most of the crowd had to get up next morning to go to school or to work." He complains that anyone "could see far more nudity in a 25-cent 'art' magazine [featuring scantily clothed women] than in this show."

The same issue of the newspaper carries an unusual headline: "Black Cat Leaps from Coffin When Opened." The article relates that "mourning relatives and friends" of a specified departed woman gathered for her funeral at the home of her daughter. When they "opened the coffin to take a last look at the deceased, out jumped a big black cat. Some thought the corpse had come to life. The black cat spread consternation among the mourners and there was a mad scramble for the open air. The cat escaped in the excitement and took refuge in the ambulance [hearse-ambulance] of the undertaker. The corpse had been prepared for burial by a local undertaking establishment and the cat somehow got into the coffin before the lid was screwed on."

On February 23 the *Independent* criticizes women of the missionary society of the First Methodist Church for stooping to "make 'monkeys' of a score of men" by persuading them to render "impersonations of various screen stars, which meant that they had to don female clothing and high-heel shoes, make improvised busts with . . . grapefruit or whatever would best serve the purpose, put on wigs, and [also] paint, powder and rouge their faces. The awkward and clown-like capers, which otherwise dignified business and professional men cut in order to enable the good ladies of the missionary circle to raise money . . . [for] spread[ing] the gospel of Christianity in benighted foreign lands, were . . .

ridiculous," though "a high school student who impersonated [glamorous movie star] Carol Lombard . . . amazed the audience with his [rare] beauty."

On March 2, 1934, horrified readers of the *Independent* learn that a prominent man who enjoyed a meal at the local Duke Inn died of poisoning because a cook used "roach powder . . . in biscuits, batter cakes, pattie [patty] shells and fritters. . . ." The young new manager of the inn then probes the death by making "an inventory of the kitchen and pantry supplies" and discovers "a quantity of roach powder in a large tin labeled Rumford Baking Powder." The son of the owner of the Duke Inn, he recently relinquished management of a hotel elsewhere to take the new assignment in Elizabeth City. The young man had shipped "odds and ends" of his pantry and sanitary supplies "by truck with instructions to the carrier that nothing was to be disturbed until he arrived in Elizabeth City. The roach powder in the baking powder tin was one of the items. . . . He explained that the roach powder came to be in the baking power tin because the bottoms of the original roach poison containers were loose and that he dumped the contents of the five or six packages in the baking power container, keeping it with his sanitary supplies, little dreaming that it would ever fall into a cook's hands." When the cook ran out of baking power, she turned to the tin of newly arrived roach powder labeled baking power. "The innocent cook used it freely, a heaping tablespoon at a time in a single batch of biscuits." Diners became ill after eating dinner at the inn on two occasions before the fatality occurred on a third night. The writer suggests that the new manager has suffered "a tough break" with the poisoning of a diner, but now he has "inaugurated new and rigid kitchen and dietary rules" and will soon restore the inn "to its former state of popularity." The writer's poorly worded conclusion diverts attention from the true victims of grave misfortune, the dead diner and his loved ones.

Keith reveals in his column of March 9 that a young unmarried "schoolteacher from a neighboring county gave birth to a baby boy in [the] Albemarle Hospital and promptly offered the baby for adoption—an offer which was quickly accepted. . . . Scores of visitors from three counties flocked the hospital, obsessed by morbid curiosity, to have a look at the pathetic young mother and her child. One would have thought they were circus freaks, judging from the way visitors starred at them. . . . Naturally, she could not go back and teach again in the same school where she had been employed, so she stated her intention of leaving this section and going elsewhere to try to get another job and make a new start."

Keith expresses disgust that "gossips and scandalmongers" shout the case "from the housetops, coloring and distorting the facts, as usual. And the only person whom the talk can harm is the innocent child, who must grow up and live in this community. The girl has certainly paid the price of her indiscretion and should be made to suffer no more. Holding this unfortunate girl and her lover up before the world as a consequence of sin could not conceivably serve as a deterrent to the practice and prevent a recurrence of such a misfortune. So why not drop it, you gossips, and bear this case in mind before you make too free use of your wagging tongues in the future." No doubt, the highly blemished and self-righteous "gossips" described by Keith renounce him by citing fierce biblical denunciations of unwed mothers and their offspring and gleefully quote from the fifth book of the Old Testament, King James Version, that the "bastard shall not enter into the congregation of the Lord" (Deuteronomy 23:2).

On April 10 the rival *Daily Advance* describes two cheerless developments, first, the construction of a controversial "death chamber wherein homeless, friendless dogs will meet their fate" and, second, the opening of a city "dog pound wherein stray dogs which have no license tags will be kept. . . ." The City Council has decreed that wandering dogs lacking license tags must be impounded and then claimed within five days, or the canines will be offered for sale, but any caged dogs not attracting purchasers "will be placed in the tight little death chamber, gas will be administered, and the unfortunates will die a presumably painless death."

Two days later the newspaper reveals that thirteen impounded dogs awaiting "sale, rescue by their owners, or death in the gas chamber . . . [have] tunneled their way to freedom," choosing "open air rather than death by asphyxiation" and sparking "general rejoicing in canine circles. . . ."

The following day, April 13, the *Advance* reports that the new dogcatcher cannot perform his job properly because his prisoners "won't stay put and everybody cusses him and even children stone him." The previous afternoon saw him "ganged [attacked] when a bunch of boys, most of them 12 to 15 years old, registered their protest over [his] taking of a dog or some dogs." One of the boys "even stoned" him. That night he faces an additional ordeal when the boys return, break into the pound, and liberate "six of seven dogs incarcerated therein." The next morning "a prominent but irate citizen" stamps into "police headquarters voicing threats to 'use a shotgun'" the next time the dogcatcher lures his dog from his lawn.

Saturday, April 14, sees the same newspaper carry an eye-catching headline: "Young America on Warpath." The commentary begins: "Young America is on the warpath" against any "unfortunate person attempting to enforce the dog law in Elizabeth City." The "dog pound stood wide open today after about 150 boys and girls, supposedly from Elizabeth City High School, stormed the pound Friday afternoon between 12 and 1, freed three dogs incarcerated therein and departed victoriously after calling to Jailer Johnnie Anderson that they would free his [human] prisoners too if the prisoners wanted to get out." Local officials fall silent in the face of "the most unpopular law" in the history of the city.

On March 22, 1935, Keith reports via his crowd-pleasing column in the *Independent* that Elizabeth City has witnessed "one or more schoolteachers each year . . . running around with pupils after school hours." He suggests that a current female teacher "goes to parties and dances with her pupils, smokes before them and with them, and permits them to call her always by her first name or by her nickname. She has displayed a more or less open interest in at least one senior boy [an eleventh grader], and . . . she was not exactly discreet in her relations with another boy on a recent trip with a number of pupils."

One week later Keith relates that a twenty-five-year-old "male member of the high school faculty" can be "seen day and night in the company of one of the senior girls, who is about sixteen." He mentions that this romance has become a juicy "topic of conversation among the high school students."

In the case of the young male teacher and the senior girl, apparently Keith does not know the entire story. Several reliable adults described this unblemished romance to me during my boyhood. A native of Elizabeth City and a fresh college graduate, the brilliant teacher begins instructing the girl when she reaches the eighth grade, then counted as the freshman year of high school. At that time, according to several of her contemporaries, she professes her love for him, and he for her. The two agree they cannot date for several years but promise to remain loyal and true. They often make discreet plans to "run into one another" at some local soda fountain on a Saturday morning or afternoon and share an out-of-the-way table while enjoying a soft drink and pleasant conversation. They wait several years before appearing together at concerts or parties and finally marry three weeks after she completes college. One of their children becomes a close friend of mine.

On September 6, 1935, the *Independent* splashes the front page with an inscrutable story about a "local Armenian watchmaker . . . found murdered on a lonely road in Virginia week before last. . . ." Virginia police officers question a ninth-grade student after discovering his "name on a piece of paper" in the slain man's office. The *Independent* describes the young man as wholesomely "clean-cut" and provides no clue why his name appears among these possibly significant office papers.

The youth, son of a prominent family living in a beautiful house three miles north of Elizabeth City, confesses to the murder. The *Independent* jolts readers with a sensational account of his story: "On Saturday night, August 17, shortly before midnight, the youth was lounging on a downtown street corner, as many rural youths are wont to do on Saturday nights. . . ." He stated that the watchmaker "approached him and offered him $5 to drive him to Norfolk. Considering this an easy way to earn $5, he consented, and they left town around midnight," but "a few miles across the Virginia state line," the man asked the young driver to turn from the highway and stop the car. The ninth grader told of pulling onto a side road and parking the vehicle. When he "flatly refused" the man's sexual proposition, "the watchmaker drew a .32 caliber pistol" and threatened to shoot unless he complied. "The boy, according to his story, grabbed the gun and a struggle ensued." The watchmaker "fell in the road dead, shot thru the head." The newspaper then suggests that the watchmaker has propositioned many young men in the area and that "any male jury will believe the boy and sympathize with him. . . ."

The *Independent* quotes an outraged prominent citizen, who thinks the youth "'ought to be given a medal for killing'" the man unless his story somehow collapses in court. No questions appear in print about the young man's credibility or about his pistol silencing of possible conflicting testimony. His father spends days "rounding up evidence" to damn the slain man as "bestial," but no person publicly expresses regret that the dead man will not be present to defend himself. Moreover, the newspaper stirs readers' emotions to the boiling point with numerous lurid expressions such as "improper and unnatural advances of the most revolting nature."

On November 22 the *Independent* adds a new twist. The youth not only ran from the scene of the murder but also "caught the first bus to Elizabeth City Sunday morning, borrowed a clean shirt from a friend, and then . . . [returned] home and told his parents he had spent the night with a friend at the Y.M.C.A." His intention to remain perpetually silent about the murder collapses when the police find his name on the piece of paper during their investigation.

One week later the newspaper transfixes readers by relating that a Virginia "jury . . . deliberated only 35 minutes" before acquitting the youth. The defense made every effort to portray the watchmaker as "an utterly despicable type of person, whose murder was wholly justified and was a blessing to the community [Elizabeth City] in which he lived." One witness even reported seeing the watchmaker "on a dark pier at Norfolk one night" engaged in "sexual relations with three sailors" but offered no explanation for his own presence on the deserted pier at nighttime. The testimony of the trial proved so graphic that "all spectators were barred from the courtroom during the presentation of evidence, and women were excluded even during the attorneys' arguments." The young man immediately resumes his life as a ninth grader, while the slain watchmaker lies in an untended grave.

On November 29 the *Independent* attempts to prick the conscience of the community with a front-page story of innocent childhood suffering. "Here in Elizabeth City, just across the railroad tracks, there lives an eight-year-old boy who cannot attend school and who seems doomed to a life of sorrow, tribulation, and perhaps crime—and all because of a tragic circumstance over which he has absolutely no control. The boy's family is white, but he is a mulatto." His "family is very poor and has been more or less dependent upon charity for many years." The newspaper relates that his "mother sold herself" to "a fairly well-to-do Negro farmer," now deceased, who fathered him. The mother "denies that the little boy's father was a colored man," insisting that "he was a Syrian," but "a good look at the boy is convincing evidence that he has some Negro blood in his veins...."

A prominent local man recently saw the lad and asked him why he doesn't attend school. "'I don't know, answered the boy,' hanging his head as tears welled up into his eyes. 'They won't let me go to the white school, and they won't let me go to the colored school.'" The *Independent* laments that "society here in the South doesn't know how to help such cases." The newspaper explains that North Carolina law mandates school attendance "from seven to 14 years of age. This mulatto boy is eight years old and is therefore required by law to go to school. His mother wants to enter him in the white school," but the county welfare agent, "knowing what he does about the case, does not dare sanction this step for fear that it might give rise to a serious situation. On the other hand, the boy's mother says she would cut his throat before she would see him enter a colored school.... Must this innocent mulatto boy, born of a white mother, grow to manhood without having even a year of schooling, simply because of the baseness and poverty of his mother?" If members of society permit this boy to grow to manhood "hated by his own family, denied an education, and shunned by both races," they can expect him "to develop into a surly ignorant criminal.... Here, indeed, is a problem for society, and society here in the South seems not to know how to handle it."

Keith regales the reading public with a juicy piece in his column on January 10, 1936. "A young married woman was telling some of us the other night how she woke up one morning and discovered that her pretty younger sister was sleeping in the twin bed with her husband. The girl didn't know how she got here, and the man couldn't explain it either. All had been on a party the night before, so they surmised that the mistake was unintentional. The wife accepted the explanation."

Among the tidbits Keith offers on February 7, two must have caused considerable comment. First readers encounter an unrestrained youth: "The young man . . . thought it was a grand idea to expose himself under the traffic light at Main and Road Streets [but] decided, after spending an hour or so in jail, that it wasn't such a good idea, after all." Then Keith reveals the existence of a shady establishment said to have been particularly popular with high school boys: "They tell me there's a downtown place of business which has become hardly better than a house of prostitution. Boys and men stop their cars in front of the place and blow their horns, and out pops a girl in nothing flat. I have even been told that one toot brings a blonde, two brings a brunette, and three brings a red-head."

W. O. Saunders Unveils the Hypocrisy and Sins of the Ruling Elite. On August 14, 1936, the newspaper publishes a letter to W. O. Sunders from George Washington Paschal, professor of Latin and Greek from 1896 to 1940 at Baptist-founded Wake Forest College (later renamed Wake Forest University). "All my family—wife, six sons, four daughters and I have been enjoying your paper for years; in fact, some of my sons turn down all other papers, secular and religious, such as the *New York Times* and *Biblical Recorder* and *Nation,* until they have read the *Independent.* Often I feel called upon to share the joy I find in reading one of your editorials with my friends," particularly the president of the college, Dr. Thurman D. Kitchin. "It is no little advantage for young people in their formative period to read [the words of] . . . an editor who stands unflinchingly for the right, denounces evils and shams, thinks clearly, writes simple idiomatic English, and is sincere and unafraid and directs his thoughts not by expediency but by conscience."

For three decades W. O. Saunders carries on a war with much of the ruling elite of Elizabeth City, exposing the misdeeds of many shrewd and ruthless men who gather ostentatiously in church every Sunday morning. He echoes Voltaire in attacking religious corruption and hypocrisy. On June 30, 1933, he blasts Christian evangelists for scornfully labeling vast regions of the planet "the heathen East" and for identifying this faraway expanse with "poverty and ignorance," warning that such remarks are a "manifestation of sounding brass and tinkling cymbals [referring to 1 Corinthians 13:1]."

He suggests that "Christian nations own the earth not because they have followed the teachings of the meek and kindly peacemaker of Nazareth, but because they ignored and defied the teachings of Jesus and conquered the earth with rifle and cannon." In conquest, "the Christian soldier relies solely upon his superior murderous arms." We Christian nations "take the Old Testament with its god of rapine, murder and lust for our guide and pay lip service merely to the Great Teacher whose rule was love. . . . One will find the Christ spirit more clearly understood in many of our so-called heathen lands today than in America or Europe."

On July 7, 1933, W. O. Saunders boldly wields his pen in support of a local drive for horseracing and betting, an issue to be settled at the polls. "In countries that have had far greater social experience than we have had in America—in countries more civilized in fact—horseracing and betting on the horse are not considered social evils. The races in Great Britain are approved by the King [George V] and Queen [Mary], and these royal and distinguished personages, both of whom are devoutly religious, enjoy attending the races. If thousands of Britishers lose their shirts betting on the races, it is their private business. If they didn't lose their shirts betting on the races they would lose them in some other way." Ordinary mortals have few outlets from "the grim realities of life" and must "get religion, get drunk, chase a new skirt or get into a game, or they would go daffy." Members of the clergy incorrectly assume "that the world is going to the devil every time any new avenue of amusement and recreation . . . open[s] to the people."

Despite his strong editorial on behalf of local horseracing and betting, the newspaper reports, on July 14, that "churches of Pasquotank County went to war with the World, the Flesh, and the

Devil" and won the battle not to permit pari-mutuel betting on horse racing by just "23 votes" when voters "turned out or were dragged out to the polls on the burning issue."

Three months later, on October 27, 1933, the *Independent* describes an ugly episode of prejudice. The Yong Men's Civic Club had planned "a series of ten musical concerts in Elizabeth City this fall and winter.... Negro musicians were to present five of the programs and white musician were to present five," with the performances characterized as "music of a higher class, ranging from the better ballads" to "spirituals, sacred music, and classics." The newspaper relates that the expense of bringing the concerts to the public "would be borne by a small group of patrons," including Governor J. C. Blucher Ehringhaus (a native of Elizabeth City), Judge Isaac M. Meekins, W. O. Saunders, and Dr. Walter W. Sawyer (my great-uncle).

"James E. Norman, a talented young Negro musician, pledged the support of all the colored musical organizations in the city and promised further to bring to Elizabeth City . . . the Hampton Institute band, [the Hampton] symphony orchestra . . ., and the renowned Hampton glee club, which sang before and was favorably received by several monarchs abroad in 1930." With the Young Men's Civic Club having been "promised the use of the Carolina Theatre for the concerts," the blueprint seemed virtually complete, and "the first program was planned for November 5. Then the owners of the theatre learned that Negroes were to hear the concerts from the theatre balcony, entering the balcony by means of the fire escape . . . to avoid contact with the white people. They promptly announced that their lease forbids them to allow Negroes to occupy seats in any part of the theatre. This clause was iron-bound and could not be violated, they said. This turn of affairs dismayed the concert committee...."

The committee then sought permission to use the commodious auditorium of the First Methodist Church, the spiritual home of my Grandmother Emma Sawyer Dunstan. The newspaper praises its "splendid organ" and "large balcony which could accommodate the Negroes." Yet the Methodist Board of Stewards vetoed the request on the sole basis "that the musical concerts 'would not be the sort of thing to be held in a church.'"

Their argument "was an excuse and not a reason, the Civic Club thought."

W.O. Saunders writes a blistering editorial, dated November 3, under the arresting headline "Christ in Negro Hearts." He begins by reminding readers that the proposal by the Young Men's Civic Club for a "series of inter-racial concerts" has led to an unfavorable response, with "the city's most desirable auditoriums barred to them . . . . No one will ever know how the colored people in Elizabeth City felt about this manifest repulse to their race. Negroes do not wear their hearts on their sleeves. But here is what the Negroes did about it: They got together in Mt. Lebanon [AME] Church [large brick Gothic Revival style edifice erected in 1905 on Culpepper Street] Sunday night and voted to lend themselves to the programs sponsored by the Civic Club, giving freely of their talent and cooperation, with the understanding that members of their race would seek no admission to the concerts. They would sing their folk songs and their spirituals for the white folks; even though members of their own race will not be permitted to sit in the galleries. Here then is a genuine manifestation of the Christ spirit that should make white Christians bow their heads in shame. Blessed indeed are the meek. And there may have been an ominous meaning in the words of Jesus when he said, 'They [the meek] shall inherit the earth' [quoting from Matthew 5:5]."

One week later Keith adds his assessment of the matter. "When I was a boy in knee pants I attended Sunday School regularly" at the First Methodist Church but intend to "steer clear of the church" in the future. "My principal reason is the narrowness of the church, as perfectly illustrated by the action of the Board of Stewards recently in refusing to allow the use of the church auditorium for a series of Sunday afternoon free musical concerts. I will resent that action to the end of my days, and . . . it has not heightened my opinion of the church and religion."

On November 17, 1933, W. O. Saunders asks in an editorial how can Christians claim "that God did not reveal himself" to other religious groups such as Zoroastrians, Hindus, Buddhists, or Muslims but "revealed himself to the Jews thru Moses and to Christians thru Christ? If God didn't do this, then did not God Almighty take a long chance in getting His message over to the rest of the world first thru a small company of Jews and later thru a militaristic group styling themselves Christians?"

W. O. Saunders often attacks practices few others question in the 1930s. On March 2, 1934, he writes of "condemned men . . . counting the hours in the death cells in the State Prison in Raleigh, waiting for the electric chair to end their lives." He pleads with the state officials to take "North Carolina out of the business of legalized murder." Meanwhile he criticizes capitalism as an unjust system and praises socialism as a far better way. On May 4 he advocates a "socialized state" and argues for abandoning American capitalism, a system that reaps colossal profits, "exploit[s] the masses at every turn, and in many instances resorts to the most despicable knavery, skullduggery, and ruthlessness to keep itself on top of the social heap." He accuses capitalists of "operating their machines only part-time in order not to produce more goods than can be sold at a [huge] profit. . . ." With "the first appearance of a surplus, they throw millions of workmen out of employment to become charges upon the cities, counties, states, and federal government."

He turns to the scene in Elizabeth City and reports, on April 12, 1935, that the pay of laborers in local lumber mills, owned by individuals of wealth and power, "has been cut from 24 cents to 12½ cents an hour" and their work week increased from 40 to 55 hours. They now receive "$6.88 for a week of 55 hours, against $9.60 a week" they took home under the old 40-hour week. On May 3 he addresses this calamity through an editorial: "Hundreds of white and Negro laborers in local lumber mills and yards are reduced to the barest subsistence in a time of rising food costs. The purchase of shoes, clothing, and other necessities of life are out of the question. And these same mill hands have to pay [dearly] for the waste lumber that they buy from the mills for heating and cooking, the same as other people. Thank God they won't need any heat thru the summer and . . . will not need much fuel to cook the little food they can buy on their present wages. . . . [President Franklin D.] Roosevelt has promised that none will starve. Many of those now struggling to keep a shelter over their heads and feed their families on present wages are . . . facing slow but sure starvation."

The following year, on July 10, 1936, the newspaper reports that "two young ladies" solicited funds from the named president of a large and prosperous local lumber company for the President Roosevelt reelection campaign. Word of his chilling response quickly spreads. No, indeed, "he wouldn't give one cent to help elect Roosevelt but . . . would give two thousand dollars to help bury him." The newspaper suggests this man not only possesses "the social and economic morals of a flea or bedbug" but also votes Republican, the party bringing "him and his company to the very brink of bankruptcy and suicide in 1929." With Roosevelt in office, his company "has recovered and is making money. . . . And now this smug, sumptuously fed and ungrateful beneficiary of a progressive and humane government snaps at the hand that feeds him. He ought to kiss the hand of Franklin D. Roosevelt."

On June 21, 1935, W. O. Saunders reminds readers that "the *Independent* has never waited upon public opinion to take a stand for its concept of right. For instance, the *Independent* supported Mrs. Margaret Sanger's birth control movement twenty years ago when it was one of the most unpopular movements in America [and a frequent target of conservatives], even daring to bring Mrs. Sanger to Elizabeth City in 1916 to address the women of this city and section in defense of her work. . . .

"The *Independent* took up the cudgels against the Ku Klux Klan at a time when that organization of racial hatred and bigotry had captured the imagination of the South. The Klan never obtained a foothold in Elizabeth City. Locally, the *Independent* has fought political graft and religious bigotry in season and out of season, until people point with pride to the fact that Elizabeth City is one of the cleanest and most liberal-minded towns in North Carolina. Necessarily, the *Independent* has made many enemies. But its bitterest enemies most often respect it."

W. O. Saunders opposes lengthening the school year from eight to nine months in an editorial dated August 16. "The State school term is eight months, and any normal child . . . can . . . learn everything . . . our schools can teach in . . . eight . . . months." Moreover, "a large percentage of the pupils in our public schools" would be "incapable of assimilating an education if they went to school twelve months a year. But we are going to have a nine-month term in Elizabeth City if we don't watch out," for the teaching forces possess "a shrewd and powerful organization; they know what they want and . . . usually get it."

On December 20, 1935, he turns to the myth of Saint Nicholas. "Sooner or later every child learns the truth about Santa Claus, and the disillusionment may turn a child's healthy credulity to morbid cynicism. Certainly the child's faith in many things that his parents and elders have taught him is rudely shattered when . . . he learns that Santa Claus is fiction. If the grownsters have lied so glibly about Santa Claus, then what faith may a child place in their pronouncements about God, the angels, and a heavenly hereafter?" The child suffers upon discovering "that Santa Claus is a myth rather than a fact. He would be spared this suffering if we explained to him in the beginning that Santa Claus was a jolly make-believe old gentlemen" who represents Jesus' "lesson [in Acts 20:35] that it is more blessed to give than receive."

Addressing the principle of giving, W. O. Saunders writes about one of his own boyhood birthdays "that everyone had forgotten." He becomes consumed with "self-pity" but suddenly realizes that the one person who "deserved a gift" on his birthday was the mother who had brought him into the world. "Acting on a glad impulse, I . . . spent the only dime I possessed for a piece of decorative glassware for my mother. . . . I think that was the happiest birthday of my life."

On February 21, 1936, he turns to the legends surrounding George Washington. He describes Washington "as the most misunderstood and over-rated character in American history. So many myths have been built up about Washington that American youth to whom he is held up as a pattern must despair of making any effort to try to live up to the exaggerated ideal. George Washington was not a statesman, he was not a great soldier, he was not a scholar, [and] he was not a great humanitarian. In him were mingled none of the elements of a poet, a philosopher or an artist. He was a . . . land-hungry Virginia aristocrat with a love for fox-hunting, liquor, and women, and who wore a No. 13 shoe [referring to an old unscientific notion that male foot size corresponds to penile length]." Despite noteworthy limitations, George Washington "was proud, he was earnest, he was fearless, he was honest, he was punctilious, [and] he was sincere."

W. O. Saunders criticizes those who make an "idol" of the American flag in an editorial dated October 29, 1936. "Muddle-minded patrioteers with no spiritual code, no high moral concept and ignorant of the true traditions and ideals of their country, have made a fetish of a flag. They worship the flag and effectually ignore or spurn the Constitution, of which the flag is but a symbol."

On November 24 he reminds readers of the great number and pitfalls of "puppy-love marriages" in Elizabeth City. "Any pair of 14-year-old high school students who think they are in love and feel the urge to marry can hop in a car, drive [roughly fifteen miles] up to South Mills, tell a couple of lies, sign a health certificate and a marriage license, pay the justice of the peace eight dollars, and be back in Elizabeth City as man and wife within 45 minutes after leaving town."

Despite W. O. Saunders' hints of peril, apparently some of these youthful marriages prove successful. Keith employs his column on May 14, 1937, to express "admiration for a young matron of our town" who "was only 15 years old" and a resident of Weeksville in southern Pasquotank County when she married in the early spring of 1935, but "she continued to attend high school until her graduation two weeks ago tonight. And during most of that two years she lived in town and commuted to the Weeksville school five days a week, eight months of the year. That's what I call a spunky girl."

W. O. Saunders editorializes on December 29, 1936, about predictions of future gasoline shortages. "Within recent years there have been alarming reports of the possibility of exhausting our oil fields upon which the automotive world depends," but "science is going to take care of that." Science has already "gone far in developing alcohol for automotive fuel . . . [made] from potatoes and other produce grown on our farms" and "now promises us an automobile carburetor that will give us 160 miles to a gallon of gasoline, instead of the 18 to 20 miles that we are . . . so proud of" today. "Think of motoring from Elizabeth City to Washington on two gallons of gas!"

He never hesitates to attack corrupt politicians or negligent health care providers. His newspaper, now published daily and known as the *Daily Independent,* horrifies readers on January 4, 1937, with detailed information about a tragedy occurring on New Year's Day, when a friend of a gravely ill youth calls "the dean of the medical profession in Elizabeth City" and pleads with him to "'come out right away.'" According to the caller, the physician replies that the youth's "'family quit using me as their family physician several years ago, so I can't take this case.'" Alarmed at this coldhearted response, the frantic friend explains that the youth had fallen into "'a dying condition and needs attention." Now indignant, according to the report, the physician snorts, "'I can't help it, I'm not coming,'" and then ends the conversation by "slamming up the telephone receiver...."

Precious time elapses before another physician can be located. He arrives "a minute or two" after "the dying youth" has taken his last breath. The grievous loss prompts W. O. Saunders to launch an editorial attack on the deplorable negligence of "the very dean of the medical profession in Elizabeth City.... The conduct of a physician who brutally refuses to make available his services to a dying man; who brutally refuses to come to the aid of a family in dire distress and rejects their tearful appeals for his help in a tragic moment, can not be too bitterly condemned. The attitude of such a physician is damnably inexcusable and a stigma upon his profession." The said man "should be deprived of his license and his own profession should shun him. God have mercy on his soul!"

The heated issue of abortion appears in the newspaper from time to time. W. O. Saunders often employs two fictitious characters called the Bank Clerk and the Soda Jerker to express views he hesitates to voice in his editorials. On January 30 the publisher-editor uses the words of the Bank Clerk to express his own views on the subject: "'Theologians, ethical medicos, and prudes have made the subject of abortion so frightful that everybody shies at the subject, leaving it shrouded in mystery and providing a racket for the unethical practitioner.... It is authoritatively estimated that there are 700,000 to 1,500,000 abortions performed in the United States annually, for which women pay 100 million dollars. The price ... ranges from $25 to $100 in Elizabeth City, to $50 to $2,000 in metropolitan centers like New York. And, as these operations are performed hurriedly and clandestinely by ignorant midwives or indifferent doctors, the death rate from septic poisoning is frightful, and thousands of women are physically impaired or invalided for life.'"

The Bank Clerk continues: "'And yet abortion is a simple operation that if performed by an ethical physician with sanitary precautions should be neither dangerous nor uncomfortable. And instead of costing an extravagant sum, such an operation performed by an ethical physician with legal sanction should cost not more than five or ten dollars. . . . Here will be the last great battlefield for woman's rights, for until [a] woman's right to refuse to have an unwanted child is recognized at law, so long will woman be a vassal, subject to masculine whimsy and masculine exploitation.'"

On February 1, 1937, W. O. Saunders castigates a Baptist minister in Lockhart, South Carolina, for denouncing the recent birthday ball "held in honor of President Roosevelt . . . as 'pagan and sinful.' And then this Baptist declares that 'God was not pleased with the birthday ball,' and 'a nation-wide epidemic of infantile paralysis [polio] followed.' There's a jackass who should be yanked out of his pulpit and punished for slandering God Almighty. Imagine a god [becoming] so displeased with anything as to give vent to his raging wrath by twisting and deforming the limbs of innocent children!" Unfortunately, "thousands of hicktown and backwoods gospel peddlers still preach that sort of gospel. And they wonder why a modern world turns away from them with contempt. . . ."

On February 13 he expresses amazement that "there are millions [of people] in these United States who believe they can inherit eternal life by submitting to some form of baptism and eating a bit of bread washed down with a thimbleful of wine."

On April 14 he suggests "the flimsy dressing of the modern American woman has influenced the . . . increased consumption of fuel for home heating" because "here in America women have practiced the striptease act until even in bitter cold weather the younger set wear but a few ounces of clothing under their fur coats. A flimsy silk dress over a chemise [loose-fitting undergarment hanging straight from the shoulders] and panties is the fashion. And woe unto the old-fashioned male who would dare suggest to a modern young miss that she should wear long drawers to avoid goose bumps and stave off colds!"

A week later, W. O. Saunders endorses a proposal by Charles Francis Potter, prominent Unitarian minister and theologian in New York City, calling for "the legalization of 'mercy-killings' in the United States. The minister would make it lawful to put to death" among others, "the incurably sick to whom life is a slow torture." The editor suggests that readers should "concede the humaneness and soundness of the proposal. Who has not looked upon some old person, helplessly bed-ridden and racked with pain, doomed to linger for perhaps months and years without hope of relief except in death, and not felt . . . regret that the misery of that helpless victim could not be ended by the administration of chloroform or some other lethal drug? But such is our revulsion against willful manslaughter that we push such thoughts from our minds. It requires courage of a high order for a prominent ecclesiastic to openly espouse a proposal to which most of us shame-facedly subscribe in the secret recesses of our hearts and minds."

W. O. Saunders firmly rejects euthanasia for anyone wishing to endure long-term suffering, pain, or confinement to bed: "We have in mind an aged woman, victim of a paralytic stroke, unable to serve herself in any capacity, confined to a bed from which she will never rise. But she endures her confinement and suffering without a murmur of complaint and exhibits a cheerfulness that is an inspiration and a benediction to her family and neighbors. Who would seal the death warrant of that angelic woman?"

On April 29, W. O. Saunders complains that "women must have beauty aids no matter what the cost. Most of the women one meets on the streets of any American town or city today would be frights but for their make-up. Take their powder and rouge and lipstick away from them, and millions of women would be utterly drab and colorless. . . . The best and most enduring beauty treatment is an abundance of fruits and green vegetables in the daily diet, and brisk walking with bared head in the rain. But . . . [because] a large number of women refuse to be practical, we thank our stars that they can buy artificial ornamentation in drug stores or at the hands of beauticians."

In an editorial dated May 10, W. O. Saunders discusses proposed Congressional restrictions on firearms. "From Colonial times it has been the tradition of the frontier-born American to enjoy the unrestricted use of firearms. To early settlers, shotguns and rifles were as essential as axes and hoes. . . . But out of this ancient freedom has come a promiscuous distribution of dangerous weapons that imperils much human life. Crimes of violence are fostered by the easy access to dangerous weapons." The proposal before Congress "is based on the English law which makes it a criminal offense for any person to purchase, acquire, or possess any firearms or ammunition without a certificate issued by the chief police officer for the area in which such person resides. This is not enough of a precaution in a land in which police officers are too often in league with criminals. Over here the applicant for a firearm permit should expose himself to the scrutiny of a judge and jury."

Four days later W. O. Saunders praises "Elizabeth City High School" for deciding "to dispense with an imported speaker for its graduation exercises and leave the oratory to its own student graduating class." Speakers from other cities seldom offer messages surpassing those delivered "by the students themselves." Moreover, an "imported speaker who might have something important and interesting to say" must "pull his punches lest he offend someone in his audience. And, after all, it is often an imposition upon prominent men to drag them back and forth across the state to make tiresome addresses to commencement audiences," populated largely by mothers and fathers who attend "not so much to hear a speech as to see their own children strut their stuff."

He recommends in a May 26 editorial that employers hire youths graduating from high school and college, but only those "who are eager to work . . . and can be trusted." W. O. Saunders complains that too many new degree holders work halfheartedly after "getting on somebody's payroll," yet he finds a role model for recent graduates in "a young man who went into a chain store in this town several years ago and applied for a job. He was told no additional help was needed. 'Very well,' he said; 'I've got to be doing something, and if you'll let me work for nothing until something turns up, I guess my old man will take care of me.' The manager of the store didn't know what to say to that, and the boy took off his coat, rolled up his sleeves and went to work. In three weeks he was on the payroll and in a year or such . . . was the manager of a store. And the last we heard of him he was still going up in the world."

On June 10 he reminds readers of the ravages of the Great Depression and asks them to show compassion in their remarks about a recent suicide. "It is hard for a man who has by years of industry and thrift amassed a competence, to see his life time savings slip away from him in a succession of business reverses. Depressed by frustration and defeat, his health suffers. The will to live gone, he succumbs to diseases that he might easily have resisted if his affairs were in better shape. Such a man finds himself facing dire poverty in his old age; uncertain of a roof over his head; dependent upon charity; deprived ever more of the comforts and pleasures of life to which he had become accustomed in all the years of his prosperity. Sick in body and mind, tired and hopeless, seeing only gloom and misery ahead, no wonder he seeks escape in a suicide's death. And so another citizen of our town ended his life this week. Be charitable in your comments . . . , for it is not given us to know how many deaths he died before he fired the shot that extinguished the frustrated life that dogged him."

W. O. Saunders usually proves principled and compassionate but occasionally echoes the prejudices voiced by large numbers of his fellow citizens. Anti-Semitism flourishes in North Carolina newspapers, with people often justifying their bigotry by citing harsh attitudes against Jews in the New Testament. Judging from W. O. Saunders' editorial on American Jews, dated July 19, 1937, anti-Semitism enjoys a strong footing in Elizabeth City during his heyday. Although the *Independent* has reported numerous atrocities against the Jews in Germany and elsewhere in Europe during the 1930s, the publisher-editor now demonizes certain members of this population in the United States. He suggests that too many "grasping, avaricious, bumptious, unscrupulous individuals" inhabit American Judaism. "In avoiding and trying to ignore the offensive element" spreading through their religion, perhaps "the better class of Jews have so removed themselves from their offending brethren that they can no longer influence or impress them. If this is true, it is a sad day for the future of Judaism. One offending Jew in a community can make life harder for the genteel Jews who are an asset to their town."

Edward Enjoys a Promising New Beginning in Elizabeth City. As noted, when the ravages of the Great Depression cost Edward his prestigious career in Manhattan's financial district during the spring of 1933, he returns to Elizabeth City. Emma, his mother, not only entrusts him with the management of her extensive real estate holdings but also hands him generous funds to open his own business alongside the Norfolk and Southern Railroad tracks on Skinners Avenue (also spelled Skinner's Avenue and Skinner Avenue on early maps but later rechristened Hughes Boulevard).

On September 8, 1933, the *Independent* carries an informative front-page article about the launching of the firm under the striking headline "A New Fuel Co. With an Old and Familiar Name" and offers positive commentary: "A new wood and coal company makes its bow to the Elizabeth City public today, the Dunstan Fuel Co., Wm. E. Dunstan proprietor. Mr. Dunstan is the son of the late W. E. Dunstan, for many years identified with the Crystal Ice & Coal Co. The Dunstan Fuel Co. will handle numerous grades of coal and a full line of pine and hard woods in fuel lengths. Their yards are located on the Norfolk Southern R. R. near the Elizabeth City Hosiery Mills. Mr. Dunstan was formerly with Bradstreet's commercial agency in New York City. Bradstreet's was merged with R. G. Dun & Co. last spring, leaving Bradstreet's employees to find new locations. Mr. Dunstan returned to his old hometown."

The same issue carries a large eye-catching advertisement informing the reading public that the Dunstan Fuel Company will open today and will offer "A New Deal for Coal Consumers," with an ample stock of both coal and wood. The advertisement invites readers to contact the proprietor by calling telephone number 178. Everyone expects the business to prove profitable. After all, coal-burning furnaces heat the hospital, courthouse, schools, department stores, and larger houses of Elizabeth City. Moreover, countless smaller houses use coal-burning fireplaces or heating stoves.

On November 10, 1933, the *Independent* publishes a lengthy favorable article about Fleetwood, Edward's older brother. "E. Fleetwood Dunstan, son of Mrs. W. E. Dunstan of this city, is making quite a name for himself these days as chairman of [the] municipal [bonds] committee of the Investment Bankers Association, according to reports carried in the financial sections of New York newspapers. Mr. Dunstan, an official of the Bankers Trust Company . . ., will make a financial talk over broadcasting station WJZ [then on the air in the New York City area] next Tuesday evening at 7:15 o'clock. . . . Mr. Dunstan made a speech recently at the annual convention of the Investment Bankers Association at Hot Springs, Va. The *New York Times* gave his speech considerable space. . . . "

The *Independent* reports on May 11, 1934, that the Democratic primary campaigns have begun and that Edward has announced his candidacy for the Board of County Commissioners. On June 1 the newspaper assesses each candidate for the various offices. "In Elizabeth City Township, the Commissioners race promises to be interesting, with four candidates in the field" for two seats, including "Edward Dunstan, a young man, whose recommendations include degrees from Duke and Harvard Universities and experience in Manhattan's financial district." The *Daily Advance* announces the election results on June 2. Edward has finished last, with 1,003 votes, 145 shy of a second-place showing and a seat on the board.

Undaunted, he runs for the City Council the following year. The *Advance* carries the news in a front-page article dated April 10, 1935. "W. E. Dunstan of West Church Street today announced his candidacy for city councilman from the third ward. He is the first candidate to make official announcement for the city election to be held here May 14. . . . Mr. Dunstan is a popular young business executive of Elizabeth City. He is president of the Dunstan Fuel Company, president of the Elizabeth City Real Estate Board, member of the Chamber of Commerce-Merchants Association, a Rotarian, and president of . . . [his] First Methodist Sunday School class. . . . A graduate of Elizabeth City High School, Mr. Dunstan continued his education at Duke University, where he graduated in 1929. He is a graduate of the Harvard School of Business Administration. In 1930 he went with the

Municipal Bond House in Wall Street, where he stayed for two years. He then spent one year with Bradstreet's, after which he returned to Elizabeth City. He is 26 years of age and makes his home with his mother on [West] Church Street."

The same day, the newspaper publishes an adjoining article about Edward's election as president of the local real estate board. "W. E. Dunstan, president of the Dunstan Fuel Company, was elected president of the Elizabeth City Real Estate Board last night at a meeting in . . . the Virginia Dare Hotel Arcade [a skylighted two-story atrium enclosed by commercial stores and offices]. . . ." Edward and others then delivered brief "talks on the problems of real estate and on the duties of the officers of the board. . . ."

On April 12 the *Independent* runs an eye-catching article about Edward's recently announced candidacy for the City Council under the front-page headline "Young Dunstan Tosses Hat in Another Ring." The anonymous writer begins: "Undismayed by his failure to win a seat on the Board of County Commissioners last year, W. Edward Dunstan, local fuel dealer and realtor, this week tossed his hat into the municipal political ring and announced himself a candidate in the Aldermanic race in the Third Ward. Because his mother, Mrs. W. E. Dunstan of West Church Street, owns scores of tenant houses in the city, young Dunstan has a vital interest in the manner in which the local tax dollar is handled. He first got the political 'bee' a year or so ago, when he announced himself a candidate for the office of County Commissioner from Elizabeth City Township. Considering the fact that he was not very well known here at the time, he made a splendid run. . . . He is now attempting to gain a seat on the City Council. . . .

"He is president and director of the Elizabeth City Real Estate Board, president of Dunstan Fuel Co., president of a local Sunday school class, member of Sigma Chi [social] and Alpha Kappa Psi (commercial) fraternities, member of the Rotary Club, member of the Elizabeth City Country Club, and member of the local Chamber of Commerce-Merchants Association. . . . Mr. Dunstan's announcement was the first in this year's municipal election, and now that the ice is broken other announcements are expected momentarily. The election will be held [in just thirty-two days,] on Tuesday, May 14."

W. O. Saunders publishes, on May 10, 1935, an article from his own pen about the seventeen candidates for the Board of Aldermen. He regards most as deplorable figures. He identifies one candidate, for example, as the offspring of a "late old-line political Boss" and a brother of a convicted criminal "of unworthy memory." This family's "influence in Elizabeth City politics has always been bad." Then the publisher-editor enthusiastically recommends his own son, "Wm. Keith Saunders, a last minute offering," who "doesn't rate high with crooked politicians, shysters and outlaws. He is an intelligent, civic-minded youngster, endowed with a passion for good government and can be trusted." W. O. Saunders offers a ringing endorsement also for the candidacy of "Wm. Edward Dunstan, a new candidate from the Third Ward." Young Dunstan "is a son of the late W. E. Dunstan, a graduate of Duke and Harvard, has had good . . . [financial and entrepreneurial] experience and is recognized as a good trustworthy businessman. He is [was] manager of much rental property owned by his mother and has an intense interest in the disposal of our tax dollars. He would make a good watchdog on the board."

Both Keith and Edward lose this bid for election. Edward drops far behind his two opponents in every ward. W.O. Saunders has characterized the man swamping Edward for the second seat on the council as a man possessing "a likeable personality" but lacking "any pronounced qualifications for the office. . . ."

Edward's Star Eclipsed by Self-Created Problems. The *Independent* provides a ready source of fascination, shock, amusement, embarrassment, information, and philosophical challenge for the Dunstan family and other citizens of Elizabeth City. Newspapers of this period and for several decades thereafter carry social columns covering the hobnobbing and pastimes of leading citizens. On July 26, 1935, the *Independent* relates that "Edward Dunstan has returned to his home on West Church Street after spending several days at the Arlington [Hotel] at Nags Head." Unless I have overlooked an entry, despite painstaking searching, Edward's name does not appear again in a local social column for several years, nor does he find himself even mentioned in a newspaper article (except on the sports page) for the next ten months.

How can these omissions be explained? Perhaps reports have circulated about one of his darker secrets. Emma had discovered two years earlier that Edward, as manager of her substantial real estate holdings, embezzled heavily from her funds. Reluctantly, she fires him. Edward continues to live on the second floor of her beautiful house. His bedroom opens onto a double-tier back porch accessible from an outdoor staircase. Thus he comes and goes as he pleases without entering the rest of the dwelling. This arrangement continues for roughly five years. During this entire period Edward turns his head whenever crossing paths with his mother and refuses to speak, though Emma overlooks her son's disgraceful conduct and makes no move to evict him from her home.

On January 10, 1936, the *Independent* publishes a lighthearted front-page article about an old tradition permitting women to propose marriage to men on leap years but never at other times. "Well, it's open season on bachelors again, and the fair damsels of the town, hunting with Cupid's darts, threaten to seriously deplete the town's supply of eligible bachelors ere the year 1936 has come to a close. The girls have waited four long years for leap year to roll around again, and now that it's here, they are ready to begin hostilities against the wary males. The girls have a good crop of unmarried males to use their lures and wiles upon this year, and some fine sport is promised. . . ." The newspaper then lists more than fifty prime candidates for the hunt. Readers must have noticed one glaring omission, Edward, offspring of a privileged, respected, and influential family.

Meanwhile many citizens of Elizabeth City snub Edward. His name never appears on the guest lists published in newspapers when prominent families host dinner parties, dances, beach getaways, cocktail parties, and other activities. Respectable ladies brusquely decline to date him. His evening life revolves around dark recesses on the fringes of society. Although W. O. Saunders had strongly recommended him for a seat on the Board of Alderman, people of his own generation know Edward all too well and whisper of his unrestrained conceit and egotism, distorted view of women as personal playthings, refusal to acknowledge mistakes, habit of making idle threats, and proclivity to blame others for self-created problems.

On May 22, 1936, Edward finally sees his name in print once again when the *Independent* publishes an article about homing pigeons, used since ancient times as reliable flying messengers trained to return home. "This sport is still in its infancy in this vicinity at this writing, but the enthusiasm is running high, and breeders are getting in line daily." The piece relates that Edward Dunstan and others "have already established lofts [pigeon houses] and started raising young birds. . . . In the near future these fanciers will organize a local Racing Club and have races between their respective lofts. . . . As early as the time of King Solomon, 3,000 years ago, the sport of flying homers was well established," and "these swift couriers of the sky . . . have been used in wars as long as history has been recorded. . . . These little sky racers are even used to bring pictures in from steamships. Only last fall the pictures of the Rose Bowl football classic [in Pasadena, California] were hurried to Southern Methodist [University in Dallas, Texas] by homer pigeons." Edward's pigeon house stands in his shunned mother's backyard. Years later Uncle Garland converts the building into an attractive bungalow and lives there for several years.

Although Edward has been virtually ignored by local newspapers for months, he continues to advertise his business on these same pages. His frequent advertisements feature an adorable smiling baby who "Doesn't Smoke Or Go Out Nights," an allusion to the excellent characteristics of the coal ("Every Lump Burns Up") sold by Dunstan Fuel Company.

Edward Threatens the Independent. In 1925, Keith Saunders and Edward Dunstan played alto horns together in the Elizabeth City Boys' Band, though detesting one another, and eleven years later the young journalist catches his old schoolmate off guard. Edward's advertisements in the *Independent* end abruptly after Keith employs his column, on June 5, 1936, to ridicule his old enemy. "Those of my readers who have played golf with Eddie Dunstan probably are convinced that he is a cussing piece of machinery. But 'you ain't heard nothing yet,' according to Garland Dunstan, his brother [home from Duke University for summer vacation]. Garland says he was awakened the other night by the tallest piece of cussin' he ever heard. Eddie, it seems, had come home late from a date and just after getting upstairs had gone to the johnnie [bathroom], where he unsuspectingly sat down on a toilet seat that had just been painted that night unbeknown to him. And they say he hasn't got it all off yet."

One week later Keith gives readers a biting follow-up. "Edward Dunstan, young Elizabeth City fuel dealer, is the latest to threaten to bring suit against the *Independent*. Young Dunstan has threatened to 'wreck' this newspaper unless certain statements made in these columns last week are retracted and an apology made. The item that was so utterly objectionable to Dunstan was a humorous yarn appearing in this column." Keith then regales readers by quoting his earlier remarks about Edward and next turns to the new controversy.

"'The whole thing is a lie from beginning to end,' stormed Dunstan last Thursday afternoon, a few hours after the *Independent* appeared on the streets. 'And you knew it was a lie [told by Garland] because you asked me about it, and I told you it wasn't true.'

"'Unless you publicly apologize next week and state that the article was untrue, I will have to take the matter to court. I already have seen two lawyers, and I know I have a good libel suit against you. If necessary, I will spend $10,000 to wreck the *Independent*, and I've got it to spend, too.'

"'I am a Sunday school teacher, and your statement that I curse profusely damages my reputation and my character. Furthermore, that article has greatly disturbed my peace of mind. I haven't been able to go ten feet on the street today without being kidded about it.'

"'You can make an apology and a retraction next week, or you'll have to face the consequences.'

"Indeed! How interesting! Mr. Dunstan, it appears, is one of those persons who 'just can't take it.' Over a joking matter which the ordinary person would laugh off, he becomes incensed to the point of threatening a libel suit. All I can tell him is to go ahead and sue.

"The trouble is that Edward Dunstan is not half so important as he thinks he is. Educated at rich Duke University and snooty Harvard, and schooled in the traditions of Wall Street, where his older brother is an important figure, he considers himself head and shoulders above 95 percent of the people in his knowledge of business and economic and political science. He thinks he is 'hot stuff.' In my opinion, he is what some people vulgarly call a 'horse's rosette.'"

In his column of June 9, Keith again addresses the matter of the wet paint on the toilet seat but with a softer and more conciliatory tone. "Eddie Dunstan, I understand, had been kidded unmercifully since I wrote him up in this column last week. Fellows around town have been calling him up and asking if he might be interested in some quick-drying paint, or in a new and effective paint remover. I hear he has been 'taking it' much better than he took the kidding that followed the first write-up. Maybe he has learned a worthwhile lesson."

6

Edward Mesmerized by Miss Ida Powell Fuller

The October 1, 1936, issue of the rival *Daily Advance* describes Edward rushing to defend his alma mater from charges leveled by the writer and social critic Ernest Seeman in the September 30 *New Republic*. Mr. Seeman had managed the "Duke University Press from its inception [in 1925] until his [forced] retirement after ten years of service." The newspaper summarizes his article in the *New Republic* with colorful statements suggesting that "Big Business dictates . . . educational policy" at Duke. Moreover, wedded to capitalism, the university administration of "ultra-conservative ranks" opposes "labor condition improvements" and dismisses progressive-minded faculty members. Mr. Seeman describes "'the Duke Chemistry Department'" as "'little more than an extension laboratory for the Liggett and Meyers Tobacco Company. . . .'"

The newspaper relates that local "Duke alumni have showed varying degrees of wrath and amusement over the story in the New York liberal weekly. . . . After reading it carefully, Edward Dunstan, young business executive whose pen has at times scratched lustily in defense of the status quo, decided the question he would like answered to be: 'Who is Ernest Seeman, anyway?'" Suggesting that Seeman had been fired as editor of the press, Edward then "exclaimed, 'The charges in the article may be true. I don't know. You can dig up the same facts about . . . Yale, Harvard, [and] Princeton, which have big endowments of stock controlled by wealthy persons. In my opinion it's an article by a disgruntled and dissatisfied fellow who lost his job. . . .'"

Ernest Seeman had aroused the ire of William Preston Few, conservative president of Duke University, for supporting disgruntled liberal students voicing strong concerns about

American labor conditions and the plight of workers. Mr. Seeman had provoked the Duke administration also by helping to found the popular Explorers' Club that coordinated many outings, including weekend trips to the mountain and the coast, the latter an inviting spot for swimming, though the campus handbook for female students required them to live under strict social regulations and even prohibited them from "swimming or bathing in any public places...." Thus Ernest Seeman lost his post at Duke.

Meanwhile, still smarting over Keith's newspaper remarks in June, Edward refuses to advertise in the *Independent* until 1937. His advertisements in the *Daily Advance* vary in design and message. Frequently, he runs one with this confident slogan: "We Don't Sell Everybody—But—Everybody We Sell Is Sold."

Edward Excels as Tax Supervisor. On March 3, 1937, the *Daily Advance* carries the bold front-page headline "Edward Dunstan Is Named by Board as Tax Supervisor." The commentary begins: "At a call meeting Wednesday morning, the Pasquotank County Board of Commissioners appointed Edward Dunstan as tax supervisor to be in charge of the plans for revaluation of property, which is supposed to begin next Monday. . . . One form of personal property that the commissioners believe the taxpayer is failing to list is his car radio [optional equipment on most automobiles in 1937].... The revaluation program is supposed to take 30 days. The commissioners want enough list takers at the courthouse to question each man, particularly about car radios and heaters [also optional equipment]. . . . The listing places for houses [on the tax forms] may be left blank" for dwellings "valued at $300 or less. . . . The members [of the Board] said they would be disappointed and surprised if the revaluation did not give the county a sizable increase in tax revenue."

Two days later, the *Daily Independent* adds: "With the quadrennial reassessment of property in the county scheduled to take place this year, as the first since 1927, and listing of taxes to start April 1, hardly thirty days remain in which to cover the entire county and city for a new appraisal...."

On April 7 the *Advance* splashes the front page with an article about Edward's progress and offers a positive assessment. "The speed exhibited by taxpayers of Elizabeth City and

Pasquotank County to list and revalue their property since the books opened at the courthouse April 1 has necessitated the acquisition of an extra lister, according to County Tax Supervisor W. Edward Dunstan. . . . Supervisor Dunstan is dividing his time between lending a hand at the listing place and . . . touring all over the county with the assessors. Dunstan . . . expressed the opinion that the work would be accomplished by the end of the month, when the books will close."

W. O. Saunders publishes an editorial the same day in the *Daily Independent* about the tax revaluation, cautiously complementing Edward and his team of twelve list takers and tax assessors. "One has but to observe the work of Edward Dunstan's crew of tax assessors to be impressed by a seeming desire of the assessors to try to get real property in Elizabeth City on the tax books at something approximating its real value. If Mr. Dunstan and his board succeed in ironing out a lot of the inequities in previous tax listings and get anywhere near a just valuation of Elizabeth City and Pasquotank County real estate, they will have rendered a great service to taxpayers collectively. But if they achieve any such result they will be damned and double damned by many individual taxpayers who have been getting away with murder. The way of the tax assessor is beset with thorns and thistles."

On April 15, 1937, the *Daily Advance* runs a front-page article under the eye-catching headline "Tax Listing Goes Along With Speed." The newspaper relates that despite the necessity of detailed writing and calculating by the tax assessors, Tax Supervisor "Dunstan said the taxpayers were being taken care of as rapidly as they appeared at the courthouse to revalue their property. . . ."

Miss Ida Powell Fuller Enhances the Weeksville Entertainment Committee. After Edward digests this commendatory article, perhaps he reads the one just below about "the mammoth fish fry [scheduled] at [nearby] Weeksville [on] Tuesday [April 20] at which State Commissioner of Agriculture W. Kerr Scott [future North Carolina governor and United States senator] will be the principal speaker. . . ." Newspaper readers anticipate flawless planning for such merry festivities and learn that "Miss Annie Marie Jackson and Miss Ida Fuller make up the Weeksville entertainment committee. . . ." On April 20 the *Daily Independent* provides additional information about the spread, "which will consist of fresh fish, deliciously fried and accompanied by cornbread and all the other trimmings that go with fish. . . ."

The following day sees the newspaper praising "Misses Ida Fuller and Annie Marie Jackson . . . for their work in arranging the dinner and the program," including music and other entertainments. Edward has never been presented to Miss Ida Fuller but will become absolutely mesmerized by her personality and bearing eleven months later.

Keith's Saucy Comments about the Revaluation. Edward's diligence as Tax Supervisor pays welcome dividends. The *Daily Advance* informs readers on April 26 that the Elizabeth City Rotary Club has reelected him treasurer during "the weekly luncheon in the main dining room of the Virginia Dare Hotel. Dunstan was the only officer reelected." The Rotary International had been founded in 1905 to support worthy charities, ethical standards in business, and international friendship. During the 1930s Edward's name appears frequently on the sports page of local newspapers as a player for the Rotarians on the City Softball League.

The *Daily Independent* soon announces, on May 26, 1937, that "Mr. and Mrs. E. F. Dunstan of New York are visiting Mr. Dunstan's mother, Mrs. W. E. Dunstan. . . ." With Edward still cold-shouldering his mother, Fleetwood and Anita must have joined him for lunch once or twice at the Virginia Dare Hotel or elsewhere during their stay in town. Edward certainly does not share any meals with them at Emma's house on West Church Street.

On June 8 the *Daily Advance* updates readers on the tax listing. "Supervisor Dunstan estimated yesterday that the total tax increase in valuation on the tax books this year will be above $1,000,000. One of the big contributing factors to this increase was Dunstan's idea of obtaining from the motor vehicle bureau a complete list of automobiles in this county and advertising the fact that automobile owners who failed to list their cars would be subject to a penalty. Many automobiles that had never before been listed were listed this year, Dunstan said. Also, a check-up disclosed the fact that a good many pieces of property listed as vacant lots are actually lots with houses on them. A good many new homes and business structures contributed further to the increase."

Ten days later the *Daily Independent* describes the conclusion of the revaluation. "Completing Pasquotank County's 1937 tax books yesterday, County Tax Supervisor Edward Dunstan announced that the property revaluation this year was primarily responsible for an increase of more than one and one-half millions of dollars in property valuation. . . . Numerous factors contributed to the . . . increase . . . this year, not the least of which was an increase of 445 houses and lots and an increase of 323 automobiles. A good many of the automobiles were new ones, but many of them were old ones which had not been listed previously. A good many of the houses and lots had previously been listed as vacant lots, although houses had been standing on them for several years."

Edward must have become livid the same day upon turning from the front page to read Keith's comments about the revaluation in his column. "Edward Dunstan, who has just completed the county's 1937 tax books, says: 'I've seen so many figures during the past month that I doubt I will even want to look at a figure on the beach.'" Keith gleefully adds, "And I doubt that."

Edward now desires a beach vacation and makes reservations at the Arlington, a Nags Head resort hotel known for serving delectable meals and attracting many free spirits from other cities and states, people without reputations to uphold locally. The entire guest list at the Arlington for the week of July 11-18 appears in the *Daily Independent* on July 21. Fewer than twenty married couples have registered. The twenty-one men vacationing as bachelors or without their wives include Edward. The guest list names twenty-three single, divorced, widowed, or married-but-unaccompanied women. The Arlington has long been one of Edward's favorite ocean-front playgrounds. With a cocktail in hand, he stakes out a position on the lower or upper level of the hotel's wraparound porch and employs his easy charm to make temporary conquests. No doubt his lustful activities quickly reach Keith's alert ears.

W. O. Saunders Suspends Publication of the Independent. Keith and other members of the newspaper staff soon experience a heartbreaking blow, for August 14, 1937, sees W. O. Saunders suspend publication of the undercapitalized *Daily Independent*. He has attracted insufficient local advertising for his controversial newspaper to survive as a daily. Elizabeth City will never be the same after this shattering of his lifeblood and purpose in life. Even fierce enemies reminisce about his long publishing career, profound principles, and daring activities.

Many people comment about the day, in the summer of 1929, when W. O. Saunders strolled down a blistering Fifth Avenue in New York City wearing tailored silk pajamas, with a light green necktie, a panama hat, and a pair of sandals, rather than a heavy suit. Reporters and photographers trailed him for several blocks and circulated his image in the metropolitan papers. After the photographers and reporters dispersed, his costume attracted no special notice from pedestrians. He had noted that women wear featherweight dresses in torrid weather, but men swelter under pounds of perspiration-trapping suits. He failed in his attempt to persuade men to wear pajamas for street wear during hot weather but certainly attracted the attention of the reading public. With the unfortunate demise of the boisterous *Independent*, Elizabeth City must suffice with the *Advance*, a newspaper fattened on the support of powerful local business and political interests and lacking W. O. Saunders' distinct affinity for ordinary people.

Elizabeth City Enjoys a Brief Visit from President Roosevelt. On Wednesday, August 18, 1937, four days after the suspension of the *Independent*, President Franklin Delano Roosevelt passes through Elizabeth City on his way to Roanoke Island for the initial performance of *The Lost Colony*, the acclaimed outdoor drama created by playwright Paul Green to mark the 350th anniversary of the birth of Virginia Dare, first child of English parentage born in America. W. O. Saunders had published an editorial about the event on August 13: "The president's special train consisting of a number of sleeping cars, two dining cars, and baggage cars, and carrying a host of congressmen, newspaper correspondents, and secret servicemen," should arrive at the Norfolk and Southern Railway Station "early Wednesday morning and, after breakfast on the train, the distinguished party will motor up Elizabeth City's mile-long, elm-shaded Main Street to the dock where the president and his party will embark on C. G. [Coast Guard] patrol boats for Roanoke Island." You may be certain "that Main Street will be cleared of all parked cars on that auspicious morning and . . . that every foot of porch and sidewalk space along the line of the procession will be packed with a mass of humanity drawn from many counties."

The appointed day sees Garland Dunstan directing the Senior Boy Scout Drum and Bugle Corps, a musical marching unit performing at civic functions. The members have been charged with greeting the president on West Main Street. Decades later, on the evening of November 25, 1994, I visited Uncle Garland at his home on Rivershore Road in Elizabeth City, seeking his comments about the presidential visit. As we sat by the fire, I recorded his account of that red-letter day in 1937 when President Roosevelt passed through town. Uncle Garland began with a brief history of the Drum and Bugle Corps, organized by Keith Saunders and others. My uncle had served as drum major of the popular group that not only played before one president and two governors but also "participated in the opening of several bridges in North Carolina."

He reminisced about his early band training that ultimately led to his position as drum major at Duke University. "I gained my experience as a drum major from [the] National Guard Camp at [the seaport of] Morehead City, where my brother-in-law, Marvin Harrison, who had married your Aunt Adelaide, took me three years in a row. . . . I hung around the [military] band [to acquire the necessary skills]. . . . Through that [experience] I became the drum major of the local Drum and Bugle Corps. . . ."

Then Uncle Garland turned to the presidential procession that created bold headlines on August 18, 1937. "Mr. W. T. [William Thomas] Culpepper had recently built his [Colonial Revival style] mansion on Main Street, and we knew the parade would pass that way. Meanwhile President Roosevelt had come down from Washington . . . on a special train . . . . Members of the Drum and Bugle Corps, about thirty-five strong, rose early that morning and headed for the passenger station, but the Secret Service seemed uneasy about throngs of people gathering there. So, we proceeded to Mr. Culpepper's home. His unusually large yard on West Main Street possessed wide open spaces where we could perform properly and be seen by the president. . . . We played several numbers while waiting for the parade to arrive at our location. The president rode in an open touring car, part of a long motorcade that proceeded down Main Street toward the Pasquotank River. . . . We struck up the military bugle call 'Ruffles and Flourishes' when the presidential car reached the Culpepper house [about 9:30]. President Roosevelt apparently said something to the driver because the motorcade stopped, and he waved to us. His gesture gave me the opportunity to salute him, and I did.

"We played two numbers, 'Hail to the Chief' and John Philip Sousa's march 'Semper Fidelis'. . . . He smiled and then gave the signal for the motorcade to proceed. I can still visualize the president with his [seersucker suit and] Panama hat pushed up around the edges [in a manner familiar to millions of Americans] and the ever-present cigarette holder in his mouth. . . . He waved to us again and clapped when his car took off. . . . He left from the dock at the foot of Main Street [for] . . . Manteo on a Coast Guard cutter to see *The Lost Colony*," with many local people, including Carroll and Annie Sarah Abbott, following him on yachts, cabin cruisers, and smaller pleasure boats.

"Instead of returning [to Elizabeth City] on the Coast Guard cutter at nighttime, the president came by car. . . . We had heard rumors that he couldn't walk but didn't know the truth [because no photograph or discussion of his difficulty ever appeared in the press]. . . . We members of the Drum and Bugle Corps rushed to the train station that evening and grabbed an ideal spot to see him arrive from Manteo. And we had to wait and wait and wait. . . . A large crowd of young people slowly gathered around us in the moonlight. We sat on the pavement and passed time by singing songs but jumped to our feet when the sirens came screaming down Main Street after midnight. President Roosevelt waved his Panama hat as the hundreds present roared their approval. His driver parked close to the train. . . . Secret servicemen pressed all around the car, but we stood our ground.

"The president smiled and looked directly at us because he recognized our uniforms . . . and . . . remembered that we had played for him. But what deeply impressed me was that he wouldn't let anyone help him. . . . He slid down from his seat onto the floor of the car [to straighten his legs and engage the braces that allowed him to walk]. And he put his arms on both the front and the back seats and then lifted himself up. . . . He walked slowly from the car with the help of two aides. Several secret servicemen helped him navigate the high step onto the train, and he climbed the final steps with crutches. We coaxed him to wave to us from a window by shouting, 'We want the president! We want the president!' Roughly thirty or forty minutes later his train departed for Washington, but we cheered and yelled for him until the last car disappeared from sight. . . ."

Approximately 10, 000 people had lined Main Street that morning to see the president slowly pass. Apparently Elizabeth City suffered only one serious accident during the fifteen-minute parade. When a young boy, Fred Markham, took the short walk from his house to the parade route, he left his Florida-purchased pet alligator in a large glass jar in his yard. Fred returned to the horrible discovery that his beloved alligator had perished from direct exposure to the blistering August sun. To this day, members of the family continue to speak about Fred's sorrow over his alligator's roasting demise.

Edward Locks Horns with His Younger Brothers and Serves a Squab Dinner. On August 25, 1937, the *Daily Advance* relates that "Forrest and Garland Dunstan . . . spent the weekend at Nags Head." The two brothers often enjoy vacationing together at the William E. Dunstan Cottage. Duke alumnus Forrest has returned home for the summer from Chapel Hill, after completing his second year of law school at the University of North Carolina. A loyal son, he has given Emma the benefit of his company for the months of June, July, and August. Forrest spends much time also with his charming childhood sweetheart, Miss Isabella Patricia Jennette, known to friends and family alike as Isabelle. Meanwhile his younger brother, Garland, has completed three semesters at Duke and served as drum major of the university band but, away from home, establishes an unfortunate pattern of sleeping through his morning classes. His grades suffer. After the Christmas holidays of 1936, Garland leaves for New York State to enter Poughkeepsie Business Institute (not to be confused with Eastman College, his late father's alma mater in the same city, closing in 1932 as a victim of the Great Depression). Poughkeepsie Business Institute, located at 32 South Cherry Street, attracts prominent young men of Elizabeth City saddled with marginal records at Carolina, Duke, or Wake Forest.

Garland and Forrest have been the best of friends for roughly two decades, though experiencing traditional sibling spats from time to time. As young men, judging from their conversations with me over the years, they hold fire-twirling Edward in scorn and usually give him a wide berth. Yet Forrest and Garland occasionally fall into disagreements and seek a personal alliance with Edward. Whenever the three brothers in Elizabeth City quarrel, each writes copious letters to Fleetwood defending his own point of view. Fleetwood never loses, not for a moment, the respect and adoration of his three younger brothers. From my boyhood perspective, Edward loved only one person, Fleetwood, without reservation.

The *Daily Advance* publishes an article about Edward's church on December 2, 1937. "The Board of Stewards of the First Methodist Church . . . [recently] elected officers for the new church year. . . ." Edward has relinquished his duties as Sunday school teacher but now acquires the position of secretary of the board. He has gained some stature in the influential business and professional community from his exemplary service as Tax Supervisor, but his name never appears during this period in the social column, identifying local people invited to dinner parties and participating in other lighthearted or cultural activities, with one bizarre exception. Edward has lost his earlier enthusiasm for keeping racing pigeons, purchased at a handsome figure, and decides to empty his pigeon house. On March 2, 1938, the social column portrays him entertaining several gentlemen at the home of a friend on West Main Street with a fresh "squab dinner"!

Edward and the Elizabeth City Dunstans enjoy a banner year in 1938. He runs an advertisement for Dunstan Fuel Company in the *Daily Advance* on January 24, 1938, under the confident headline "No Recession, Just Confession." His confession reads: "The sales of our company are currently 20% above last year, and [the sales] for the full 1937 calendar year were 25% above 1936. We are indeed grateful for this faith from our many customers, and we sincerely expect to continue . . . [supplying] only the finest quality fuel in the future."

Edward Catches Sight of Miss Ida Powell Fuller. Friday evening, March 4, 1938, sees Edward enter the Elizabeth City High School gymnasium to attend a semifinal basketball match for the Albemarle Tournament. The playing teams include the girls of Central High School, located just outside Elizabeth City, who trounce the girls of nearby Weeksville by a score of 19 to 6. The *Advance* reports the following day that spectators demonstrated unusual exuberance. "Lusty rooters and yelling backers accompanied their teams to the big show yesterday, and . . . they nearly filled both the downstairs and upstairs of the high school gym."

Edward's roving eye catches sight of Miss Ida Powell Fuller, who cheers for the Weeksville basketball team as enthusiastically as any student. Captivated by her stunning beauty and zestful spirit, Edward asks those around him to identify the fair damsel. Several of them know Miss Ida Fuller and tell him she hails from Franklin County, more than one hundred and fifty miles west of Elizabeth City, and has been teaching English and history to high schoolers for the past six months at the tiny village of Weeksville in southern Pasquotank County. The talented and vivacious Miss Ida already has earned respect in Weeksville and Elizabeth City for her musical and intellectual gifts. Her name has appeared several times in the newspaper for enhancing banquets and educational-cultural programs with her trained soprano voice. Edward returns to the gym for additional tournament games in an intense quest to catch another glimpse of the spellbinding Miss Ida.

She begins to hear from friends in Weeksville that Eddie Dunstan of Elizabeth City has voiced keen interest in making her acquaintance. At first she suspects, correctly, that he might be an untrustworthy lothario and ignores the long-distance overtures, but ultimately curiosity trumps caution.

She tests the waters by going, with a friend, to a Sunday morning service at the First Methodist Church. She marks the date, March 27, 1938, and other dates in the unfolding drama on her calendar. Miss Ida knows that Edward, as a small-town businessman, probably will be present at church. After the service he eagerly arranges to be presented to her and expresses much interest in becoming better acquainted. Moving in for the kill, Edward sends flowers on Thursday, March 31, and telephones on Sunday, April 3. No one warns Miss Ida of the danger. Her closest school-teaching friends in Weeksville come from other locales and know nothing of Edward's unsavory reputation among principled women.

Edward and Miss Ida soon begin dating. He probably supposes she might represent his last chance to acquire a respectable spouse and musters his best courtesy in her presence. She finds him attractive in numerous ways. Edward enjoys a gift for reciting entire passages of lofty verse. He possesses an enviable education from his early association with his brilliant father and from his years at Duke and Harvard. Besides, his striking legacy includes descent from distinguished families, among them Dunstan, Fleetwood, Vaughan, Sawyer, and Herrington. She learns that his powerful great-great-great grandfather, John Dunstan, who died in 1726, served as Naval Officer and Collector of Customs in Colonial Carolina for the Lords Proprietors (distinguished gentlemen and nobles holding Carolina as a proprietary colony) and the Crown of England. Valuable documentary evidence about the career of John Dunstan dots the Colonial records (as noted in volume 3). Exercising authority from Edenton, then the Colonial seat of government, John Dunstan enjoyed oversight over a vast region of the "Province of Carolina . . . North and East of Cape Fear" (William L. Saunders, ed., *The Colonial Records of North Carolina*, 10 vols. [Raleigh: State of North Carolina, 1886-1890, vol. 2: p. 497]).

7

David and Zenobia and Miss Annie

Edward discovers that Miss Ida Fuller enjoys an equally notable lineage. She tells him the colorful history of her family early in their association. I will hear the story many times as a child, here reconstructed from memory, letters, interviews, memoirs, family records, deeds, college archives, historical works, and newspaper accounts.

Miss Ida's paternal grandfather, William David Fuller, born 1829, enjoyed prosperity as a successful planter in Franklin County, located in the northeast-central section of North Carolina. He marries Martha Frances Kearney before the Civil War. Fighting for the Confederacy, William falls into the hands of Union forces in March 1865. The Northerners release their starving, wounded prisoner at the end of the toxic war, but he never recovers his strength and dies six months later of dreaded smallpox. With no experienced family adult available to supervise farming, Confederate money worthless, former agricultural slaves deserting a sinking operation, and fields unplanted, the comfortable Fuller assets entirely evaporate after his death.

William Fuller's widow and two young children, nine-year-old David Thomas and seven-year-old Mary Susan, bravely fend for themselves under extremely demanding circumstances. They live for two years on the substantial farming acreage of Martha Frances Fuller's brother. Young David now faces an arduous dawn-to-dusk round of cultivating and reaping crops and tending chickens, cows, and hogs but gains invaluable experience in the process. His mother soon recognizes his extraordinary skills. In 1868 Martha Frances Fuller borrows twenty-five dollars from her brother and immediately makes a successful bid during an auction at the courthouse for a substantial tract of land near the community of Pocomoke in southwest Franklin County.

Young David Supports the Family. Martha Frances earnestly counsels twelve-year-old David, nicknamed Davie, "Son, you have become the man of the family, and our very lives depend upon your ability to support us." She expresses absolute confidence in his natural talents and innate gifts, though her mind clouds with private misgivings about his backbreaking new responsibilities at such a tender age. David inventories their assets. Their sole possessions consist of little more than the land, a mule and plow, several trunks of tools and household goods, and one or two chests of threadbare clothes. He sets out with youthful ardor and confidence to honor his beloved mother's charge. She has entrusted him with a sacred mission, and he intends to succeed in providing for his family while creating a rural paradise.

Young David rides his mule roughly six miles northeast to the village of Franklinton, where many adult freedmen, most with vital farming skills, have come seeking better jobs. He introduces himself as Mr. Fuller and interviews a number of former slaves on a street corner. One by one, he hires agricultural workers to tend the land he now possesses. He then assembles the chosen men and solemnly pledges to help them cut timber and build cabins for themselves and their families.

David, his mother, and his sister continue residing with his uncle at first, but he envisions owing a vast estate complete with a comfortable country house and a great complex of agricultural buildings. The first months prove taxing as the twelve-year-old boy struggles to supervise adult men, clear fields, build structures, make ends meet, and bring in a successful crop. His astonishing ability quickly wins the loyalty of the agricultural workers and the admiration of neighbors. Soon everyone—old and young, poor and rich, colored and white—calls him Mr. Fuller. For the next seven years Mr. Fuller works tirelessly to build a thriving agricultural enterprise and succeeds far beyond expectations.

David Builds a Plantation. After amassing a plump savings account by selling surplus crops and animals, young David sets his sights on relocating to Moulton in north-central Franklin County. In 1875 he travels to Moulton and acquires a generous expanse of land, purchased for $259.50, according to the deed.

Many men working for him at Pocomoke ask to come with him to Moulton   He pictures his mother and sister and the wives and children of his current agricultural laborers moving to the new location after he constructs sufficient dwellings to accommodate everyone. Meanwhile he sets his sights on assembling a much larger work force.

Saddling up, nineteen-year-old David firmly seats himself on a horse and speeds the roughly seven miles southwest from Moulton to the county seat of Louisburg, named for the ill-fated French king Louis XVI, seeking a skilled crew with firsthand agricultural wisdom to farm the land he now possesses. Many colored men with crucial experience come face to face with him as they crisscross the heart of town looking for work. He shares with them his dream of building an extensive plantation and eventually possessing all the land visible from the vantage point of his future house. He assures those men singled out to join his agricultural enterprise that he will help them cut timber and erect cabins for themselves and their families. They, in turn, will help him build a simple two-story cabin of hewn timber as temporary quarters for his mother, sister, and himself.

David employs some men as wage earners to tend the acreage set aside for his personal use, others as tenant farmers. The emancipation of slaves has entrenched the agricultural concept of tenant farming. All the men understand they will own neither the land they farm nor the dwellings they inhabit. The tenant farmers will pay David either cash or part of their crop as rent. Upper-rung tenant farmers pay cash for rent and supply their own tools, seeds, fertilizer, and farm animals.   Bottom-rung tenant farmers report to David as sharecroppers. They rent their land for a substantial share of their crop. David supervises them closely and supplies their tools, seeds, fertilizer, and farm animals. Meanwhile, after the harvest and the selling of crops, upper-rung tenant farmers pocket far more cash than sharecroppers. With time and experience, however, sharecroppers can advance to the upper rung. Then they will pay cash for rent and personally pocket more cash from the sale of their crops. Wives of all the men will assist David's mother as housekeepers, cooks, and poultry keepers, and some will help in the fields during annual periods of sowing and reaping. In time, bystanders will often see many mule-drawn tall carts crowding dirt roads on Saturday morning while hauling an abundance of produce from Fuller acreage to market in Louisburg.

David selects a pleasant site for his future permanent house and begins building cabins in the vicinity. The cabins closest to this central site serve as dwellings for men working the land he has reserved exclusively for his own use. They toil strenuously from daybreak until sunset for their wages. Cabins at a greater distance house the hardworking tenant farmers. Near his own original dwelling, the two-story cabin, David begins constructing an attractive permanent house and an imposing complement of outbuildings, ranging from several barns and stables to special structures used for stripping and curing tobacco. The vast complex includes a chicken house, smokehouse, distillery, carpentry shop, and well house, the last protecting the water supply and providing an ideal thick-walled spot for keeping milk and butter cool.

David creates a virtual village of families knit together by close social and economic ties, with the members of the community depending upon one another for their very survival. Almost everything necessary to sustain life exists on his plantation, including a commissary, or store that sells provisions. David gives credit when members of the community lack funds to buy from his inventory of flour, cornmeal, molasses, coffee, meat, fatback, lard, salt, castor oil and other medicines, needles and thread, clothing, shoes, snuff and other forms of tobacco, kerosene, matches, and many additional items. The tenant farmers and other workers possess insufficient cash to purchase much kerosene as fuel for lighting their dwellings and usually say their bedtime prayers soon after nightfall. For years, David employs kerosene lamps and candles for his own family but eventually installs a generator to bring the marvels of electricity, including lighting, to the plantation.

Through farming, David bonds with nature and the thick carpet of earth beneath his feet. He excels in the careful and responsible management of the land. His chickens and cows produce an abundance of eggs and milk, while his hogs grow fat roaming his wooded land. He plants countless acres of tobacco as a cash crop. He harvests also a dazzling array of cotton, corn, wheat, beans, peas, Irish potatoes, sweet potatoes, tomatoes, collards, turnips, cabbages, cucumbers, melons, and squash. His roses perfume the fresh country air. He takes pleasure in walking beside forest-lined streams where sunlight filters through high leafy canopies. He observes bees sipping nectar from dewy flowers. His orchards become laden with apples, peaches, and pears. Wild grapes and blackberries dot his land. David's strawberries ripen into scrumptious delights, and he nurtures pecan and black walnut trees.

His honey locust trees bear fragrant flowers and long brown pods containing seeds embedded in a dark sugary pulp. The seeds, edible raw or cooked, offer a rich source of protein and can be roasted for use as a coffee. The nutritious pulp suggests the taste of molasses. David often employs the pods to make savory locust beer for home consumption. One old recipe for brewing locust beer specifies breaking a large quantity of pods into pieces and combining them with sliced apples in a sizeable crock and then covering the mixture with gallons of boiling water. The amount of water used determines the strength of the beer. The preparer next spreads a clean cloth over the container and waits for the mixture to become lukewarm before adding one-half ounce of brewer's yeast (baker's yeast will suffice) and two cups of molasses. The home brewer leaves the container undisturbed for three or four days of fermentation and then strains the locust beer through clean muslin for immediate serving or bottling.

Additionally, David produces distilled alcoholic beverages. He makes some of the best apple brandy in the county by crushing apples in a cider mill and later distilling the fermented juice. Meanwhile he distills whiskey from fermented grain mash, made with corn, rye, or barley. He keeps a plentiful supply of alcoholic beverages to offer guests and to consume for personal enjoyment after a long day of work.

David has perused books on residential architecture and consulted other successful planters before designing and constructing his pleasant house of comfortable proportions, invigorated with modest Victorian elements. His land provides much of the needed building materials. Whenever he and his permanent staff of workers find spare time, they erect the foundation and framing. They haul stones from creek beds for the sturdy foundation. They bring down trees to build the heavy timber framing and scoop out great masses of red clay to bake into bricks for the chimneys, creating a fish pond at the excavation site. David commissions stonecutters to provide exterior stairways and fireplace hearths. His mule-drawn wagons haul clapboards, roofing materials, window panes, cement, plaster, nails, paint, stain, and other items from Louisburg. The rising David Thomas Fuller House occupies a lovely tree-shaded site approached from a winding county road by a new cedar-lined private avenue. The cedars grew tall and stately and give the avenue a touch of grandeur.

The large two-story house, flanked by massive exterior chimneys, possesses a prominent center gable, which David combines with a traditional gable roof to create a harmonious triple-A roof. The spacious porch, whose robust pillars carry stylish decorative brackets, opens through a pair of glass-paned doors onto the clean lines of a plastered central hall running nearly the length of the house and giving access to the parlor and other rooms. Opening the six doors of the hall creates a cross breeze that relieves the heat of summer. David finishes all rooms with wainscoting, or decorative wooden facing applied to the lower expanse of an interior wall. Moreover, he creates a hall stair that rises in a straight flight and exhibits handsome wainscoting on the wall side. The stairway gives access to the second-floor hall and bedrooms.

A one-story rear wing of the house contains the rectangular dining room, where spacious windows pierce the two longer walls and provide cooling breezes in summer. The kitchen forms a detached structure standing far enough behind the dining room to safeguard the main house against fire. Cooks carry food along a covered walkway, decorated with flanking latticework, from the kitchen to the dining room. Fireplaces with wooden mantles and stone hearths warm the dining room, parlor, and other living spaces during chilly days and nights. The restrained decorative details of the interior create a harmonious home environment signifying the partial Fuller recovery from the Civil War.

David and Zenobia. By the early 1880s David lives the life of a well-to-do country gentleman with the means to choose his own destiny and the power to influence local affairs. Having amassed sufficient wealth to support an expanded family comfortably, he seeks the hand of his distant cousin Zenobia Fuller, who lives near Mapleville, several miles south of his own community of Moulton. On December 16, 1885, twenty-nine-year-old David Thomas Fuller marries twenty-five-year-old Zenobia Ann Fuller, regarded as late marriages at the time for both the bridegroom and the bride. They pose in fashionable attire for a photographic portrait, with David seated and Zenobia standing, her left hand resting gently on his right shoulder. People seldom smile for the camera in the nineteenth century. Yet handsome and serene-faced David seems to eye the future with boyish confidence. Zenobia wears dainty flowers in her hair but offers the camera an almost grave expression.

The marriage brings both spouses much happiness. Zenobia gives birth to a boy, William David, called Willie, on November 16, 1986, and a girl, Martha Ann, called Annie, on May 10, 1888. Her next pregnancy proves exceedingly difficult and leads to nine days of torturous labor before she delivers a girl, her namesake, in mid-September 1890. Depleted, Zenobia clings to life several days, until September 24, and her infant daughter lives but a few months before following her mother into the earth. Inconsolable, David remains a widower for the next sixteen years. Meanwhile his mother, now sixty-two, skillfully guides the upbringing and education of her two surviving grandchildren.

David as a Widower. Judged by the standards of the ruling class of his day, David proves a model of integrity and honor as a widower. He consistently attends church every week. Sunday afternoons often see David at the reins of a horse and buggy, carrying his mother and children to visit other prominent planter families, including the Tharringtons, Cottrells, Perdues, Guptons, and Parrishes.

Over the years many noteworthy true stories about him have reached my ears from his children and grandchildren. Once, when serving as a juror on a capital case—the defendant has been charged with murder—David holds his ground for acquittal against the strong pressure of eleven other jurors insisting upon conviction.

His courage leads to a hung jury. Later, evidence comes to light proving the innocence of the accused, and everyone realizes David's valor has saved a human life.

On another occasion when selected for jury service, David watches the ticking courtroom clock creep forward and realizes the trial will extend beyond one day. Storms howl outside and make the local dirt roads treacherous. Thus the jurors face an uncomfortable night sleeping on the courthouse floor. Someone informs a local furniture dealer, "Mr. David Fuller must sleep in the courthouse tonight." The merchant immediately dispatches a wagon from his store to send David bedding and a three-quarter mattress (then a standard size extending three-quarters the width of a double mattress). David refuses to sleep in comfort while other jurors experience a night of misery and asks local friends and acquaintances to provide blankets and sheets for creating pallets, or temporary small beds on the floor, for the benefit of his colleagues.

The most memorable story about David, conveyed to me by four of his children, regards his medical skills. Bites from snakes and particularly from rabid animals pose a critical danger to nineteenth-century farming people living in isolation from professional medical services. Folk medicine at the time extols the use of the so-called *mad stone* to counteract the rabid or poisonous effects of animal and snake bites. The typical mad stone fits in an adult palm and takes the appearance of a porous stony mass. Extremely rare, mad stones form occasionally in the stomachs or intestinal canals of large herbivorous animals such as deer. David travels a considerable distance to acquire a mad stone during the last quarter of the century, with an eye toward curing family members or neighbors afflicted with dangerous animal or snake bites. His tan-colored stone possesses a textured surface and bears many black dots.

Word quickly spreads to adjoining counties and beyond that David holds one of the highly prized objects. People come from far and wide in buggies and wagons bearing loved ones bitten by presumably rabid animals or poisonous snakes. He gives all patients medical care without charge and immediately begins treatment after bedding white patients in his house and colored patients in the dwellings of his farming associates. David first boils the mad stone in milk. He then applies the hot stone to the wound. The stone falls off after becoming filled with poison, so I am told, and he repeats the process of boiling and applying as often as necessary. After hours or days of treatment, the mad stone will no longer adhere to the bite, indicating the elimination of all poison. The cured patient then returns home. Apparently David never loses a single medical guest during the treatment process.

David and Miss Annie. Meanwhile David's acreage has continued to expand as he amasses one tract of land after another until he can no longer see their limits from his house. By 1905, Miss Annie Elizabeth Mangum has called at the prosperous Fuller plantation. Educated at neighboring Louisburg College and certified as a teacher, she seeks to rent quarters from David, whose dwelling stands conveniently near a one-room schoolhouse where she has accepted a teaching position. Martha Frances Kearney Fuller, his mother, enthusiastically approves the idea. She looks forward to Miss Annie Mangum's company and knows no gossip will sully the family, with a mother present under the same roof as her son and his new boarder. Besides, David exceeds her age by almost nineteen years.

The Fullers learn that Miss Annie, as most people call her, reached adulthood under comfortable circumstances in the city of Durham, roughly fifty miles southwest of Moulton. She describes spending her girlhood in a spacious Victorian house on Mangum Street, named for her family. She mentions that the Mangum House stands across the street from Trinity College (later becoming the East Campus of Duke University) and once slept at least ten family members: the father and mother (George Arnold Mangum and Mary Elizabeth Powell Mangum), their seven children, and one of George's brothers. A surviving late nineteenth-century photographic portrait shows five family members standing and five seated on the lawn in front of their attractive vine-draped porch, all stylishly attired in tailored dresses and suits.

David and his new border discover several common interests such as discussing family histories. Miss Annie's parents knew their lineage. Her late father, George Arnold Magnum, who died in 1899, had told his children of their Mangum heritage extending from time immemorial in England. Family records show that Miss Annie descended from Virginia-born William Mangum I, who obtained a choice eighteenth-century land grant from John Carteret, Earl Granville (1690-1763), one of the eight Lords Proprietors of Carolina.

The initial eight Lords Proprietors, distinguished courtiers, had acquired the Province of Carolina from King Charles II, in 1663, as a proprietary colony. The proprietary era lasts until the colony transfers to the protection of the Crown, in 1729, and gains a much closer relationship to the King and Privy Council, though Lord Granville retains his share of Carolina. Endowed with the substantial grant from Lord Granville, William Mangum creates a prosperous agricultural complex in a district of British America (Granville District) forming the upper part of present-day North Carolina. Later, the Granville District becomes divided into counties and then, at the time of the American Revolution, the Granville estate loses the district.

William Mangum's acreage in the Granville District lies in the area ultimately forming Warren County, North Carolina, bounded on the north by Virginia and the south by Franklin County. The grant from Lord Granville describes William Mangum as a planter of Saint John's Parish. One of his sons, Miss Annie's distant uncle William Mangum II, counts himself among the Loyalists to the King of England and fights for the British in Georgia during the divisive Revolutionary War, only to spend his final three decades as an exile of vastly reduced circumstances on tiny Morris Island, off the southwestern tip of Nova Scotia.

Continuing, Miss Annie tells David of her direct descent from William Mangum I and then turns to trace the Powell lineage. As the Mangums, the Powells originated in England. Mary Elizabeth Powell Mangum descended from Robert Powell, her paternal grandfather, who had arrived from England in the late eighteenth century.

Miss Annie learns that her new landlord, David, knows his own lineage. His first direct ancestor in British America, Ezekiel Fuller, came from England and settled in Isle of Wight County, in southeastern Virginia. Ezekiel dies in 1723. His son Timothy moves to Granville County (located in the Granville District) and fights in the French and Indian War (1754-1763), a conflict seeing

France and its Indian allies pitted against England and its colonies. Timothy's grandson Daniel settles in Franklin County and begets William, David's father. As noted, William dies only six months after the last gasp of the Civil War, leaving behind a scorched and ruined family, but young David springs to the rescue and brilliantly restores Fuller vigor and assets to a glimmer of antebellum luster. When seeking lighthearted pastimes in the isolated countryside, David and Miss Annie often regale each other with stories about their relatives and family trees. David's mother helps fill any gaps in his memory.

David tells Miss Annie the story of Zenobia's tragic and untimely death. Does she tell David about her former beau, Mr. Douglass, whose photograph she keeps until the end of her life? Handsome and endowed with wavy light hair, Mr. Douglass sits for the camera around the turn of the century wearing a fine vested suit with high lapels, while his neckwear consists of a stiff wing collar and four-in-hand tie. His fashionably tailored jacket gives him a professional square-shouldered silhouette. How did Miss Annie and Mr. Douglass meet? Did heaven reach down to earth for them? Why did they part? Did they still catch themselves remembering? The answers to these questions remain forever lost in the impenetrable mists of time.

Miss Annie's early photographs reveal a seemingly serious but sophisticated and stylish young lady opulently arrayed in embroidery and lace. Sitting for a hand-painted oval photograph as a student at Louisburg College, blue-eyed Miss Annie wears an elegant lace-trimmed cream silk gown, no doubt buttoned at the back, with very high neck. Her light brown hair has been brushed up on the sides and probably coaxed with a curling iron into soft waves around the head.

Miss Annie and David find much tranquility spending time together. Ultimately, he proposes to Miss Annie, after seeking permission from her mother. As noted, George Arnold Mangum had died in 1899. Family and friends witness their dignified marriage in Durham on October 31, 1906. The *Franklin Times*, anchored in Louisburg, alludes to the wedding in a lighthearted front-page piece penned on "Oct. 29, '06," but not published in the newspaper until November 2: "Mr. D. T. Fuller's friends and neighbors will be shocked, but not surprised to learn of a recent attack of heart trouble, and [he] will leave on Tuesday, the 30th inst., for Durham to see a specialist, who has been in charge of his case for some time. They [his friends] will be more surprised to learn that she will return with him, as he thinks his case requires her whole undivided attention. Good bye, Davie."

Annie Elizabeth Mangum had celebrated her thirty-first birthday precisely eight weeks before the wedding, and David Thomas Fuller will reach his fiftieth birthday in a mere sixteen days. He always addresses her as Miss Annie, and she him as Mr. Fuller. Apparently the marriage offers both husband and wife great contentment. Miss Annie gives birth to their first child, Mary Susan, on September 25, 1907. Only four months later David mourns the death of his beloved mother, the indomitable Martha Frances Kearney Fuller, though memories of her steady encouragement rush back to comfort him.

Miss Annie's counsel and good judgment prove invaluable to her husband in the coming years as he continues expanding the David T. Fuller Plantation into a noble property. December 18, 1909, sees Miss Annie give birth to fraternal twins, George Duke and David Thomas, Jr. She brings forth another boy, Walter Erwin, on May 21, 1912—five weeks after the disastrous Titanic sinking—and the final Fuller child, Ida Powell, on June 2, 1914.

Walter, who has enjoyed two years of babyhood free of any personal shipwrecks, becomes quite jealous at the birth of Ida. Kindhearted David soothes the toddler by taking him to Louisburg and buying him a fine hat for church. Delighted, little Walter nicknames his prized acquisition the Preaching Hat, drawn out to Pre-e-e-e-aching Hat. He drives Miss Annie to distraction by calling out from his bedroom every night, "I want my Preeeeaching Hat! I want my Preeeeaching Hat!" Finally, an exasperated Miss Annie temporarily expands her vocabulary with an indecorous word, laughingly telling her husband, "Give the boy his damn Preeeeaching Hat before we all lose out minds."

The five children grow strong on the products of the earth around them. For amusements, they explore the Fuller plantation; play games, and coax adults into telling the glorious stories of bygone days.

Lamentation for David. David drives himself relentlessly not only in operating his plantation but also in expanding his holdings with new tenant farms and numerous agricultural animals and buildings, virtually an empire by the standards of a modest rural county. At this time electric power lines do not reach rural areas. Thus David electrifies his home and barns by installing a large Delco Light Plant, a reliable generator driven by an internal combustion engine. The Delco, according to exuberant newspaper advertisements, "brings city conveniences to the farm and takes much of the drudgery out of farm life." Now David has electricity available for household and farming purposes. He starts the Delco, and the entire family becomes mesmerized by the stunning glow of light bulbs and electric lamps.

To achieve a bountiful harvest of surplus crops, sold for cash, David constantly encourages his farmers. They exert Herculean labor, for the stiff red clay of Moulton proves difficult to plow and requires abundant manuring and diligent pampering. Such measures succeed in tapping the earth's natural power to produce a copious yield. On-the-run David often bolts breakfast and lunch and skips on sleep.

After twelve years of marriage to Miss Annie, he develops stomach cancer and becomes gravely ill but lingers until June 20, 1919, when he dies at the age of sixty-two years and seven months. On June 27 the *Franklin Times* carries his long obituary on the front page, referring to David initially as Dr. D. T. Fuller, thereby saluting his many years serving others through the healing arts:

"Dr. D. T. Fuller, one of Franklin County's most prominent and substantial planters . . . died at his home on Friday morning . . . after an illness of several months. . . . He was a kind and devoted husband and father, indulgent in all things that were good. He was a neighbor whose companionship, advice, and kindness were always abundant and appreciated by many. He will be greatly missed in his community. . . . He took much interest in the public matters of his neighborhood and gave freely of his time in the prosecution of things of public benefit. Mr. Fuller was a man whose friendship was appreciated and whose hospitality was always free and of the most royal kind. Mr. Fuller gave much of his time for many years to the interests of public schools in his district [by] serving on the school committee [school board]. . . ." He leaves two surviving children from his first marriage, "Mr. W. D. [William David] Fuller . . ., member of the Board of County Commissioners of Franklin County, and Mrs. J. F. [Joseph Ferril] Parrish" (his first-born daughter, Martha Ann), as well as five children from his second marriage, "Masters George, David, and Walter Fuller, and Misses Mary Susan and Ida Powell Fuller."

"The funeral services were held at Corinth [Baptist] Church and were conducted by his pastor," in collaboration with three additional ministers who arrived from "South Boston, Va. The remarks by the ministers were . . . appropriate, complimentary and deserving, showing a life well spent. The interment . . . in the church cemetery" featured "the beautiful and impressive Masonic ceremony," as conducted "by Sandy Creek Lodge with the assistance of many visiting Masons from . . . Hendersonville, Louisburg, and many other neighboring lodges. Possibly the largest crowd of friends and relatives" ever assembled at Corinth Church came "to pay a last sad tribute to the deceased man," now resting beside Zenobia. "The floral tribute was profuse and beautiful. . . . The bereaved family has the sympathy of the entire community."

Miss Ida Powell Fuller has celebrated only five birthdays at the time of her father's untimely death and later in life possesses but one clear mental image of him. Perhaps a pivotal event in her life, she remembers crying when her mother punished her for some trivial misbehavior. The dying David, whom she calls Papa, struggles from his bed to comfort his youngest child. He holds Ida gently in his arms and soothes her with a gentle touch: "There, there, my precious little one, your mother is so strict with you. Now stop crying and make your proud father smile." This treasured memory of Papa often calms Ida in later times of unpleasantness.

Ida finds another source of cheer in her much older half-siblings, who live with their spouses several miles away but often come to the plantation for visits. She addresses William as Brother Willie and Martha Ann as Sister Annie. Meanwhile Fuller housekeepers and cooks teach Ida to employ terms of endearment for her brothers and sister living at home. She addresses Walter as Bralt (for Bro Walt) and addresses the twins similarly, Br'george (for Bro George) and Br'dave (for Bro David). She addresses Mary Susan simply as Sister. As a young child, spunky Ida frequently joins Walter, two years her senior, for play and other activities. The two enjoy dressing up in adult clothing. A surviving snapshot from around 1919 shows Ida wearing a delicate lace dress and classic dark straw hat, while Walter sports long trousers, collared shirt, head-swallowing touring cap, and four-in-hand necktie extending well below his waist. They stand barefoot before throngs of bushes and betray complete satisfaction with their showy splendor by grinning from ear to ear.

8

Miss Annie Shows Grit and Becomes a Power in Franklin County

After David dies in 1919, Miss Annie wears black clothing for years as a sign of mourning but faces her new status as widow of a country squire with unyielding courage and determination. She resolves to play a greater role among the powerhouses of Franklin County by combating the smothering restrictions then imposed on Southern ladies.

First, she ensures that the rich tapestry of fruitful activities on her sprawling plantation will continue providing a comfortable life for her family. She hands an overseer considerable authority over the entire agricultural establishment. Miss Annie possesses scant interest in housekeeping or preparing food and retains her large staff of maids, cooks, and gardeners, all drawn from the farming families on the plantation. She charges twelve-year-old Mary Susan, who enjoys wielding authority, with directing the household staff in her absence. Second, she secures a crucial telephone by paying the phone company a pretty penny to run a line several miles to the plantation. Miss Annie possesses the only telephone within five miles in any direction, and the instrument proves invaluable in giving her a stronger voice in county affairs and summoning help in emergencies. Third, she acquires a good source of transportation. Although completely inexperienced as a driver, Miss Annie purchases a new motorcar and takes the wheel with the intention of driving forward but accidentally shifts into reverse and slams into her house.

Rather than attempting to operate an automobile again, she informs her nine-year-old twins, George and David, they will serve thenceforward as her chauffeurs. This period of light-handed government oversight sees countless people operating motor vehicles without drivers' licenses. George and David express delight at their newfound responsibility but then discover they lack the height to touch the automobile pedals with their feet or to see above the steering wheel. Their mother immediately arranges for the pedals to be extended to reach their feet and directs the twins to observe the road by looking through the steering wheel. The boys take turns driving Miss Annie and other family members on Fuller outings. They visit relatives near and far in North Carolina and Virginia. Miss Annie always sits beside the designated chauffer and peppers him with instructions about the proper driving speed (*slow*) and the correct operation of the vehicle (*cautious*). In these days before the widespread adoption of electric starters, someone always cranks an automobile by hand to start the internal combustion engine. The motor often fires suddenly and kicks the crankshaft back. The twins break their arms more than once while cranking the family car.

Many decades later Mary Susan pens several pages of her reminiscences about life on the plantation. She tells of the Fuller children using two terms of affectionate respect, Aunt and Uncle, for older people of color. From time to time Mary Susan mentions Aunt Beck, one of the most beloved cooks preparing meals for the family. Mary Susan relates that Miss Annie always steered clear of pots and pans, for she "never had any experience with cooking and knew very little about what went on in the kitchen." Aunt Beck not only created superb meals for the family but also brought nutritious food from the plantation kitchen to the agricultural workers. Mary Susan describes the hardworking cook often trudging to a large tract of Fuller land called "the Tucker place," located "two miles from home . . . , with a basket of food on her head and [carrying] a gallon of buttermilk for the colored men working in the . . . fields. . . ." Mary Susan adds that Aunt Beck "slept upstairs with us after my father died" but outlived him by only one year.

She then describes a treasured memory of David Thomas Fuller springing from the time a Raleigh physician "set up an office in the Louisburg Hotel to remove tonsils. Papa took me on the buggy [for a tonsillectomy]. It started raining that afternoon. With [Papa carefully putting] the buggy curtains up and [nestling me in lap robes and other snug articles] . . . of cover, I stayed warm and dry."

After David died, according to Mary Susan, Miss Annie employed home remedies for curing or relieving disease, and she mastered a hefty medical book to gain sufficient skills for treating every member of the plantation community. Physicians came to Moulton "for emergencies only," though we Fullers "went to the dentist," who had established his office on the upper floor of a building in Louisburg. "We took a [box] lunch to eat while we waited for each other [in the dentist's office]. One of the boys [once] dropped the box, and boiled eggs went rolling down the steps...."

During a severe influenza epidemic the entire Fuller family became seriously ill and stayed together "in one room upstairs on three double beds." Miss Annie asked one of the men on the plantation to bring "a box of oranges [to the sickroom]. That is about all we ate...." Then one of the cooks, whom the Fullers affectionately called Aunt Lizzie, "cooked an opossum. She knew we would not eat [opossum] ..., so she said, 'Aunt Lizzie has brought up a duck.' I guess we all ate a little."

Returning to the subject of doctoring, Mary Susan describes the use of "the mad stone ... to draw out the poison from snake [and] dog bites.... People would come from miles away" for this vital treatment without charge.

Mary Susan often mentions the Fullers gladly sharing their blessing with others. Many of their pastors at Corinth Church attended Wake Forest College, located in the nearby town of Wake Forest (but later moved to Winston-Salem and later still rechristened Wake Forest University). These young men repeatedly "said they never could have gotten through school" except for the kindness of "the Fullers and others who loaded the car down with farm produce" to spare them from outlaying much money on groceries. Mary Susan adds that "food was always plentiful" on the plantation because "a large orchard and garden" provided "fresh, dried, and canned fruits and vegetables" as well as "homemade cider vinegar by the barrel, sweet potatoes by the hill, [and an abundance of] pickles and preserves. Chickens, hogs, and cows supplied fresh and cured meats [plus] butter [and] eggs."

Miss Annie as a Forceful Matriarch and Officeholder. Meanwhile, when women finally achieve the vote with the ratification of the Nineteenth Amendment, taking effect in 1920, Miss Annie becomes a power in the political and civic affairs of Franklin County. She sponsors candidates for office mirroring her progressive viewpoint. The twins drive her from one meeting to another. While she discusses proposals and policies affecting the county or the region, the boys play outside in good weather and sit quietly beside her on cold or rainy days. Miss Annie enjoys the respect of her fellow Franklin County citizens. They seek her advice on innumerable matters. She serves on various committees and proves a strong advocate for strengthening public education. A remarkable trailblazer, Miss Annie enters the first echelon of women gaining elective office in North Carolina when voters propel her to membership on the Franklin County Board of Education, in 1935, and she serves without opposition until retiring eighteen years later, five months shy of her seventy-eighth birthday.

An avid reader, Miss Annie encourages her children to digest literary masterpieces. She tolerates but seldom applauds their enjoyment of popular amusements. They relish playing cards, yet Miss Annie seizes the proverbial "devil's books" at the tiniest quarrel over a game and tosses them into the flames of a fireplace or kitchen cookstove. She brooks no opposition to her authority.

She expresses no fear about residing in a large country house without the protective presence of a man. She ignores cooks and housekeepers who whisper about seeing two feminine ghostly presences—a young adult and an infant—in her dwelling. She always keeps a loaded pistol by her bed. If she hears the slightest mysterious sound interrupting the haunting nocturnal calls of whippoorwills, she squanders no time investigating but raises a window and fires several shots into the night sky. Everyone within earshot comments knowingly, "Miss Annie just heard a noise!"

Miss Annie takes comfort that several families on her plantation live within shouting distance. She has formed close bonds with all members of the Fuller agricultural establishment. They bear numerous surnames, including Debnam, Powell, Foster, and Eaton. As noted, her children always call the older women

Aunt and the older men Uncle. The farmers and their families address the Fuller children as Miss Mary Susan, Mr. George, Mr. David, Mr. Walter, and Miss Ida. Few tenant farmers possess buggies. Most of them place chairs in their mule-drawn wagons for carrying their families to church.

One of the most beloved tenant farmers, Uncle Ned, has established the custom of knocking on Miss Annie's back door soon after dawn each New Year to wish her good luck, reflecting an old British tradition that a household visited initially by a man on January 1 will enjoy twelve months of good fortune. In the meantime one tenant farmer' son, a lad called Zoo, forges a close bond with George and remains his best friend for life. As boys, Zoo and George can snub the rigid and heartbreaking segregation then plaguing North Carolina, for they live on an isolated and self-sustaining enclave ruled by a powerful matriarch who abhors the prevailing abuse of colored citizens and welcomes the warm friendship.

One tenant farmer's wife, Aunt Ida Debnam, serves as the nursemaid to the Fuller children. She showers them with affection, and they love her dearly. She beams one Christmas morning when Walter squeals with delight to find that Santa Claus has left him an engraved pocket watch. As he warms himself by the fire, he calls Aunt Ida to come examine his new timepiece. Walter's hand slips as he hands her the treasured gift, and his watch shatters on the stone hearth below. Aunt Ida and Walter weep. She cradles the heartbroken boy in her arms to comfort him. Everyone present knows that Miss Annie does not readily excuse carelessness. She tells Walter that perhaps Santa Claus will bring another watch next year. Until then, he must ask other people for the time or organize his daytime activities by observing the movements of the sun.

Impish Ida and Her Playful Siblings. The Fullers often drive roughly four miles east to a spot on Sandy Creek gracing the small unincorporated community of Laurel, site of a water-powered gristmill called Laurel Mill. Gristmills effectively harness nature's energy by grinding corn and wheat into cornmeal, grits, and flour. Complete with a wide dam nesting above impressive rock formations, Laurel Mill possesses an undershot water wheel powering belts and gears to turn the massive stones grinding the grain. The grist mill at Laurel serves as an essential agricultural resource during Ida's girlhood and young adulthood but later operates only sporadically and finally closes at the end of the twentieth century.

In the 1910s and 1920s, inhabitants of Franklin County gather at Laurel not only for grinding their grain but also for picnicking, swimming, fishing, and baptizing. The young Fullers enjoy scampering over the large boulders and roughly horizontal rock surfaces rising from Sandy Creek. They spend long hours swimming in the cool flowing water.

Whenever Sandy Creek becomes swollen and turbulent after heavy rainfall, the Fullers remain by the shoreline rather than venturing into the churning trap of deadly currents. On once occasion the little daredevil Ida tempts fate by ignoring this sound principle and finds herself pulled under the treacherous water. A strong swimmer on an outing with his family risks his life diving for her. For many years Ida retains vivid memories of her heart-pounding brush with death yet never relinquishes her passion for swimming.

She couples her thrill-seeking nature with a mischievous side. Once when a young girl comes to the Fuller house for a day of play, Ida suggests exploring the attic. She challenges her trusting friend to enter a dark attic storage room alone and immediately slams and latches the door on her. Ida returns to the ground floor, leaving her stunned prisoner to her fate. Fortunately for the terrified youngster, the Fullers inquire about her whereabouts and immediately rescue the girl from the dismal windowless chamber. No doubt rock-ribbed Miss Annie devises suitable punishment for Ida's rascally deed.

Ida's brothers sometimes rival her in exhibiting an impish side. On one occasion when swimming at Laurel, the three unaccompanied boys dare one another to walk the four miles home in naked splendor. George, David, and Walter strip off their bathing suits and head for Moulton. The boys grin widely and wave conspicuously at everyone passing their way on buggies, wagons, automobiles, and trucks. The young scamps have become quite pleased with themselves by the time they finally turn into the tree-lined private avenue leading to the Fuller house. Miss Annie sees them coming from the porch. "I think you have lost your minds," she says in a calm even voice, "but I have an effective treatment to restore your sound judgment."

She lines the boys up and administers a heavy dose of castor oil to each and sends them to bed for the rest of the day to cure their deficiency in good sense. Tucked away in their beds on the second floor, the brothers hear two sets of muffled laughter from below as Miss Annie regales Aunt Ida with the tale of their daring birthday-suited adventure.

The Fuller children enjoy telling and retelling both factual and fanciful horror stories. One true story they whisper to one another—always out of Miss Annie's earshot—concerns an unfortunate neighboring girl. In her early teens, she pens a farewell note to a friend explaining her intention to commit suicide. The girl foresees her rigidly conservative parents expelling her from their home and never again uttering her name after discovering she carries a child. She envisions living wretchedly as a homeless and unfed wanderer and hearing vile, heartless people label her a *whore* and her infant a *bastard*. To avoid the strong possibility of suffering unbearable persecution, she takes her life by jumping into a well on the family farm. Miss Annie unsuccessfully attempts to shield her sons and daughters from news of such heartbreaking calamities, but her children possess their own channels of information and know far more about the secrets of Moulton than their mother can possibly imagine.

Perhaps their favorite true story concerns a young girl of the region being pronounced dead after a sudden and severe illness. Her grieving parents leave a dazzling jeweled ring on her finger when burying their beloved daughter in a church cemetery. Grave robbers come after dark for the valuable ring. When they open the coffin in chilly night air and roughly attempt pulling the ring from her finger, the girl suddenly emerges from a deep coma. Frightened and confused, she sits up and calls for her parents. The grave robbers flee and abandon her to the damp, gloomy graveyard. She recognizes the shadowy church and stumbles to her nearby home along an inky country road. Her mother and father scream in terror when she steps through the unlocked front door. Moments later they rejoice—realizing she lives—and they begin piecing together the bizarre story of her exhuming. She makes a complete recovery. Needless to say, her happy parents never bring charges against the would-be robbers who saved their daughter's life.

The practice of embalming bodies still remains rare in rural settings. More than one family has buried loved ones sliding into deathlike comas. The Fuller children learn in horror that one of their distant relatives suffered this fate. The truth comes to light when the family moves the deceased from one resting spot to another and discovers he had roused and desperately struggled to claw his way out of his underground prison.

Chilling true stories circulate of certain people of great wealth being buried with working telephones to avoid the ghastly possibility of a live entombment. A number of nineteenth-century souls alleviated their fright over live burial by having their coffins equipped with pipes leading to the surface of the ground. The undertaker tied a cord to one of the big toes of the deceased and then ran this so-called toe string through the open end of the pipe to a bell above the grave. The entombed person coming out of a coma needed only to wiggle the appropriate foot to ring for help.

Ida proves a pack rat and collects everything imaginable. Her preserved childhood mementos include her photograph album, crammed with snapshots and documents. She probably begins assembling the album in 1923, the year of her ninth birthday, judging from the dates written below the first photographs. She captures images of many well-groomed relatives and friends, all scrupulously attired in stylish hats and clothes down to the smallest detail.

One snapshot, inscribed "Out for a ride," shows young Ida decked in a pretty dress falling below her knees. She sits in her small personal buggy and holds the reins of her dappled pony. She often pilots the attractive vehicle along winding dirt country roads not only to explore natural settings but also to visit friends and relatives. Moreover, the pony carries her for weekly sessions with her voice and piano teachers, for Ida possesses the power to produce magnificent song and has shown an early appreciation for classical music. Ida demonstrates an unquenchable thirst also for reading and learning. Her fascination with literature slowly evolves from her early childhood.

The year 1920 sees six-year-old Ida begin her formal education in the nearby one-room school on Fuller land. Two ladies, Miss Valentine and Miss Hollingsworth, serve as teachers and border at the Fuller home during the short school year. One of them teaches the first, second, and third graders. She customarily gives Ida's small first-grade class a period of instruction and then suggests a classroom assignment such as neatly printing the letters of the alphabet. While completing the assignment, Ida listens carefully as the teacher instructs the second graders and then the third graders, thereby accelerating her own pace of learning. She absorbs considerable knowledge in a compact school year. Two years before Ida entered the first grade, the voters of North Carolina had approved a constitutional amendment extending the minimum school term to six months.

Four of the Fuller siblings complete their elementary education in the same one-room building and then attend high school, Mary Susan at Louisburg High School and the middle trio at the small new Gold Sand School, roughly six miles east of their home. Ida, the youngest child, spends her final elementary years and the entirety of her high school years at Gold Sand. The Fullers and other white children ride over dirt roads on a rickety wooden school bus to Gold Sand School. The vehicle rattles and groans under the weight of the young passengers and possesses insufficient power to climb the steepest hill along the way. Rain or shine, the boys scramble through the door and push the bus to the summit for the last leg of the journey.

Children of the rest of the Fuller faming community walk to their own educational facility, gaining instruction through the seventh grade. They keep complaints to themselves but cannot hike the long distance to a colored school offering higher grades, and the county provides no transportation for them.

Ida enjoys her days at Gold Sand. A surviving photograph shows her standing with a group of other elementary students on an outing with their teacher, Miss Elizabeth Johnson, who apparently has not noticed a clowning boy dangling his hand over the head of a girl in front of him. As an elementary student, Ida joins several clubs and sings solos in numerous musical programs.

In the meantime Ida pursues an active social life. One day when illness prevents her from attending school, a fellow student writes her a surviving but now tattered and fragmentary letter lacking a signature. The unknown young man, who trusts "sending this by Walter," has employed lined school paper for stationery. He carefully folds his effort and pens the address on the back, "Miss Ida Fuller at Home." He confesses "how much we missed you" at school today and cannot wait for some prearranged gathering "next Sun. night." The author warily promises to send another message "if I don't have to apologize to Ruffin [Ruffin Harper, Ida's current boyfriend] for this letter" and then adds an amusing, "P.S. If you don't get this, let me know, and I will write again." Ida permanently saves his affectionate and unguarded letter in her photo album as a prized keepsake.

About this time another potential and unknown suitor compliments Ida with a warm note, from which she clips and saves only fifteen words cautiously expressing interest in her: "I do think she is a mighty nice girl, but I know one much nicer." Jubilant Ida has written the single word "me" to indicate the identity of the "much nicer" young lady.

The Fuller Children Forge Ahead Socially and Educationally. Ida's sister and brothers carve out their own social niches. Mary Susan preserves a spotless reputation and calm demeanor attracting respectable and lofty-minded individuals to her circle in high school and later at Louisburg College and Meredith College. In contrast, young George relishes the company of chatty older women and begins courting one of his high school teachers. In the 1920s such matters generally remain under family rather than government jurisdiction. Miss Annie expresses scant concern over the affair and stoically ignores any resulting gossip. She takes satisfaction in knowing George will not impregnate a young girl and predicts he will seek greener pastures in college. Her lustful son has formed liaisons with several older women by the time he completes high school at the age of seventeen, in 1926, and enrolls at North Carolina State College (later renamed University) in Raleigh. He returns home after falling quite ill and, after recovering his health, decides to forego college. He builds his own country store with an attached bedroom where he usually sleeps. Young George soon persuades another teacher to become his sweetheart, and she gladly helps him decorate the bedroom.

His amiable fraternal twin, David, avoids passionate entanglements until he meets the love of his life as a student at old Wake Forest, long before the respected institution moved from its original campus in the town of Wake Forest to the city of Winston-Salem. Yet the extensive Fuller agricultural land sees the dawn of new courtships. Teenage Walter seeks and finds innumerable romantic adventures not only in high school but also as a student at State. Earlier, in 1927, young Walter, then fourteen or fifteen, stands before Ida's camera while steadying Lulu, one of the Fuller horses, by holding her bridle and caressing her neck. An attractive young girl named Lessie Davis, gracefully decked in a dark dress, perches sidesaddle on Lulu's back and seems to bask in the protective presence of Walter. His handsome face and fashionable attire must have charmed Lessie and any other visitors arriving that day at the Fuller home. He sports a natty Gatsby—the cap whose name derives from the F. Scott Fitzgerald novel (published 1925)—and a fine sport coat, white shirt, four-in-hand necktie, ankle-length trousers, and laced leather shoes.

Ida Stars at School and Braves the Great Depression. By the eighth grade, 1927-1928, Ida has begun performing in school plays. Additionally, she enjoys a major role as a soloist for a Christmas cantata at Gold Sand on December 23, 1927. The following year she attends a banquet of the Young Tar Heel Farmers, presided over by her brother Walter, president of the club. Ida's two surviving report cards document her excellent grades under Miss Lillie Harper, her teacher in both the eighth and ninth grades.

In the tenth grade, her junior year, Ida plays the female romantic lead in Lillian Mortimer's *He's My Pal* (Chicago: T. S. Dennison and Company Publishers, 1927). Lillian Mortimer has become a successful American playwright and wins popular acclaim for this comedy-drama in three acts. Ida's stylish character, Lark, dominates the stage as a "lovable but frivolous" eighteen-year-old classic beauty living in a bustling California town. Mysteriously, she had lost her true love one year ago. He seems to have vanished from the face of the earth. Lark possesses no clues about his fate. She attempts to put the past behind her by accepting a proposal of marriage from likable young Wally, now embarking upon a lively career in advertising. Lark hides her deep heartbreak by planning elaborate interior furnishings for her bridal home.

When Wally's best friend, Roger, arrives for a visit, the audience makes two stunning discoveries. First, Roger has suffered the loss of his right arm saving Wally's life. Second, Roger and Lark—unknown to Wally—know each other intimately. Roger comes into focus as Lark's lost love. Lark and Roger profess undying devotion for one another, but he plans to catch an evening train, alone, as the honorable course of action. Yet Wally discovers that Lark loves Roger. Wally quickly packs his bags to leave town, freeing Lark to marry Roger, to whom he owes his life and feels a tremendous sense of obligation. Moreover, Wally sacrifices his reputation to push Roger and Lark together. He persuades unselfish young Mona, who secretly has been "looking at him with her heart in her eyes," to tell Lark a clever falsehood, that Wally has run away after falling in love with Mona and she with him. These rapidly unfolding stratagems have the intended effect of pushing Roger and Lark to the altar.

As the play unfolds, stock characters prance across the stage. A brutally sharp-tongued wife finally realizes that she has "been an ungrateful woman" ruining the life of her "wonderful, smart husband. . . ." Conforming to the open bigotry then abounding throughout the nation, the playwright adds an incompetent Negro cook, Smudge, described as "a typical lazy darky . . . who drawls her words," exemplified by "de cake am cut, an' de ice cream am served."

In the meantime Lark and Roger enjoy three months of wedded bliss. Then Wally suddenly returns and proposes to Mona, who appeared in the first act as "an ugly duckling" but has gained three important assets—a new sense of confidence and poise, a "pretty summer dress," and a fresh face painted by a "beauty specialist." Wally now realizes how deeply he loves Mona. She mistakenly believes he pities her and refuses to enter a loveless match. After the usual comedic misunderstandings, Wally finally clearly expresses his love for Mona. Ecstatic, she accepts his proposal. Then an enthusiastic Lark and Roger lead the others in circling the happy couple and singing "Here comes the bride" as the curtain falls to ringing applause.

May 1930 sees Ida attend the Junior-Senior Banquet, where twenty-five students and teachers sign her program and hear her offer the traditional junior toast to the seniors. Those present enjoy a multi-course dinner, beginning with grapefruit cocktail and ending with Washington pie, actually a double-layer cake with a raspberry jelly filling and a confectioners' sugar topping, when prepared according to the classic recipe, but variation include a custard, chocolate, or cherry filling and a whipped cream topping.

This scrumptious dinner belies the onslaught of the ravaging Great Depression, then striking Franklin County with particular economic severity. Although people throughout the county have drastically curtailed their spending, this period sees Miss Annie escort fifteen-year-old Ida to a smart ladies' apparel shop in Louisburg to enhance her wardrobe with a new dress. Ida tries on several and finally finds one pleasing to both mother and daughter when someone rushes into the shop shouting that the bank has just closed. Miss Annie pales but utters only five words, "Ida, take off the dress." The Fullers remain land rich but have become instantly cash poor. Their bank in Louisburg eventually reopens, yet depositors never regain full restoration of their old checking and savings accounts.

Ida reaps much pleasure from belonging to the Bordeaux Club, whose members gather for banquets, musical programs, book reviews, addresses, and intellectual exercises. During the second half of her senior year, in 1931, the club sponsors a formal debate on the provocative proposition that "women are superior to men." Miss Annie leads the three-woman team affirming the proposition, while three men, all schoolteachers, offer the opposition. The arguments must have been lively and entertaining. Ida saves the club program in her photo album but fails to note the winning team, though few ladies or gentlemen ever achieve victory crossing verbal swords with Miss Annie.

When Ida attends the Junior-Senior Banquet of 1931, her contemporary and half nephew Edgar Fuller, son of Brother Willie, offers the toast to the seniors. That evening Ida must have mentally coupled bitter-sweet yearnings for her protected past and optimistic dreams for a starry future. As one of the sixteen students in her class, she sits with the other seniors at their final school function before commencement marks their successful conclusion of the eleventh grade.

Not yet seventeen, Ida has earned the highest academic rank in her class. Gold Sand High School names her valedictorian. She focuses on composing a challenging and memorable valedictory address for commencement exercises. Ida has become an excellent and convincing public speaker by 1931, having mastered the technique of writing and memorizing her remarks long before making a presentation. She always stands before her audience with only a small note card, discreetly folded in her palm and marked with a few key words for a quick glance to prod any unexpected gaps in her memory. At her graduation, Ida challenges those in attendance to dodge narrow and doctrinaire individuals, welcome intellectual challenges, and dedicate their lives to the service of others. These three principles will guide her through every triumph and pitfall of life.

9

Ida Denied a Career in Music

Miss Annie had advanced a sizeable sum of money to Louisburg College before the hideous tidal wave of the Great Depression swept across the landscape. In 1891, the college had become the property of the ruthless, tobacco-moneyed Dukes, but the family retreated from financial support in the early twentieth century by handing ownership to the North Carolina Conference of the Methodist Church. Louisburg College survives. A venerable private institution for young ladies, the college stresses responsible citizenship and intellectual growth. Miss Annie's keen interest in education and the arts often brings her to the beautiful campus perched on the oak-shaded summit of the highest hill in Louisburg, roughly seven miles southwest of her Moulton home.

On April 10, 1931, she pores over stunning news in the *Franklin Times* that Depression-battered Louisburg College faces the possibility of "a permanent shutdown" or other calamity. When anxious top college administrators admit to Miss Annie they cannot repay the debt, she decides to recoup part of her loss by enrolling Ida, and they acknowledge their obligation to cover the tuition, fees, meals, and housing. Meanwhile the trustees decide to admit young men, beginning the following September, boldly attempting to double enrollment and save the institution.

Students seeking academic laurels have long flourished at this small junior college that opened in 1857 on the grounds of an older academy founded in 1814. Despite the urgent financial difficulties wrought by the Depression, resolute Louisburg College perseveres in stressing gracious standards of behavior and well-toned instruction. Students dress stylishly and modestly for classes and meals. Ladies wear dresses and gentlemen wear coats and neckties in the dining room—adorned with elegant palm trees—

where polite servers bring delicious meals to the linen-covered tables. Everyone here observes strict rules of dining etiquette.

On September 9, 1931, Ida hails the beginning of her first year of college. The *Franklin Times* carries an enthusiastic article, published on September 11, describing young gentlemen registering alongside young ladies at a miraculous "full swing" and cautiously foreseeing new days of prosperity despite many financial difficulties "experienced the earlier part of the year."

Ida Flourishes at Louisburg College. Ida quickly becomes a popular figure on campus. Other students admire her ready wit and intellectual skills. She desires to concentrate on music, but Miss Annie insists on a more practical course of study in the wake of the devastating Depression. Thus Ida majors in English and minors in music. She particularly relishes her classes in music, English, German, and French. Her study of French and German proves beneficial for reading international literature and achieving correct pronunciation when singing pieces composed in those languages. The college guides Ida toward becoming accomplished also in singing Italian and Latin classics.

She steadily acquires greater poise and technical brilliance in the development of her voice as a fine instrument. A charmingly nimble soprano, she had begun studying voice under a music professor at Louisburg during her senior year (eleventh grade) at Gold Sand, and she performed alongside college students when the campus opened its doors for a public program in piano, voice, and reading on Tuesday evening, February 10, 1931. On that occasion the college even showered her with the honor of singing a solo, "The Nightingale has a Lyre of Gold" (arranged by the English orchestral conductor Sir Henry Joseph Wood from a song by the syphilis-ravaged English composer of German descent Frederick Delius).

By the opening of May 1933, Ida has almost completed requirements for her diploma from Louisburg. A trove of documents in the Louisburg College Archives attests to the celebration of at least four major campus events during the month. May 6 sees the college present an elaborate May Day Festival, with Ida serving as the pianist. The production features a host of familiar literary figures, exemplified by Alice in Wonderland,

Mother Goose, Humpty-Dumpty, Little Jack Horner, Old King Cole, Little Boy Blue, Simple Simon, and Mary Had a Little Lamb. Each figure gathers about the throne of the Fairy Queen and endeavors to bring her joy by introducing a band of entertainers such as tumblers, elves, and May Pole dancers.

On May 12 agile-voiced Ida sings in the Spring Concert of the Louisburg College Glee Club, a lengthy performance ranging from Wagnerian serenades to Russian folksongs and even includes a violin concerto. Ten days later the Music Department presents the annual Grand Concert. Ida sings "Roberto, o tu che adaro," an aria from the Italian translation of German-born Giacomo Meyerbeer's French operatic classic *Robert de Diable*.

The Louisburg College yearbook, the *Oak*, includes a class prophecy for the graduating students of 1933. The writer composes a long poem revealing how each student will fare in the future. One verse trumpets Ida's gift of voice: "And then for Ida Fuller let's give a loud cheer / She's famous by now in grand opera, I hear."

On Tuesday morning, May 22, Ida attends the commencement exercises of Louisburg College. Four days later the *Franklin Times* names Ida Fuller as one of the five "Honor Students" and reports that "Dr. William Preston Few, President of Duke University," had delivered the commencement address to "the young ladies and gentlemen in the graduating class. . . ." The newspaper then summarizes his advice, including the recommendation that the graduates proceed courageously amid the wreckage of the Depression, not seeking "refuge from times like these" but "facing the future with minds open." Dr. Few advances the principle also that education "should be life-long, creative, and should fit one for an avocation as well as a vocation."

The graduating students undoubtedly shake hands or embrace with well-meant promises to maintain their friendships through letters and visits. Many of them have already made arrangements to transfer to a senior institution for the final two years of college, but not Ida. Miss Annie insists that she return to Louisburg for a final year to add a certificate in bookkeeping and shorthand to her freshly-minted diploma in liberal arts. Her mother intends to recoup every possible cent from the old unpaid loan. Miss Annie consoles Ida with promises that she may continue acquiring training in voice and piano at the college. During the months ahead Ida often seeks escape from the tedium of her business courses by strolling to nearby Cicero's, attracting patrons with an assortment of popular magazines, soft drinks, candies, and other refreshments. The Four Winds Tea Room, another frequented spot in the town of Louisburg, offers students blessed with financial resources a pleasant setting to enjoy an occasional change from the excellent fare of the college dining room.

Yet this academic year brings Ida considerable anguish. She has become devoted to two professors at Louisburg. One focuses on teaching modern languages, the other on English and art, but they have acquired notable skills also in training the voice for singing or speaking. The first professor has completed studies at institutions such as the University of Chicago and the University of Vienna, and the second at Columbia University and the Chicago Art Institute. Unknown to Ida and the other students idolizing them, the women have not only declared their undying love for one another but also vowed never to part. Then someone encounters the two enjoying a moment of unguarded affection and bolts to college administrators with explicit details. The college curtly dismisses them.

The women keep their wits in the face of shrill hostility. Two men discovered in a similar embrace certainly would have fled to prevent the possibility of a frenzied mob mutilating them or claiming their lives, but the professors possess the protection of their gender in a region still tightly wedded to the medieval principle of chivalry. They go directly to their most talented students and acknowledge their love for one another. They have decided to open a voice and diction studio in New York City and invite the handpicked students to join them as pupils. They express confidence that Ida possesses the voice and poise to become, under their tutelage, a noteworthy opera singer, perhaps even a prima donna. Blessed with an unbigoted personality, Ida expresses happiness that the two women have found genuine love and becomes enthusiastic about the possibility of joining them in New York as a pupil for an operatic career. Miss Annie instantly vetoes the proposal as foolish and impractical in the dark days of the Depression and reminds Ida of the importance of learning skills providing ready employment.

Tears for Aunt Ida. Ida privately bemoans the missed opportunity to prepare her superb gift of voice for the opera, but a far more important reason to grieve occurs about this time. She receives an urgent message to pack her bags for Moulton because Aunt Ida Debnam, her beloved childhood nursemaid and companion, has died. She rushes home and hears poignant reports that Aunt Ida had experienced wrenching loneliness after her youngest Fuller charge left for Louisburg College. Aunt Ida's biological family asks Ida to sing the funeral solo in their modest church. Mourning inconsolably, Ida fights back tears and struggles to keep her voice from breaking as she sings a heartfelt farewell over the body of one who has nurtured and guided her through the inexhaustible joys and perils of childhood. She must have wondered if any future soul will offer her even the faintest shadow of Aunt Ida's lavish and unselfish love.

Ida Graces Meredith College. In September 1934, Ida transfers to Meredith College, a distinguished private women's institution with a strong faculty and beautiful campus. Its classic buildings adorn manicured grounds near the then western edge of Raleigh, the state capital. Ida enrolls as a junior on September 11, but most members of her class had entered Meredith as freshmen and formed crucial friendships and ties their first semester. These young women view her as a stranger, an outsider, who must prove herself. To make matters worse, Miss Annie economizes by arranging for Ida to live with relatives in Raleigh during her first year at Meredith, certainly a barrier to forging close bonds with students residing in college residence halls. Miss Annie tightly controls the purse and still insists that Ida bow to practicality in Depression-era America by majoring in English rather than music.

Unlike Louisburg, Meredith reserves all performances of solos in college concerts for music majors. Ida makes the best of a difficult situation. She will sing no arias in public at Meredith but earns a coveted spot in the College Choir though the quality of her voice. She becomes an officer in two campus religious organizations and participates with other students in carrying baskets brimming with fruits, candies, and other welcome items to the ill, imprisoned, elderly, and destitute. She particularly enjoys the lectures of one of her gifted English professors, Dr. Julia Hamlet Harris, who had left Chapel Hill with an undergraduate degree and Yale with a doctorate and now serves as an adviser for the prestigious Colton English Club. Ida's name soon appears on the roll of that association. She becomes an active member also of the Astrotekton Literary Society, dedicated to the promotion of cultural endeavors. The Astrotektons have selected a rousing motto befitting their name from eighteenth-century English poet Edward Young's *Night Thoughts*: "Too low they build who build beneath the stars."

Ida participates when the College Choir presents its annual Christmas concert in Raleigh, on Sunday, December 15, 1935, following out-of-town performances one week earlier in Winston-Salem and Burlington. The program includes carols and songs from England, France, Italy, Germany, and Russia.

On February 15, 1936, the Meredith student newspaper, the *Twig*, carries several advertisements of interest to the college community. The Permanent Marcel Shop in the Capital Club Building not only offers a shampoo and finger wave for fifty cents but also administers "spiral permanents" and other fashionable hair styles "to suit your taste or requirements." Another advertisement beckons students to a film about a recklessly wayward playboy making amends, *Magnificent Obsession*, playing at the S-T-A-T-E and starring Irene Dunne and Robert Taylor. Meanwhile moviegoers look forward to the coming attraction about a fugitive gangster holding intellectual luminaries and others hostage at a dilapidated service station, the acclaimed *Petrified Forest*, based on Robert Sherwood's play, part thriller, part parable, and enlivened by the stellar acting skills of Leslie Howard, Bette Davis, and Humphrey Bogart. The film makes Humphrey Bogart a star.

On May 25 the *Twig* reminds readers of the upcoming May Day celebration, scheduled for Saturday afternoon, May 2, "in the grove on Meredith campus," with "two hundred and fifty colorful characters and dancers. . . ." Participants will enact "the pageant of the Sleeping Beauty . . . for the entertainment of the May Queen and her court." Spectators always look forward to the grand finale of the celebration: "After the pageant will follow two parts of the May Day program which are invariable from year to year and without which no Meredith May Day would be complete—the drill of the Queen's Guard, composed of sixteen juniors, and the May Pole dance, in which eighteen sophomores take part" in elaborately decorating the pole with streamers while dancing in delicate flowing gowns. The first-rate Meredith College Archives preserves a brief color film of the May Day celebration for 1939, including several seconds of the precision drill of the Queen's Guard and the superb May Pole dance.

Ida's college graduation nears as May 1936 dwindles. She participates in the annual Class Day Exercises honoring the seniors. The Meredith College *Quarterly Bulletin*, for June 1936, describes the graceful festivities, held on May 30: "A large crowd" watched a revered tradition unfold as "white-clad sophomores marched in double column down the hill . . . carrying . . . two great chains of daisies on their shoulders." Next "the seniors came down the same path," wearing "lace dresses of lavender and yellow. They passed between the lines of singing sophomores, and then both classes marched to their" appointed places for additional ceremonies and songs.

The following day, Sunday, May 31, the Meredith graduates hear the baccalaureate sermon, "The Sovereignty of the Coming World," delivered by Dr. E. McNeill Poteat, Jr., respected in progressive circles as a poet, scholar, writer, and liberal-minded pastor of Pullen Memorial Baptist Church in Raleigh. Commencement exercises occur on June 1, the eve of Ida's twenty-second birthday. After the academic procession, with seniors, faculty members, and others entering the College Auditorium to the strains of Wagner's *Tannhauser March*, Dr. Bernard Chancellor Clausen, pastor of the First Baptist Church in Pittsburgh, Pennsylvania, and the author of several popular books on religion, delivers the commencement address.

Ida still misses her friends and professors at Louisburg, but she can take pride in her accomplishments at Meredith, and her name appears on the Honor Roll for 1935-1936. The college yearbook, the *Oak Leaves*, depicts her in a complimentary light:

"Ida is another of the Louisburg College girls who have made good with us. She has acquired quite a large number of friends. Her perseverance, industriousness and conscientiousness spell but one thing—success."

Ida Launches a Promising Teaching Career at Weeksville. Ida returns to Moulton for the summer but prepares to move coastward after the principal of Weeksville High School in southern Pasquotank County invites her to join the faculty as a teacher of English and history, beginning September 1936. Apparently virtually everyone in Weeksville soon adores Miss Ida Powell Fuller both as a person and as a teacher. She proves superlative in the classroom. She quickly revives and soothes tired students by singing to them for one or two minutes. They usually request "The Crocodile Song," whose original author remains unknown. Ida always sings her favorite version of this old standby:

>O, she sailed away on a sunny summer's day,
>On the back of a crocodile.
>"O, you see," said she, "he's as tame as he can be,
>I'll float him down the Nile."
>
>The croc winked an eye as she waved them all goodbye,
>Wearing a happy smile.
>But at the end of the ride, the lady was inside,
>And the smile was on the crocodile!

Ida has rented a room at Weeksville from Jarvis and Geraldine, an outgoing husband and wife celebrated for their impressive qualities and assets, he as a business owner and civic leader and she as a magnetic social leader. They own a handsome spacious house and rent several rooms to local teachers. Ida greatly enjoys their company.

Meanwhile she becomes an avid reader of the two Elizabeth City newspapers, the rip-roaring *Daily Independent* and the staid *Daily Advance.* On Friday, November 13, 1936, the social column of the *Independent* reports that Ida and another Weeksville teacher, her friend Lois Herring, will motor with Jarvis and Geraldine to Chapel Hill for the weekend to attend the Carolina-Duke game. The names of the four often appear in social columns. On December 24 the *Independent* relates that several "teachers at Weeksville High School have left to spend the holidays with relatives," including "Miss Lois Herring, who has gone to Greenville," and "Miss Ida Fuller, who is visiting in Louisburg" and Moulton.

The following year, 1937, unfolds under ever-deepening clouds chilling local and national events. On February 1 the *Daily Independent* alerts readers to new threats by publishing an alarming article from the United Press. The depraved German Führer (leader) Adolph Hitler now loudly warns "that each nation must be the judge of its own armed needs," a grave impediment to international concord, and he scoffs at the League of Nations as a worthless organ of peace.

Many Pasquotank County residents seek relief from worsening international developments by attending local school celebrations. The *Daily Advance* chirps serenely on March 19, 1937, that "Weeksville High School staged last night a mother-daughter, father-son banquet in the new gymnasium with marked success. . . . There was music too, with Miss Ida Fuller of the faculty, accompanied by Miss Annie Marie Jackson, in a solo number. . . ."

In the early spring, the Weeksville community focuses on the upcoming visit of new State Commissioner of Agriculture W. Kerr Scott, to be celebrated with a lavish fish fry. As noted, local newspapers applaud his speech of April 20, promoting North Carolina agriculture, and praise also Miss Fuller's musical contributions before the enthusiastic throng.

Although Ida spends most of the summer at Moulton, the *Daily Independent* reports on August 6 (eight days before suspending publication) that she has returned briefly to Weeksville to visit Geraldine and Jarvis. September 1937 sees the school year begin on an optimistic note. Yet on Saturday, November 6, Ida's idyllic tenure at Weeksville comes to an abrupt end.

She and Lois have accepted an invitation from Geraldine to enjoy a quick shopping spree in Elizabeth City. Geraldine takes the wheel. Two days later the *Daily Advance* covers the disastrous ensuing mishap: "The bone in her [Geraldine's] right foot fractured near the ankle as [a] result of an automobile wreck on the Weeksville highway four miles from Elizabeth City late Saturday afternoon." The newspaper adds that Geraldine, "wife of a prominent Weeksville merchant, was . . . getting along as well as could be expected at Albemarle Hospital. Contrary to rumors," Geraldine's "foot has not been amputated. Her Oldsmobile 1936 sedan turned over three times when it left the road on a curve about 4 o'clock Saturday. Five other occupants, including her two small children, two Weeksville schoolteachers and a Negro maid, escaped with only superficial injuries. The teachers were Miss Lois Herring and Miss Ida Fuller."

The "driver of the only car near the accident" told the investigating highway patrol officers "that he had pulled over to the side of the road, off the pavement, because his gas gave out. He said the . . . car [driven by Geraldine] passed him, swerved and upset, turning over three times before it came to a rest. The car was headed toward Elizabeth City. Its top and body were badly smashed in the upset, and the door opposite [beside] the driver was torn completely off, the highway patrolmen said."

This toned-down account omits much pertinent information. Geraldine has exceeded the speed limit to make better time. She swerves her automobile sharply into a triple-somersault when she sees the other car on the side of the highway. The battered door torn from her car catches and virtually severs her foot during the process. When Geraldine's car stops turning, she holds her dangling foot in disbelief and cries, "Look, Ida." The other horrified passengers see that her foot seems connected to her leg by only a few threads of flesh and mangled bones. When Jarvis rushes to her hospital bedside within the hour, she pleads with him not to allow physicians to remove her foot. Against unanimous medical advice, he insists her wishes be honored. The reattached foot heals improperly and gradually poisons her body and mind. Geraldine virtually withdraws from society. She often stays in her bedroom and sits in a chair facing the wall. She cannot muster the will even to look at cherished old friends who come to pay their respects. Her house takes on a somber and discordant atmosphere.

In a bizarre twist, she brings a suit against her husband. The *Advance* reports on May 10, 1938, that "Geraldine . . . holds her husband . . . responsible for the accident on November 6 in which her foot was crushed. She is suing him for a total of $29,300 in a suit entered here by her attorneys. . . . She charges that her husband did not keep in proper condition the brakes and running gear of the car she was driving at the time of the accident, and that the defective condition of the brakes was the cause of the crash. . . . Her right ankle was lacerated in the accident, and she claims she will never recover the full use of her right leg so as to be able to walk as before the accident."

When the matter finally comes before the court, Ida and the other passengers reluctantly testify that Geraldine had been speeding. Years pass before Geraldine finally consents to the removal of the deteriorating, swollen foot. To the delight of her family and friends, Geraldine then regains her old poise and charm and reclaims both her strong marriage and her vital role as a luminary of Pasquotank County.

10

Edward and Ida

In the grim months at Geraldine's house after the automobile wreck, Miss Ida Powell Fuller seeks academic employment away from Weeksville and secures a teaching contract for the following September, an appointment at the town of Plymouth, roughly sixty miles southwest of Elizabeth City and beautifully situated on the southern shore of the Roanoke River. In the meantime she continues her local teaching duties.

As noted, Sunday, March 27, 1938, sees her make the acquaintance of Edward Dunstan, prosperous young owner of Dunstan Fuel Company in Elizabeth City. On Friday night, April 8, just days after Ida begins dating Edward, she performs in a comedy-mystery at Weeksville. Edward must have been present. Four days later the *Daily Advance* carries an article about the presentation: "Ardent applause from an enthusiastic audience was the response given to . . . [Jay Tobias' 1933] play *Hobgoblin House* [staged] by the P.T.A. of Weeksville School on Friday night. Time and again the members of the cast were obliged to hesitate for the hilarious laughter in the audience to become subdued.

"Ghosts and headless phantoms stalked about during the course of the play, creating a weird, eerie atmosphere. The plot involved the disposal of an inheritance and the discouragement of so-called puppy love. . . . Upholding the most important parts of the serious side" of the performance "were Miss Ida Fuller and Miss Ina Brothers. Miss Fuller's representation of an old maid type with a determined mind and a determined tone of voice" proved "as strong as the blows that she administered to the cheeks of the young men wooing her nieces. Miss Brothers . . . added to the spooky atmosphere of the play by her effective narration of ghost stories. Due to inclement weather and bad roads, many people in this vicinity have requested that the play be presented again on Thursday night, April 14."

On Friday, April 15, 1938, Ida must have been present to see Edward hit a homer playing softball. The *Advance* announces the following day that his team, the Elizabeth City Rotarians, "trounced the All Star team in a fast moving softball game Friday evening. . . . The score was 20 to 12."

On Monday, May 2, the Rotary District Conference meets in Elizabeth City. As a Rotarian, Edward maps out a newspaper advertisement for Dunstan Fuel Company under the warm headline "Welcome Rotarians!" The *Advance* carries an editorial the following day praising Rotary for "elevating every worthy occupation to the plane of a profession" and for creating "a world fellowship of men" dedicated to promoting "understanding among peoples that leads to peace." The newspaper characterized Rotary "also as a promoter of wholesome and rollicking fun" that allows "the tired business and professional man to let himself go and play the boy now and then." The *Advance* relates on May 5 that the "farewell luncheon given in the ballroom of the Virginia Dare Hotel" saw the principal speaker "exhort all Rotarians to apply the motto of their organization: Service above Self, to their business and social life."

Miss Ida finds the smooth charmer Edward fascinating and regrets having signed a contract to teach at Plymouth. He had sent her flowers from Mildred's Florist on Saturday, April 16, the day before Easter Sunday. She attends church with him the following day and marks this Easter celebration on her calendar.

About this time Edward invites her to join him one cloudy night for a pleasant restaurant dinner but on the return to Weeksville stops his car at an isolated roadside tomb possessing a tall monument. He dares Miss Ida to jump the drainage ditch beside the road and touch the old gravestone. Lithe and fearless, she bounds across the ditch and runs to the marker. Edward immediately speeds several hundred yards down the dirt road and extinguishes his lights, leaving Ida alone in the pitch-black darkness, but she refuses to panic and assumes the prankster will return for her. In a moment he backs up and opens the passenger door for her in a show of pretended gallantry. She laughs with him over the mischief but should have viewed her temporary abandonment in a more serious light.

In the meantime Ida enjoys her final days at Weeksville High School. She sings Charles Wesley's popular eighteenth-century hymn "Jesus, Lover of My Soul" in a duet with another teacher during the baccalaureate service, on April 24, and she performs her final official duty at Weeksville by attending commencement exercises three days later. Wistfully bidding Miss Ida Fuller farewell, the graduates look forward to beginning their careers or enrolling in college, and the younger students anticipate revitalizing their spirits during the next four and one-half months of summer vacation.

On May 9 the *Advance* reports that Weeksville will lose four teachers who "did not apply for another year," including "Miss Ida Fuller, high school English and history" and "Miss Lois Herring, first grade." Lois has enjoyed teaching in the village despite several classroom tribulations such as discovering a first grader tugging on what appeared to be a lollipop stick. She tells amused friends of asking the boy to remove the candy from his mouth. He pulls out the tail and then the body of a dead mouse! Meanwhile Lois has experienced difficulty sleeping at Geraldine's troubled house and gladly returns to Greenville to plan her upcoming wedding to popular Robert Crutchfield, known to friends as Crutch, who has served during the past year as the principal of Weeksville High School. Lois complains to friends about the Elizabeth City banker giving her a ride to Greenville just before the wedding—"he kept mistaking my knee for the gear shift." In the meantime Ida has decided to pursue postgraduate studies during the summer at the University of North Carolina. First, she returns to Moulton and spends several weeks with Miss Annie.

Edward's Offbeat Love Letters. Ida and Edward exchange many handwritten letters during the coming months. She saves his efforts, usually rushed, though he keeps only one of hers. His first letter to her, postmarked Wednesday, May 4, 1938, and written on Dunstan Fuel Company stationery, bears the envelope address "Miss Ida Fuller, Louisburg, N.C." and on the left side "RFD

[Rural Free Delivery] #3." His words to "Dear Ida" thinly disguise his whiny-braggadocio-insensitive personality: "I really should write this on a typewriter as I know that this will be soaking wet from perspiration. I have just come from the 'end' of the Rotary Convention, and I never have been so hot. At the last luncheon we were packed in like sardines. . . . I sent you a Daily Disappointment [*Daily Advance*] yesterday so you could read [about] all of those speeches I've been making [to the Rotarians]—just think what you missed by 'I wanna see ma-ma [Miss Annie].'"

He cannot resist gloating about finding a replacement date during her absence: "I had a most unusual experience last night by having a date with a girl from London, England. Her father came over to speak to us [at the Rotary Conference], and she and her mother came, too. I had dated girls in N.Y. who were born in foreign countries, but most of them had been in this country a good while and you couldn't get them to talk about their customs, etc. This one talked so much that we only danced about one-third of the time, and I listened to her the rest. Can you imagine?"

He then turns to prearranged plans for visiting Ida: "I don't know whether or not I know how to get to your house [in Moulton], but maybe your neighbors are good directors. At any rate, if I don't get lost, etc., I shall be there when the gong sounds 8:30." Following his usual pattern, he omits any complimentary close and simply signs the letter "Edward."

He plans a long weekend with Ida. Accordingly, on Friday afternoon, May 6, Edward leaves his business in the hands of an able assistant several hours before closing time. He returns home and changes clothes. After motoring for more than four hours before reaching Louisburg, Edward takes the wrong road and heads in the wrong direction until arriving at Franklinton, about seventeen miles southwest of Moulton. He notices a lady sitting in a rocking chair on her porch and asks for directions to Moulton. She smiles and replies, "You must be going to pay your respects to Mrs. Fuller's daughter." Her remark greatly impresses Edward. He soon realizes that virtually everyone in Franklin County either knows the steadfast Miss Annie or knows her name.

He finally pulls into the beautiful cedar-lined avenue leading to the David Thomas Fuller House. The weekend proves restful and immensely enjoyable for both Edward and Ida. The cooks in the Fuller household have prepared a bountiful evening meal to celebrate Edward's visit. Keen-eyed Miss Annie forms an estimate of him quickly. At bedtime, after Edward retires to his comfortable guest room, she describes him to Ida as a *sport*, or one living a carefree, extravagant life.

Saturday morning sees Ida guiding Edward around the Fuller plantation and introducing him to several of the farmers and their families. After lunch, the two stroll on the tree-shaded campus of Louisburg College and visit the old gristmill at Laurel. That evening Edward drives Ida roughly twenty-five miles southwest to the small town of Wake Forest for dinner at the establishment of Miss Jo Williams. Ida saves a card from the restaurant: "Miss Jo Williams Invites you to make her Dining Rooms your headquarters during your stay in Wake Forest." On Sunday morning, May 8, they attend services at Corinth Church, the spiritual home of the Fuller family. That afternoon Edward begins the return drive to Elizabeth City. Ida accompanies him as far at Gatesville, where she will spend several days visiting her sister, Mary Susan Fuller Woodall, and brother-in-law, Wilbur. F. Woodall, a popular Baptist pastor with the spiritual care of a flock in Gates County.

Edward's next hurried letter, written on Tuesday, May 10, 1938, begins with the salutation "Dearest Ida" and possesses a warmer tone than his earlier effort: "Well, here it is less than 48 hours since I've seen you and it seems like 48 days! What am I going to do for & with the next 300 hours? If you hadn't . . . come part . . . way with me the other night, I don't know how I would have made it. . . .

"I have been doing some heavy courting this afternoon. Took a young lady horseback riding—(12 yrs. old, the girl, not the horse). I . . . see in the *Daily Advance* that [Geraldine] . . . is suing Jarvis for $29,300 for negligence in allowing her to drive a car with improper brakes, etc. Does that mean that you & Lois have to testify? I suppose I'd better stop as I know you're busy with the baby (lucky baby) [he refers to the son—then called Wilbur Junior—of Mary Susan and Wilbur]. However, I'm just a baby, too, so please think of me a little. . . . . ." Edward signs the letter without a complimentary close. He then draws a stick figure beside his name and writes, "P.S. This is a picture of me. Now how about [sending me] one of thee?"

One week later Edward writes "Dear Ida, I am sorry I didn't make a carbon copy of my last epistle to you since it was 'so much like me' [apparently quoting verbatim from her most recent letter to him]. I would like to find out how I really am," for that information "might have lessened my ego. . . ." Turning to another irritant, Edward notes that his "clever little ode and drawing failed to even so much as bring forth a snapshot." He adds the earthy and haughty remark, "I drew the right leg & foot a little long to imply—to myself—that I was 'sticking my foot in it' (or don't you have that expression in Moulton?). . . . Will see you about 8 PM Saturday night if nothing happens. . . ." He closes with a few lines of verse: "No ode or picture, will I pen / Just my Love, to you I'll send. / I know the meter is not so hot / But what it takes, 'I just ain't got.'"

On Monday, May 23, the day after returning from Moulton, Edward writes Ida a snappish and disjointed letter covering a number of points vexing him. He sends also several newspaper articles to support his assertions. He insists, "I don't really brag as you claim I do. . . ." Then he proceeds to boast about his accomplishments: "My talk at [the] Rotary Club [as the County Tax Supervisor in the spring of 1937] stated taxables to increase $1,000,000 & [the] article concerning the tax rate showed $1,554,036 actual increase. . . ."

He then adds, "I'm an inventor" and includes a long undated newspaper article to back this claim: "W. E. Dunstan . . . was coming back from Nags Head last night, and cars going the other way kept blinding him. He couldn't see a thing. Kept running off the road, and didn't like it a bit. . . . He reached in and pulled out his sunglasses and everything was fine. Said today the thought he'd make a couple of hundred thousand Jewish flags [offensive term for dollars] out of his idea. He'd have dark glasses put on the windshield at night." Several of his acquaintances demanded a cut of the profits for suggesting refinements such as the shade should come down only at the approach of another car. "'That's 95 per cent gone,' moaned Mr. Dunstan. 'By the time they take out the three per cent sales tax, I'll feel like a two-cent piece.'"

When turning in the same letter to several whispers Ida has heard about his laziness, he pleads for sympathy: "I formerly was a hard worker but since my mother fired me [more than] 4 ½ years ago, I have been in the doldrums—but—since I've met you 'Life Begins at 30' [the age he will reach in late November and a reference to the 1935 comedic movie Life Begins at Forty, starring Will Rogers]."

Edward has informed Ida some time earlier about Emma stripping him of employment, but the slick rascal never discloses his crime of embezzlement. He slyly depicts his mother as an autocratic shrew who fired him for overstepping his place by suggesting profit-making improvements in her real estate empire. Nor does he tell Ida that he has not spoken to Emma once during this entire period. He always describes himself as a dutiful and loving son striving to appease a heartless and hurtful mother. Inexperienced with men of deception, Ida remains unaware that Edward has spent his entire life blaming all his shortcomings and failures on one woman after another.

On Saturday, May 28, Edward begins a letter with the warm salutation "Dearest Ida." He writes from his Elks Lodge on East Fearing Street: "You can now see by this stationery that we do something at the Elks Club other than drinking and gambling [such as composing letters]. However, from the looks of your friend [Edward names a prominent young man then present] . . ., he probably has had a drink. Mine was iced tea. The 'B.P.O.E.' . . . [the letters beneath the Elk decorating the letterhead] means Best People on Earth [actually Benevolent and Protective Order of Elks (an American fraternal order and social club founded in 1868)]!" Edward then struts across the page with his pen, reminding Ida that he had served as "sports editor of the [Duke] Chronicle . . . ."

Next he berates Ida for her memory. "Incidentally, I never debated at Chapel Hill . . . [apparently she has questioned him about this boast in her most recent letter]. Your memory is pretty good on things you shouldn't remember (providing I told you that) and no good on things you should or could remember. . . . If it's ok with you, I'll be up again this week-end—June 4 [two days after her twenty-fourth birthday]—Please let me know at your earliest convenience. And please make it yes."

Ida pushes caution aside and approves his suggestion to visit her at Moulton, on the weekend of June 4-5. During his stay she casually mentions her birthday falling in June but refrains from embarrassing him by saying he has missed the celebration by only two days. Back in Elizabeth City, Edward writes to Ida on Wednesday, June 8. He begins by reporting on the recent local election. Her friend and former landlord at Weeksville, Jarvis, won a seat on the Pasquotank County Board of Education. Edward then confesses his own disappointing defeat in the election for "secretary of the Rotary Club" but, after serving as "treasurer for two years," he suggests he has "earned a little 'rest.'" Then he mentions an oversight: "I forgot to ask you when your birthday would be when I was up there so I'll have to take a stab in the dark call it the 15th. I can't be over 15 days wrong either way...."

On Saturday, June 11, Ida responds with the only letter of hers that Edward saves. She begins with the salutation "Dear Edward" and makes several remarks about his planned participation in Laymen's Sunday the following day at the First Methodist Church.

Ida then shifts to a romantic comment: "I did note the arrangement of those stamps on the letter I got from you last week. Flattering indeed, Mr. Dunstan!" Edward had turned the stamps sideways, head to the right, a placement signifying the sending of love and kisses. After expressing sympathy concerning his complaints about the hardship of transporting many truckloads of coal to customers on the coast for the coming winter, Ida turns to her impending academic session at Chapel Hill: "Next week... I shall be living at 310 Grimes Dormitory.... She then minimizes one of Edward's recent faux pas: "By changing my birthday to the 15th, you made me thirteen days younger than I really am, ... certainly... not displeasing."

Next she discusses one of her great passions, reading superb literature. "I certainly have enjoying reading Eve Curie's [definitive] biography of her mother [*Madame Curie* (1937)] this week" and "don't think the critics were too extravagant with their praise. Should I voice my opinion I might be extravagant with my praise of a certain young man, but dear me, it does seem so futile when I consider that I am rather 'Unimportantly' yours!" She signs her name just below this unusual complimentary close that probably reflects one of Edward's recent slights.

Edward replies on Thursday, June 16, and addresses his letter to Ida at the University of North Carolina: "I see they really did put you on the third floor [of Grimes Dormitory]. However . . . you can lie in bed and be nearer the moon, as you like to do. I had to go over to Manteo Sunday afternoon (to see about that darn'd coal) and stayed over at Nags Head for swimming and supper" and then "to see the moon come out of the ocean. . . ."

He mentions giving her a locket as a gift and then reveals, "I wanted to get you a ring" but found the traditional June birthstone (pearl) unattractive. "I expect to come up to Chapel Hill Saturday the 25th if the sweetest girl there will be in. Incidentally, where can you recommend besides 310 as a good place to stay. I've never spent a night there except at the Sigma Chi house & I'm not sure about that. But I am sure that I miss you!"

Despite his bold and ungentlemanly expression of interest in spending the night in her room, Edward gains the coveted invitation to visit Ida. Apparently he has become jealous over her written remarks about budding friendships with male and female students at the university. On Wednesday, June 22, he writes to caution her that summer schools attract many men who are there "to play . . . instead of study."

Edward then readdresses the question of where to stay while visiting Ida. She must have mentioned the possibility of choosing the beautiful Carolina Inn. "I had forgotten about the Carolina Inn when I wrote last week. However, I think I shall stay at the Washington Duke in Durham as I have to pass through there and may wish to drop in on Dear Ole Duke. Expect to be at Chapel Hill . . . about 8 PM. Don't date too late Friday night!"

The weekend greatly disappoints Edward. Perhaps he actually envisioned laying his head upon a pillow in 310 Grimes. He does not write Ida until Thursday, July 7, responding with only two sentences to a question from her about his eleven days of silence: "I am sure you can answer your own query very well. There is nothing 'wrong' except that I realized Saturday night week that it was bad enough to be in love with someone 200 miles away, but downright disastrous when it's all one-sided."

Perhaps she responds curtly or not at all. He finally writes again, on Monday, July 18: "I realize that in writing this note there is a good chance of getting no reply. However—here goes! I just wanted to say that if you're going to be in Chapel Hill this week end . . . , I would come up," but "please let me know at your earliest convenience."

Ida responds on Wednesday, July 20: "I am planning to be in Chapel Hill this week-end, and I shall be expecting you Saturday night." She adds a chilly "Sincerely, Ida." On Thursday, July 21, Edward replies to her note on the bottom of her own stationery: "Since I am part Scotch [inclined to frugality], I hate to see so much paper going to waste. . . . I will be up Saturday night to see the sweetest girl there, and I hope she is in a good mood. . . . This weekend will be one month since I've seen you," and this "reminds me that 'TIME MARCHES ON.'"

This weekend proves quite enjoyable for both Ida and Edward. When Edward writes a long letter to Ida on Tuesday, July 26, he turns the head of the stamp to the left, signifying a promise never to leave her, and addresses her warmly as "Darling." He begins with a discussion of the weather and other matters of local interest in Elizabeth City and then turns to his need for a holiday. "I think I'll head for Nags Head . . . in a day or two as I haven't been on my vacation this summer, and I need a little sun-tan. I wish . . . you would come down. Anyway, after such a strenuous six weeks [at Chapel Hill] you need such a rest. . . . I really did enjoy seeing you again, and I fell in love with you all over again or should I say deeper, as I haven't been 'out of love' with you since April. You are very sweet when you want to be and especially when you forget your sub-conscious feeling concerning Time, etc. Don't wait too long to write, and why not surprise me by saying you are headed for the Beach?"

Ida flatly refuses to entertain the idea of visiting Edward at the beach without the propriety of an accompanying chaperone but does make plans to visit despondent Geraldine at Weeksville, from Friday afternoon to Monday morning, August 5-8. Edward writes on Wednesday, August 3, expressing great happiness "to hear you're coming to Weeksville. Maybe [Geraldine] . . . can spare part of your time. She'd better!"

The Dinner Party Haunted by Secrets. Edward dreams that fair Ida might throw him a secure lifeline from the extreme turbulence of his life. He proposes to her on Friday, August 5, 1938, probably in the evening, but she insists on meeting his mother before deciding. Edward rashly assures Ida that his mother will invite her to dinner. He must have felt beads of perspiration breaking out on his face. Edward has not spoken one word to Emma since 1933. Late that night he persuades Garland, who has returned to Elizabeth City after completing his course of study at Poughkeepsie Business Institute, to approach Emma about hosting a dinner party honoring Ida the following evening.

In the morning Garland greets his mother with the request. He regales her by quoting warm, complimentary remarks about Miss Ida coming from several of his Weeksville friends. Emma readily agrees to Edward's plea for help, albeit through his brother. She hopes Ida might somehow bridge the tragic family rift. She immediately invites Forrest and his fiancée, Isabella Patricia Jennette, whom friends and relatives call Isabelle. Forrest and Isabelle realize Ida might prove a godsend to the Dunstan family and gladly set aside earlier plans for the evening. Emma spends the late morning with Maggie (whose surname escapes me), her personable housekeeper-cook, planning a lavish meal.

Ida arrives with Edward promptly at six o'clock. Addressing his mother for the first time in roughly five years, Edward bows slightly and says, "Mother, may I present Miss Fuller?"

Emma welcomes Ida warmly and introduces her to Isabelle, Forrest, and Garland. Ida notices Emma's regal appearance, Garland's polish, Isabelle's charm, and Forrest's charisma and extraordinary good looks. She understands why young ladies visit Forrest's church just to sit behind him and admire his wavy black locks and broad shoulders. Garland proves unusually friendly and approachable. When Emma excuses herself briefly to check on progress in the kitchen, Forrest, Edward, and Isabelle begin discussing local people, names unknown to the guest of honor. Garland immediately jumps from his seat and exclaims, "Let's become better acquainted with Ida."

A flawless upholder of social graces and standards, Garland places an orchestral record on the electric phonograph and asks Ida to dance. The three gentlemen take turns dancing with the two cheerful ladies until Maggie announces the serving of dinner.

Everyone seems in high spirits and enjoys Maggie's scrumptious meal. The animated conversation by the six people at the spacious dining table masks the terrible truth that Edward never addresses a single remark to his mother during the entire meal. After dinner, the young people continue conversing and dancing. True to their upbringing, the dashing Dunstan boys, or at least Forrest and Garland, smile brightly and carefully fashion their witty words and courteous deeds by the elegant guiding compass inherited from beloved Will.

Perhaps Garland shows Ida a clipping from the *Daily Advance*, dated June 29, bearing the unusual headline "Elizabeth City 'Rebels' Create Stir." The lengthy article describes how Southern students studying at Poughkeepsie Business Institute, including Garland, provoked quite "a stir in the Yankee stronghold when they hoisted a Confederate flag out of their dormitory." The newspaper purrs that although their act "riled an oversensitive Yankee D.A.R. [Daughters of the American Revolution] chapter" established in the city, the president of the school ultimately decided the students "were not violating any laws," and "the stars and bars continued to float in the breeze of Yankee territory." The *Advance* publishes a photograph of several of the "young Confederates," shown with their flag, and lists Elizabeth City students attending the institute: Garland Dunstan, Shell Scott, Woody Foreman, Mac Duff, and Bill Robinson. As a matter of fact, Garland had completed his course of study before the president of the institute resolved the ticklish issue in favor of the Southern students.

Ida never realizes in the excitement and pleasure of the evening, Saturday, August 6, 1938, that Edward has snubbed his mother. The truth about the abyss between son and mother fails to reach her ears for months. She has glowed in the presence of the captivating Dunstans and gives Edward his answer later that night—a resounding YES!

11

Ida's Carefully Concealed Secret

Engaged within four months of becoming acquainted with Ida, Edward desires to set an early wedding date, but his fiancée insists on honoring her commitment to teach at Plymouth in September. The two aim at late December, not long after the conclusion of the school term. Edward soon makes a show of giving Ida an elegant engagement ring featuring a round brilliant diamond enhanced with diamond side stones, a galaxy of fire smoothly cradled in a graceful platinum band, carefully selected in Elizabeth City at Louis Selig, advertised as "the most beautiful jewelry store in North Carolina." During the coming months Ida will face endless tasks completing arrangement for her coming nuptial celebration while fulfilling an increasing tide of obligations in the classroom.

Clouded Wedding Preparations. In the meantime Edward composes a letter to Ida on Friday morning, August 12, from the popular First Colony Inn at Nags Head. His salutation, "Dearest Sweetheart," reflects the warmth of the entire letter. He begins by telling Ida of his arrival at the beach "a few minutes ago, so of course the first thing I do is write to my little darling. . . . Surely wish you were here, as I miss you so much. Don't really see any reason why you can't thou. It seems like ages since Monday morning [when you left Weeksville to visit friends in Richmond, Virginia]. . . . Hope you miss me just a little bit—please say you do. I love you so much. . . ."

Edward wrestles with his fountain pen again on Tuesday, August 16, this time in Elizabeth City, but proves snappish and quick-tempered in the opening sentences: "You certainly are a prize winner when it comes to writing me. I had looked forward so much to hearing from you this week but here it is lunchtime and no letter from you in my [post office] box." He makes these remarks despite knowing Ida has been ill, but Edward does not inquire about her health until the second page: "I hope you are feeling better by now and well enough to write...."

Edward's strong anti-Northerner side shows when he mentions reading the book *A Southerner Discovers the South* (1938) by Jonathan Daniels, editor of the *Raleigh News and Observer*. "It is very good. I always enjoy reading anything that gives the South a break. I don't even like this ink as I notice it [the bottle] has a NY label." Ida must have found this remark odd. Didn't Edward once dream of a dazzling career on Wall Street? He ends the letter by again reminding the recuperating Ida of her negligence in not writing: "I have felt so upset over not hearing from you [that] I have been sitting here in almost complete darkness...."

In the meantime Lois Herring has asked Ida to play a key role in her own wedding, to Robert Crutchfield, solemnized on Saturday morning, September 3, 1938, at the Emmanuel Baptist Church in Greenville. Edward concocts a lame excuse for not attending. The *News and Observer* reports eight days later that "Miss Ida Fuller of Louisburg sang [two soaring love songs expressing eternal devotion] 'Because' [originally published 1902, with music by Guy d'Hardelot (pen name of Helen Rhodes) and lyrics by Edward Teschemacher] and 'The Sweetest Story Ever Told' [originally published 1892, with music and lyrics by R. M. Stults]."

The celebration continues with a luncheon for members of the wedding party and out-of-town guests at the home of the bride's parents. During the elaborate midday meal Ida converses with a young married couple, Elizabeth and Francis Nixon of Hertford, a lovely small town sixteen miles southwest of Elizabeth City. Elizabeth, known as Lib, had spent her girlhood in Greenville as a member of the prominent and congenial Mayo family. Lib soon will become one of Ida's most cherished friends.

During the luncheon a postman knocks on the door bearing a letter marked "Special Delivery" and addressed to "Miss Ida Fuller, c/o Miss Lois Herring, Greenville, N.C." Ida must have been astonished to receive a letter from Edward in the midst of Lois' special celebration. Edward begins with a reference to their upcoming wedding: "Don't sing too loud at Lois' big event! Wish it were ours instead. . . ." He soon turns to Ida's upcoming relocation: "I hope you know by now where you are going to stay in Plymouth [when the school year begins, on Thursday, September 8]." He has offered her no assistance in finding a suitable place to live.

Ida has moved to Plymouth and rented living accommodations from C. J. Norman by Tuesday, September 6, 1938, when Edward writes to her from Elizabeth City: "Welcome to Plymouth! I wish I were there to welcome you properly. I'll have to wait a few days I'm afraid. . . . Just wanted you to know I'm thinking of you."

The honeymooning Lois and Crutch send Ida a picture postcard the same day from a majestic spot in the mountains of North Carolina. They thank her for gracing their wedding with song. Lois includes the charming compliment "that you sang prettier Sat. than I've ever heard you."

Meanwhile Edward visits Ida the following weekend and then writes on Tuesday, September 13: "I hope you are feeling better in more ways than one by now. I arrived back in the big city without an accident, driving . . . [as you requested] about 55 [the speed limit] instead of 65. . . ." He then thanks Ida for giving him a striking photograph of herself sitting under the graceful branches of a spreading tree: "I didn't get a good 'look' at your picture Saturday night but have since then. It is the first thing I see in the morning and the last thing at night. I think I'll . . . move it to my office so I can see it all day! But if I do I'm afraid I couldn't get any work done—looking at it so much—in case there was any work (or cold weather). . . . My mother just returned from [visiting Fleetwood, Anita, and Ted in] New York last night, so I am not keeping bachelor quarters now." Ida still remains totally in the dark about Edward's hostile behavior toward Emma.

Emma Finances Edward's New Dunstan Supply Company. Emma's dinner party in honor of Ida has paved the way for Edward to reestablish at least a chilly relationship with his mother. He immediately seizes the opportunity to petition her for a sizeable loan or, even better, an outright donation of money. Emma generously attempts to end the family estrangement by transferring funds to her difficult son as a gift. Edward desires her money to expand his business. The *Daily Advance* deftly relates, on August 18, 1938, that when "Ed Dunstan promised to spend several thousand dollars" creating "a building supply . . . company" in the field behind his mother's house, neighboring "Church Street residents" voiced strong opposition. Another site he proposes to the City Council arouses the ire of residents in that neighborhood, who rightly imagine the proposed undertaking "decreasing the value of their residential property." Edward finally drops "his request . . . to start a building supply business in a residential district."

He decides to purchase a closed pickle plant on Skinners Avenue (later renamed Hughes Boulevard), with an eye toward converting this ample structure into his building supply business. The *Advance* carries a front-page article, on September 13, about his venture under the headline "Supplies Replace Pickle Industry." The newspaper informs readers that "W. E. Dunstan recently bought C. C. Lang & Sons [of Baltimore] pickle plant [earlier operated as Leitch and Helwig] and . . . plans to start a building supply business to take the place of the pickle industry now lost to the city. . . . Mr. Dunstan plans to move his fuel business [also on Skinners Avenue] to his new location and thus be able to serve building and fuel needs from the same locale. The big building he bought has a concrete floor and a railroad siding and is ideally suited for his company's needs, says Mr. Dunstan. This recent purchase culminates Mr. Dunstan's efforts . . . to move and expand his business enterprise." Edward's new venture soon opens as Dunstan Supply Company.

Forrest and Garland Embark on Promising Careers. In the meantime articles about Forrest and Garland often season the newspaper. On August 8 the *Daily Advance* runs a piece under the headline "Forrest Vaughan Dunstan Passes Bar Examination." The newspaper relates that the secretary "of the state board of law examiners said today that 53 of the 94 persons who took the examination . . . would be issued licenses. . . . Forrest Vaughan Dunstan of Elizabeth City was among those passing the examination."

Meanwhile, on August 17, the *Advance* reports that three Elizabeth City students have graduated from Poughkeepsie Business Institute: "James Mac Duff, son of Mrs. W. P. Duff; Bill Robinson, son of Mr. and Mrs. C. O. Robinson; and Garland Dunstan, son of Mrs. W. E. Dunstan." Twenty-two-year-old Garland embarks on a real estate career under the supervision of his mother.

The newspaper again pleases the Dunstan family, on September 22, by carrying a front-page article under the headline "Forrest Dunstan Now Real Lawyer." After taking his oath as a licensed attorney three days earlier, "Forrest Dunstan pulled on a sweatshirt and old trousers today and started painting the floor of his lawyer's office on the fourth floor of the Carolina Building [popular name for the Hinton Building, where the late Will, his father, maintained an office on the second floor]. Dunstan took the oath Monday at Waynesville, together with [State Senator] Ralph Gardner, son of former Governor O. Max Gardner . . ., and Jim Queen, son of Solicitor [prosecuting attorney] John M. Queen. All three studied law at Chapel Hill under Judge [Felix E.] Alley. . . ."

The judge administered the oath that inducted the young trio into office. "The latest member of the Elizabeth City bar," Forrest Dunstan shares offices with "his brother Garland, who is handling real estate. . . . Lawyer Dunstan received his A.B. from Duke University and studied law at the University of North Carolina. He recently passed the State bar exam."

On October 4 the *Advance* announces that "Forrest Dunstan, newest member of the bar in Elizabeth City, [successfully] defended his first case in Recorder's Court [a court of limited jurisdiction] Tuesday morning, but paradoxically his client lost his freedom for three months. The young attorney convinced the court that" his client, a "husky Persse Street Negro, was guilty of neither forcible trespass nor assault, the two charges lodged against him." Yet his client imprudently testified that "he had bought whiskey from the man he was supposed to have fought and had imbibed quite a bit of it," a declaration causing the court to revoke an earlier suspended sentence of three months. Recorder [Judge] W. C. Morse . . . congratulated Attorney Dunstan on his demeanor in court and the finished manner in which he conducted the case...."

Ida Teaches at Plymouth. None of Edward's letters to Ida survive from September 13 to mid-November, but he proves a constant weekend visitor in Plymouth during this two-month period. Perhaps he tells her during one visit that his extraordinary paternal grandparents, Edmund and Mary Louisa, once held sway on vast stretches of Dunstan land lying just across the Roanoke Rive from Plymouth. Edward and Ida must have found much to discuss. Ida probably tells him that Lois and Crutch now occupy a house on beautiful Franklin Street in Chapel Hill. Crutch has gained a teaching position in the Accounting Department at the University of North Carolina. Lois writes Ida, on Wednesday, September 24, showing appreciation for a handsome wedding gift: "Many thanks, my dear, for the silver. . . . I believe I'm going to enjoy keeping house. . . . I love married life. . . . The mountains were beautiful but I was more interested in my husband. How's that? I can sleep now [after the restless nights in Weeksville]."

While Lois basks in wedded bliss, Plymouth buzzes with gossip. When Ida first arrives in town she hears many lurid tidbits about a nearby woman accused of adultery and attempted murder. The *Daily Advance* had published a sensational article, on July 20, 1938, about this "unfaithful wife whose illicit love for another man led her to attempt the murder of her husband." Charges brought against her include "fornication and adultery with" a "handsome 21-year-old youth" and trying to kill her husband "by dumping box lye in his personal whiskey." Her husband declared the doctored whiskey made him feel "'awfully sick.'" The passionate young man "testified yesterday that his intimate relations with" the older woman "took place in barns and in their homes." Continuing, the newspaper relates that the woman has been incarcerated "for the adultery and fornication" until the case reaches Superior Court, but her young lover walked away scot-free "to return to his home."

Another topic of discussion in Plymouth centers on two young brothers. Their parents accuse them of flooding the yard every day by turning the handle of an outside spigot and leaving the water running. The *Advance* informs readers on September 2 that whenever the parents point a finger, "the youngsters . . . deny that they . . . left the spigot running." Finally, the mother decides to catch the culprits by observing the yard "from a back window" and watches in amazement as the boys' thirsty pony, Buck, opens the spigot with his teeth and drinks freely before walking away, "leaving the water pouring." The astounded father then invites "half a dozen men" to come to his house "and watch the performance. . . ."

Ida loses weight under the stress of teaching in an unfamiliar school, planning her forthcoming wedding, and conducting a difficult long-distance courtship. Despite increasing fatigue, she agrees to sing at a Plymouth reception honoring a prominent couple returning from their honeymoon. On October 22, 1938, the *Advance* compliments her. "Miss Ida Fuller rendered two enjoyable vocal selections" during "the outstanding social event. . . ."

Ida maps out vital details for her future married life by selecting graceful patterns of sterling flatware (Louis XIV by Towle), china (Blue Dawn by Noritake), and crystal stemware (American by Fostoria). Later, her difficult future sister-in-law Anita, wife of Fleetwood, will criticize Ida to her face for not choosing fanciful King Edward sterling flatware by Gorham to honor Edward. Anita exhibits her usual insolence by feigning moral outrage about the flatware selection. She possesses two sterling flatware services for twelve at her home in New York City and boasts to Ida about selecting one of these, Saint Dunstan by Tiffany, to honor the family name of her husband.

Ida's nagging problems accelerate with ever-worsening news from Europe and the Middle East. In terms of the Middle East, Herbert Peele, publisher-editor of the *Advance*, issues an editorial on October 26 warning of a looming maelstrom, largely springing from the "double dealing on England's part in the World War [1914-1918], when both Jews and Arabs were led to believe that England had pledged her word to satisfy their national aspirations in Palestine [British-administered territory on the Mediterranean known for its long, tumultuous history], when to satisfy both was clearly impossible. . . ." The newspaper reminds readers that the World War had seen many Arabs give their lives and assets fighting Turks on the basis of false English promises, with the United Kingdom now "reaping the whirlwind [of bitterness and mistrust] in Palestine. . . ." As a history teacher, Ida knows that the gathering storms in the Middle East and Europe—the latter now trembling before Hitler—might unleash malicious forces almost beyond imagination.

Mrs. Gregory Enters the Picture. Back in Elizabeth City, Edward scouts for post-honeymoon living quarters for his intended and himself. On Monday, October 17, a classified advertisement in the *Daily Advance* catches his eye: "FOUR ROOM furnished upstairs heated apartment; [with] private bath, entrance, [and] garage. 507 W. Church Street. Call 313-J or 734-J." He recognizes the address as that of a nearby private residence. This house, on the southwest corner of Church and Westover Streets, stands one short block from his mother's dwelling, on the southwest corner of Church and Persse Streets. Edward rushes to 507 (later renumbered 701) and speaks with the owner, Katherine (Kate) Dean Gregory, widow of the distinguished dentist Dr. Samuel Wilson Gregory.

Mrs. Gregory owns a handsome Queen Anne style residence with two impressive corner towers. The lofty pair enlivens the roofline and nicely sets off the patterned slate roof. The towers flank a pedimented double-tier central portico, pleasantly extending into a superb wrap-around one-story porch supported by Tuscan columns. Mrs. Gregory has just enclosed the second-story central porch and converted the new room into a modern kitchen with an electric refrigerator and gas cookstove.

She explains that her new tenants will enter the house through front double doors into a spacious entrance hall, opening onto the first stage of the right tower, and they will climb the elegant Neo-Classical Revival stairway, possessing an intermediate landing, to the balcony on the second story. Her renters might decide to use the windowed tower off the entrance hall as a living room, the balcony for dining, and two of the rooms on the second floor as bedrooms, or perhaps they might decide to use one of the two rooms on the second floor as a den or living room. They will enjoy a private bath on the second floor as well as a garage facing Westover Street. She intends to retain for her personal guests a second-story bedroom possessing a concealed back staircase entered from the first floor and designed for servants to conduct their duties virtually unseen. Accordingly, Mrs. Gregory's overnight guests will share the back staircase with her maid.

Mrs. Gregory will close and lock the interior doors providing passage from the entrance hall into her home. She will enter her house from the large single door on the Westover side of the wrap-around porch. Edward, known for penny-pinching on necessities but reckless spending on luxuries, dickers for weeks with Mrs. Gregory about rent. The two finally come to an agreement. On a later trip to Plymouth, he describes to Ida the beautiful home they will occupy, if she finds the quarters agreeable, and then he focuses the discussion on various details about the Gregory family.

Perhaps Edward remembers hearing as a boy that the dentist and his personable wife had lived on Burgess Street during the early part of their marriage. On Friday, October 10, 1902, the *Elizabeth City Tar Heel* announced that "Dr. and Mrs. Gregory entertained a party of friends at their home on Burgess Street Wednesday evening. An excellently arranged program of high-class music was rendered by the hostess . . . [and by] Miss Sharp and Prof. Lanier. Dainty refreshments were served."

The Gregory family soon moved into their spacious new home on West Church Street, built by the West End Land and Improvement Company. There Dr. and Mrs. Gregory enjoy a happy and stable marriage, briefly marred by an automobile mishap on January 13, 1916, leaving the dentist with broken bones and painful wounds. The *Advance* describes the trying experience five days later. Before the accident, Dr. Gregory had left by train to oversee "his farm in Camden County" and, after returning "on the night express," began "walking up Main Street" but saw "an automobile . . . coming toward him." The driver, rushing "to catch the night train," claimed the glare of oncoming automobile lights blinded him from seeing anything. His motor car struck the strolling dentist. Witnesses rushed "Dr. Gregory . . . to his home on Church Street, and [physicians provided] immediate surgical attention. . . ." The newspaper reassures readers "that his condition today is much improved."

Dr. Gregory has mended by the time his beautiful sixteen-year-old daughter, Dorothy, recites a poem during a school Christmas program, as reported by the *Advance* on December 21, 1916. Decades later, Dorothy's life will become laced with dark mysteries and unimaginable sorrows (described in volume 2).

Ida surely expresses delight to learn that Mrs. Gregory adores classical music and that her late husband enjoyed performing lighthearted musical compositions. The *Advance* had related on July 2, 1937, that "Dr. S. W. Gregory . . . has been grinding away at teeth for many years. . . . He will fill a tooth for you . . ., and if you get in a bad humor during the work, he will stop and make music for you, charging nothing extra for the extra. He has a guitar up in his office," located on the second floor of the Carolina Building, and "a wire contraption with a French harp [harmonica] attached to it." He plays by slipping "the harp apparatus over his head" and holding the guitar. On a recent day, he "started 'Over the Waves' ['Sobres las Olas,' classic waltz by Mexican composer and violinist Juventino Rosas (1868-1894)], modern dentistry forgotten."

Dr. Gregory then turned to discuss the discomfort associated with dentistry, confessing that "'pain is nothing now to what it used to be. We once did our grinding with little hatchets, chopping off big parts of the decayed tooth. That didn't help our popularity.'" He played his instruments "again—'I wish I was in Dixie'—[and] the office resounded with the melody. He kept good time with his foot, and got fancy with the harp, getting trills in the high notes with the greatest of ease. . . . It wasn't Christmas, but Dr. Gregory loves 'Silent Night' [and] . . . played it through twice. One could almost see Santa and eight sweltering reindeer [Rudolph becomes popular as the ninth reindeer when Gene Autry sings about him in 1949] swing through the July air outside the office window."

The rival *Independent* intones on July 30, fifteen days before suspending publication, that "Dr. Sam Gregory . . . soothes his patients' nerves by getting out his one-piece band outfit and playing a tune or two. This outfit consists of a mouth harp [another term for harmonica] and a guitar, with the harp fastened to a brace so he can play it with his mouth" while strumming the guitar with his hands. "Dr. Gregory mastered this stunt 40 years ago and has never tired of performing it."

On September 3, 1937, the *Advance* relates that Dr. Gregory has served as an honorary pallbearer at the funeral of another revered dentist, Dr. J. Herbert White, conducted from Christ Episcopal Church. Dr. Gregory becomes the dean of the Elizabeth City dental profession upon the death of Dr. White, born 1860, but he falls seriously ill before the end of 1937. The *Advance* relieves concerns about his health on January 12, 1938, by informing readers that "Dr. S. W. Gregory . . . is reported much improved at his home, 507 West Church Street."

On Wednesday, February 9, the newspaper jars the front page with two adjoining somber articles. The first reveals that King George VI of the United Kingdom will "make a state visit to France next June. . . . Political observers were quick to point out that the monarch's first journey outside the realm since his coronation last May would serve to balance the German Fuehrer Hitler's springtime visit to fascist Rome."

The second, an obituary, informs readers that "Dr. Samuel W. Gregory, 73, died at 6 o'clock yesterday afternoon at his home on West Church Street. He is survived by his wife, the former Miss Kate Dean, of Henderson; two daughters, Mrs. C. E. Griffin [Elsie Gregory Griffin], of Elizabeth City, and Mrs. G. Allen Ives [Dorothy Gregory Ives], of New Bern. . . . The funeral will be held Thursday morning at 11 o'clock from the First Baptist Church. . . . Burial will be in New Hollywood Cemetery.

"Forty-three years in the dental profession entitled Dr. Gregory to the distinction of being the oldest practicing dentist in Elizabeth City. Dr. Gregory was graduated with the class of 1888 from the oldest dental school in the world—Baltimore College of Dental Surgery, and he was also a graduate of Wake Forest. Like so many of his profession in those days, he first practiced from house to house, carrying his satchel of instruments with him. . . . Dr. Gregory . . . served several years on the hospital board . . ., was chairman of the School Board for a number of years," and "served on the Board of Aldermen. . . . A native of Camden County, Dr. Gregory was born . . . on October 4, 1864, during [the] latter days of the Civil War. . . . He was married in 1897 . . . to Miss

Katherine Dean of Henderson. . . . Dr. Gregory was a lover of music. He was accomplished with the harmonica, guitar, and a 200-year-old violin he owned."

Issuing an editorial the same day under the headline "To Dr. S. W. Gregory," *Advance* publisher-editor Herbert Peele warmly eulogizes the late dentist. "The death of Dr. S. W. Gregory marks the passing from the scene of another of those men who were leading spirits in Elizabeth City in the days of its most rapid growth and development, an era the like of which the town may not see again. The *Daily Advance* . . . knew him as chairman of the School Board and considers him . . . one of the best chairmen the board ever had. We knew him as a Kiwanian [member of the Kiwanis Club, a national and international service club] and as one of the most genial and popular spirits of that organization. We knew him as deacon in his church and as sincerely concerned for its healthful growth and its services in the community. We knew him as a [dental] craftsman who delighted in fine work, as the artist does.

"We knew him as a man who had music in himself and was 'moved with concord of sweet sounds' [quoting from Shakespeare's *The Merchant of Venice*, act 5, scene 1]. We knew him too as one who liked nothing better than the converse and companionship of congenial friends. He was a man, then, who lived a full and busy life . . . through its allotted span without shunning its responsibilities. The *Daily Advance* is happy to have so known him and believes that for . . . one who has lived such a life, death has no terrors but comes as a friend."

Mrs. Gregory immediately withdraws from social events for a proper period of mourning but frequently visits her daughter and son-in-law, Dorothy and Allen Ives, in New Bern, roughly one hundred and thirty miles southwest of Elizabeth City. Named for Bern, Switzerland, New Bern had served as the seat of government for North Carolina from 1746 until 1792, when Raleigh became the state capital.

The *Advance* relates on April 30, 1938, that "Mrs. S. W. Gregory has returned to her home, 507 West Church Street, after spending some time in New Bern with her daughter and son-in-law, Mr. and Mrs. Allen Ives." Nine days earlier the newspaper had announced that "Dr. Arthur Gollobin," a young dentist relocating from Virginia, "has begun practicing here in the same office used by the late Dr. S. W. Gregory."

About this time Mrs. Gregory decides that her house possesses entirely too much room for one person and employs carpenters, plumbers, and electricians to convert most of the second story into rental quarters. By the opening of summer she has resumed an active role as a member of the United Daughters of the Confederacy. The *Advance* reports on June 21 that Dorothy Ives and her two children "are visiting Mrs. Ives' mother" and adds three days later that Mrs. Gregory has attended a meeting of the United Daughters of the Confederacy. During this meeting, as described by the newspaper, members of the organization welcome the announcement that a prominent local citizen has agreed to "donate *Rise and Fall of the Confederate Government*, [2 vols., 1878-1881] by Jefferson Davis, to the . . . library" of Elizabeth City High School.

The newspaper relates on August 16 that Mrs. Gregory and her Elizabeth City daughter, Elsie Griffin, along with Elsie's husband and son, have returned from the western part of the state, where "they visited Blowing Rock, Lake Lure, Little Switzerland and other points of interest." On December 7 the *Advance* informs readers that Mrs. Gregory had left the previous day for New Bern to "spend some time visiting her daughter [Dorothy Ives]. . . ."

By this time Edward has notified Mrs. Gregory that he will rent the second floor of her house at 507 West Church Street. He lacks the faintest inkling of the huge impact she will have on his life (described in volumes 2-6).

Night of Terror. Meanwhile Edward has become a familiar figure in Plymouth on weekends. While he and Ida enjoy a long discussion about their wedding plans over a leisurely restaurant dinner on Sunday night, October 30, 1938, they remain unaware that hysteria grips much of the nation. Edward drives his fiancée home later and sees her safely inside.

The couple freezes as everyone in the house sputters about ghastly radio news flashes describing an enormous interplanetary force from Mars invading the United States. The following day the *Advance* publishes sensational front-page articles from the

Associated Press (an agency reporting and transmitting stories to teletypewriters in newspaper offices) and equally sensational articles from local reporters. The newspaper accounts reveal a nation numbed with fear.

Radio listeners in Manteo, on Roanoke Island in northeastern North Carolina, "dashed back and forth in the streets" screaming "of thousands dead in New Jersey. . . ." Countless Americans fainted or collapsed in terror. People suffered heart attacks. Many "frantic listeners" in New York City bolted from their apartments into the streets. Cadets studying at Clemson College (later renamed University) in South Carolina "fled buildings and rushed to the highway, seeking rides they knew not where." One student dashed from campus to a river, "asserting he would jump in, if the enemy's heat rays became too intense." Five students at tranquil Brevard College in the mountains of North Carolina "fainted as pandemonium reigned on campus" amid cries of a doomed "world coming to an end."

The newspaper then reveals the source of these bizarre scenes. Radio listeners experienced untold "panic and fear" over a Columbia Broadcasting System program presented as a series of seemingly "authentic news reports" of a lethal attack by "men from Mars. . . ." These radio "news reports" ran without commercial interruption and thus acquired a highly realistic quality. Many people feared that the Martian invaders might actually be the Germans in disguise.

The *Advance* identifies the person responsible for the broadcast as the American actor and producer Orson Welles, whose Mercury Theatre dramatization of H. G. Wells' novel *The War of the Worlds* (1898) created the frenzy. The newspaper adds that the Federal Communications Commission has already begun an investigation. The bogus news flashes describing a deadly Martian invasion not only spread terror but also brought twenty-three-year-old Orson Welles immediate global fame. For years, Ida expresses amazement that so many souls became hysterical over a pre-Halloween broadcast not confirmed by rival radio networks.

Western European Democracies Tremble before Hitler. Meanwhile the European crisis has worsened after Hitler acts on his ruthless plan to absorb Austria. With the intimidated and divided Western democracies desperately attempting to avoid war by appeasing the Nazi regime, Hitler advances his goal of bringing all German-speaking peoples under his rule. Thus he prepares to incorporate independent Austria into a new expanded Germany. He thrusts his forces into Austria and silences pockets of opposition. The *Advance* publishes the result on March 14, 1938: "Adolph Hitler today triumphantly entered Vienna, capital of the German state [of Austria that] he has absorbed in his greater German Reich [literally Empire]. His motorcade passed the city limits at 4:50 p.m. (10:50 a.m. E.S.T.). Fully a million shouting, flag-waving Viennese . . . greeted him," though "frantic hysteria swept through Vienna Jewry today as Austria became but a name in history."

With Hitler pushing the word to the brink of war, Americans find themselves on pins and needles. The first week of April finds many Pasquotank County residents seeking temporary escape from the threatening international scene by flocking to Elizabeth City's Carolina Theatre (welcoming white patrons) or Gaiety Theatre (welcoming colored patrons) to enjoy Walt Disney's first feature-length movie, the enchanting but disquieting animated fairy tale *Snow White and the Seven Dwarfs*.

Despite the mesmerizing effects of the film, many Americans suffer sleepless night over the increasingly disturbing news from Europe. Under the ill-omened headline "Hitler in Person Assumes Power in Sudetenland" (German-speaking western borderlands of the republic of Czechoslovakia in central Europe), the *Daily Advance* reports on October 3 that Adolph Hitler, tailing his armies, "personally assumed power over this former Czechoslovak territory in a triumphant military procession today and declared that 'never will this land be torn from the Reich.'" (The late twentieth century will see a reconstituted Czechoslovakia divided into the Czech Republic and Slovakia.)

November 1938 finds the Nazis terrorizing German Jews with mounting horrors. On November 12 the *Advance* stuns readers with chilling news describing the German landscape marred not only with vicious billboards "declaring 'Judaism is Criminalism'" but also "smashed and looted Jewish store[s] defaced with insulting signs" and symbols such as nooses and swastikas. Meanwhile the German regime continues erecting vicious "new barriers around Jews, isolating them further from the nation's cultural and economic life." Two days later the newspaper reports that the Nazis have "expelled Jewish students from all universities . . . and other institutions of higher learning in the latest move toward separation of Jews and Germans." Hitler's government has stripped German Jews of their identification as Germans, classifying them as subhuman degenerates with no claim to considerate treatment. With good reason, Jews have lost hope of Christians coming to their aid. On November 19 the newspaper describes growing Jewish fears spurred by a decree from the head of the council of Protestant churches in Germany that "the name of Jehovah" must be "erased from Protestant churches throughout Nazi Germany. . . ." The shocking order demands that "the name of the God of Israel must be obliterated wherever it is displayed in Protestant churches. The names of . . . all prophets of the Old Testament also were ordered erased. This [Christian] action" adds a repugnant "sequel to . . . the wave of anti-Jewish violence which swept Germany last week."

Ominous Wedding Bells. In this grim atmosphere Ida teaches at Plymouth and makes final preparations for her approaching wedding. Edward types a postcard to his fiancée on Monday, November 28, 1938, informing her that a "representative of the [*Norfolk*] *Virginian Pilot* just called to get your picture." Ida's serene engagement photograph (shown on the front cover of this volume) graces several newspapers in North Carolina and Virginia.

She has subscribed to the *Daily Advance* and receives each issue by mail. Early December sees her reading a number of articles in the *Advance* about Forrest Dunstan, her future brother-in law. On December 5 the newspaper announces that the County Commissioners have elected Forrest "assistant trial justice of Recorder's Court for the next two years." The following day, Herbert Peele publishes an editorial saluting Forrest and two other young "new officials taking over the duties of their respective offices. . . . Each of these officials has his record yet to make, but the *Daily Advance* has never seen a group of new officials take office in whose worthiness it felt more confidence. Each is representative of a high type of citizenship." Herbert Peele imagines "each of them . . . beginning what will be a long career of public service and usefulness."

On December 12 the newspaper headline "Dunstan Presides" introduces another article about Forrest. "Sitting on the bench for the first time, Assistant Trial Justice Forrest Dunstan . . . disposed of four simple drunk cases in short order Monday morning," with the "inebriates . . . paraded before the bar, their cases . . . heard, and judgment . . . rendered. . . ."

When Ida's teaching duties end in early December, she enjoys a flurry of bridal showers and parties at Plymouth, Weeksville, Elizabeth City, Raleigh, Louisburg, and Moulton. Edward writes on Monday, December 1, sending thanks for an unnamed birthday gift (probably his class ring from Duke that she has ordered), and he issues a dining invitation, on behalf of his mother, for Sunday at noon, "so don't make any plans for that time. . . ." He closes: "All my love to the sweetest girl in the world (sometimes), Edward."

One week later he mentions finally notifying Mrs. Gregory that we will "rent her apartment. . . ." He ends by looking forward to the wedding and honeymoon: "Less than three weeks, sweetheart, & I hope you will be just as glad as I when they're over. I can hardly believe I'm so lucky. . . ." On Tuesday, December 20, Edward writes again and encloses "a little cartoon" evoking thoughts "that in just 8 days" he will exchange wedding vows with "a very sweet little girl." The newspaper clipping shows a battered and broken groom who has been dragged to the altar by his much larger bride. She explains to the clergyman, "He changed his mind last night, but everything's all right now."

Ida envisions a wedding ceremony of restrained but joyous dignity signifying the joining of two souls for life. Many young couples living in Depression America prudently economize on their nuptial celebrations to reduce needless expense and avoid the appearance of extravagance in the midst of great suffering and want. True to her lofty principles, Ida refuses to scatter thousands of dollars in a spending frenzy and plans an inspirational wedding of simple elegance and spiritual depth, perhaps with one or two touches of splendor.

She sends Edward her written description of the upcoming wedding for his approval and suggestions. Ida intends to refine this rough draft and mail the polished version to newspapers as a guide for articles about the nuptials, to be published after the event. Edward scribbles a stunningly cruel response on Saturday, December 24, 1938, just four days before the appointed wedding date. Seething, he finds the piece entirely too showy in describing wedding decorations and appointments: "It might be all right for Lady Astor [brash Virginia-born Nancy Witcher Langhorne Astor, Viscountess, the first woman to sit in the British Parliament] . . . or some hosiery mill women. . . ." His condescending comment about "hosiery mill women," who work for rock-bottom wages under burdensome circumstances, deeply stings Ida. She still fails to grasp his scorn for anyone weathered, faded, and prematurely aged by wrenching poverty (mirroring his defiance of Jesus' instruction, as framed in Matthew 25:40, to show mercy to "the least of these"), though Ida should have accumulated clues when Edward began sneering about several of her struggling Moulton neighbors battered by the Great Depression.

His ungentlemanly and unwarranted appraisal of her rough draft extends entirely beyond the pale, but he excels in diluting his victim's anger by inflicting guilt and shame. The words he finds most objectionable ("tall cathedral candles were burning in six seven-branched candelabra") appear almost verbatim ("the setting was further enhanced by tall cathedral candles in branched candelabra") in the *Advance* on May 13, 1939, describing an Elizabeth City wedding of social prominence that all the Dunstans will attend. Despite crystal evidence laid before her, Ida still fails to comprehend that she verges on trading her sheltered birthright for matrimony to a merciless tyrant.

That evening Edward scrawls another letter to his fiancée. "I wrote to you this morning concerning the write-up. I suppose I was pretty frank in my comments, but such things have been nerve upsetters for me so long that I am easily disturbed." If Ida still remains blind to Edward's "easily disturbed" nature, everyone else in his immediate circle has suffered innumerable traumas from his volcanic temper.

He then proceeds to discuss his well-known frugality involving the outlay of small sums. "During the entire time I was in N.Y. I was continually hounded as to my spending habits. . . ." People "thought that just because my brother [Fleetwood] had a fair income that I too should have plenty" of cash to squander, "and now here in Eliz. City I am . . . continually expected to make large donations to various" causes and charities, "but I prefer to lead . . . a simple life. . . . I may have sounded . . . harsh in my morning letter," yet I will not "have a write-up of that [lavish] type. . . ." Ida's proposed wedding article has even jogged his memory of "one little girl who . . . spent all of her savings for the biggest wedding here in several years," but ever since she and her husband have shared a dismally cramped apartment with her mother and father.

Edward has unmistakably shown that any peace in his household will require absolute submission to his autocratic rule. He adds a syrupy afterthought, "I certainly miss you, precious, and surely wish these next 93 hours were over."

He promises in his final prenuptial letter to Ida, written on Sunday, Christmas Day, 1938, not to make this narrative "long" and "fussy," just a few hurried words before the wedding day. "My brother and family [Fleetwood, Anita, and Ted] arrived late last night. We expect to arrive in Moulton about 11:30—it is hard to get these New Yorkers up. They are sleeping until 10:30 today. They brought along a beautiful silver fruit bowl [as a wedding gift] for the center of the dining table. I told them that it was larger than our table!" He closes, "Will see you soon—Love, Edward."

Several newspapers in North Carolina and Virginia publish lengthy articles describing the Dunstan-Fuller wedding, with all expressions offensive to Edward stricken from the narrative. On January 1, 1939, the *Norfolk Virginian Pilot* spotlights the nuptials: "The wedding of Miss Ida Fuller, of Louisburg, N.C., and William Edward Dunstan, of Elizabeth City, was solemnized at 3:30 o'clock Wednesday afternoon [December 28] in Corinth Baptist Church . . . [near] Louisburg. The Rev. Wilbur F. Woodall, brother-in-law of the bride, officiated. . . . Simple decorations in the colors of green and white were used on the altar and chancel of the church. . . ." Music included a program of organ selections and solos before the entrance of the bridal party and continued with classical pieces during the ceremony.

"The 'Bridal Chorus' from [Wagner's opera] *Lohengrin* was used as the processional [though this musical drama weaves a tale of tragic love], and as the vows were spoken [Schumann's introspective] 'Traumerei' [Dreaming] was softly played. The bridal party left the church to the strains of Mendelssohn's 'Wedding March.' The bridegroom had as his best man his brother, E. Fleetwood Dunstan, of New York City. The ushers were George Fuller, of Louisburg, and Walter Fuller, of Hickory, brothers of the bride; Forrest Dunstan and Garland Dunstan, of Elizabeth City, brothers of the bridegroom. Mrs. Wilbur F. Woodall [Mary Susan Fuller Woodall], of Charlotte, N.C., attended her sister as matron of honor. . . . The bride entered the church with her brother, David T. Fuller, by whom she was given in marriage. She was attired in a Patou [Parisian fashion-design house founded by Jean Patou] model of Windsor blue, made Empire style [characterized by a high waistline], with shirred [gathered in decorative parallel rows] bodice. Her turban [fashionable turban-style hat], also of Windsor blue, had a matching face veil [associated with purity and modesty and adding softness to the face]. She carried an arm bouquet of red roses and swansonia [an ornamental admired for its fragrant blossoms of rich bright colors]."

Following the Dunstan-Fuller ceremony, the church empties as members of the wedding party and guests attend a reception at the home of Miss Annie, mother of the bride. The *Pilot* describes "rooms of the house . . . decorated in the Christmas motif." After the guests enjoy various refreshments, including Russian tea to curb the winter chill, the bride and groom cut the wedding cake, baked earlier in the detached kitchen behind the Fuller house. Ida has chosen a Lady Baltimore cake, a sumptuous Southern alternative to a plain white wedding cake. Cooks enhance Lady Baltimore frosting with brandy or rum or orange-lemon juice and various flavorings. Then they carefully fold a plentiful combination of chopped walnuts and dried or candied fruits into part of the luscious white frosting, making the Lady Baltimore cake distinctive. They spread the fruit-nut frosting abundantly between layers and reserve the plain brandied frosting to spread on the top and sides of the beautiful rich cake.

The *Pilot* tells also of Ida's education at Louisburg and Meredith Colleges and Edward's at Duke and Harvard. The newspaper then lists out-of-town wedding guests. Edward finds several familiar names among this group—Emma, Forrest, and Garland Dunstan of Elizabeth City; Fleetwood, Anita, and Ted Dunstan of New York City; and Marvin and Adelaide Harrison of Raleigh—though not one of his lifelong friends, fraternity brothers, or business acquaintances makes an appearance. His entire representation totals eight people: his mother (Emma), three brothers (Forrest, Garland, and Fleetwood), sister-in-law (Anita), nephew (Ted), sister (Adelaide), and brother-in-law (Marvin). Edward tempers his edgy excitement by voicing as many personal boasts as possible.

Magnetic Ida has attracted numerous friends to the wedding from North Carolina, Virginia, and South Carolina. They have known Ida since her childhood at Moulton, college days at Louisburg and Raleigh, or teaching career at Weeksville and Plymouth. Listing only people mentioned elsewhere in this narrative, Ida's many out-of-town guests include Wilbur and Mary Susan Woodall, her brother-in-law and sister, who have moved from tiny Gatesville to Charlotte; Walter and Estelle Fuller, her brother and new sister-in-law, of Hickory; Annie Marie Jackson, her friend and former fellow teacher, of Weeksville; and Robert and Lois Crutchfield, her friends and former fellow teachers, of Chapel Hill.

Later in the afternoon the bride and groom take their leave by motorcar for the wedding trip. They have not announced their destination, the historic port city of Charleston, South Carolina, and their guests probably speculate about possible spots as Edward takes the wheel and drives away. Nearing Charleston, the newlyweds see that the highway crosses a long curving bridge dwarfing everything in sight and seemingly vaulting into the clouds. Acrophobic, Edward becomes terrified about traversing the Cooper River on this dizzying span and asks Ida to operate the automobile. As she drives over the sweeping bridge giving Charleston a direct link to the north, Edward keeps his eyes tightly closed and breaks out in a cold sweat as he prays for the ordeal to end. Once they finally reach their hotel, the newlyweds enjoy the mild climate and the unique architectural and cultural splendors of Charleston. They find time also for intimate moments.

Ida Shines in Elizabeth City and Nags Head. Edward and Ida return to North Carolina in early January 1939 and begin making their home at 507 West Church Street in Elizabeth City. About six weeks later she visits the office of Dr. Joseph A. Gill, a young local obstetrician, who predicts that the stork will visit her in early October. Edward fumes at the damnable news. He has never entertained the slightest interest in having children and sharply bristles at the prospect of a birth during his first year of married life. Mrs. Gregory, whose house shelters the couple, proves genuinely caring by bringing delicious treats upstairs to Ida on business days, when Edward operates Dunstan Supply Company.

With the period of public bereavement for Dr. Gregory now behind her, Mrs. Gregory pursues an increasingly active social life. The *Daily Advance* reports on January 26 that she has been elected "third vice president" of the local chapter of the United Daughters of the Confederacy and on February 3 that she and four friends have left for Florida to "spend some time touring the state." On March 31 the newspaper relates that Mrs. Gregory and several other ladies "are attending the district meeting of the United Daughters of the Confederacy" in Plymouth. Newspaper readers learn on July 18 that she has returned to town after spending two weeks at the beach with her daughter Dorothy Ives of New Bern.

Socially correct and intellectually curious, Ida quickly becomes a popular figure in Elizabeth City and receives an invitation in late January to visit the Junior Woman's Club for its monthly afternoon meeting. The members cordially ask her to join the influential organization. The *Advance* reports on February 17 that Ida had has been named to a committee of three charged with planning a special "card party [to be] given by the club" the following week. Meanwhile, as related by the newspaper on January 26, she has joined a circle, or women's study and fellowship group, of the First Methodist Church. Readers learn on

April 29 about her recent dynamic presentation, "New Realizations of Democracy," during a circle meeting.

Ladies attending club meetings and other afternoon gatherings always don smart hats and fine gloves. Ida adores beautifully trimmed hats. No doubt she relishes an article published in the *Advance* on January 30 about popular examples for Easter 1939, including "Directoire bonnets . . ., turbans . . , and white straw pillboxes . . . with purple veiling. . . . The wimple [a delicate headcloth framing the face] will continue to flutter from streamlined turbans. . . ." Ida must have spent considerable time combing select shops to find a graceful hat for April 9, Easter Sunday.

By this time she wears her hair in an elegant French roll. She gains numerous invitations to bridge parties and continues also to pursue more serious matters. The newspaper announces on Wednesday, May 10, that Ida has read her recently completed paper on the accomplished American author-poet Eunice Tietjens to members of the refined senior Woman's Club, by their invitation. Ida must have anchored her narrative on Eunice Tietjens' autobiographical *The World at My Shoulder* (1938), recording the fascinating dimensions of her experiences in the United States, Japan, China, and Europe.

Most citizens must have been horrified to read in the newspaper the same day, May 10, that "Adolph Hitler, Germany's fiery-tongued dictator, received a lone vote for mayor of Elizabeth City in the municipal election Tuesday."

On Friday, June 2, 1939, Ida's twenty-fifth birthday, the *Advance* relates that "Mr. and Mrs. Edward Dunstan spent the past weekend at Louisburg visiting Mrs. Dunstan's mother. . . ." Meanwhile Ida looks forward to poring over newspaper articles about the highlights of a royal visit. On June 7, as war clouds loom on the European horizon, King George VI and his consort, Queen Elizabeth, arrive at Niagara Falls, New York, from Canada on the first visit to the United States by a reigning British monarch.

Several days later, as noted by the newspaper on June 13, Ida and Emma motor to Nags Head to enjoy "a house party" hosted by Adelaide Dunstan Harrison of Raleigh at the William E. Dunstan Cottage. Ida envisions cultivating close ties with Emma, her remarkable mother-in-law, and Adelaide, her personable sister-in-law. She laments the icy relationship between Edward and his mother, whom she calls Mother Dunstan, and makes every conceivable effort to heal the breach. Ida visits or telephones Emma almost daily. She enjoys her company and values her wisdom. Ida learns much from Emma about Dunstan-Fleetwood-Vaughan-Sawyer-Herrington family history.

She frequently consults her mother-in-law also about food preparation. Whenever Ida asks for a recipe, Emma replies that she has "virtually no experience in the kitchen" but will consult Maggie, her splendid cook. Edward desires his meals prepared in the distinctive regional style then prevalent in northeastern North Carolina and southeastern Virginia. He tells his wife that one Elizabeth City favorite, the boiled dinner, of English lineage, should be served once or twice weekly. Ida knows little about boiled dinners but gains valuable instructions from Emma and Maggie. The preparer blends and enhances flavors by boiling all ingredients together in one pot, including streak of lean or another cut of pork, Irish potatoes, snaps (green beans) or greens (such as collards), dumplings (cornbread made with plain white cornmeal and cooked as small hard cakes), and often rutabagas or turnips to add a keen bite. Ida masters the technique. She and her cooks produce boiled dinners equaling those of anyone in the region.

"You Will Give Birth to a Duck—Not a Baby!" July proves another busy month for the couple. The *Advance* reports on July 4 that "Mr. and Mrs. Edward Dunstan of West Church Street have returned after spending some time at Winchester, Virginia." Edward enjoys motoring to Virginia to behold the majestic Blue Ridge Mountains and pristine Shenandoah Valley and expresses much pleasure in seeing horse farms and stately houses along the way. He regards the noble mountains of North Carolina too distant from Elizabeth City for an uncomplicated and enjoyable trip and thus always shuns those breathtaking peaks.

After the mountain vacation, Ida plans a house party at the William E. Dunstan Cottage at Nags Head, away from the stifling heat and humidity of summertime Elizabeth City. The newspaper relates on July 7, 1939, that "Mrs. Edward Dunstan of West Church Street is spending some time at Nags Head with a party of friends [and relatives] from Louisburg." She has invited Miss Annie and several friends and cousins to the cottage for a week. Everyone enjoys the grandeur of the Atlantic Ocean and the relaxed informality of life at the seashore, though Ida alarms her mother by swimming frequently in the ocean, just three months before her expected delivery date. Miss Annie warns her, "You will give birth to a duck—not a baby!"

Hours of swimming, building sandcastles, and collecting seashells sharpen appetites for the simple fare usually served at the beach. Ida has brought her stellar housemaid-cook, Marie (whose surname escapes me), to prepare meals and keep the cottage clean and comfortable for the guests. Marie turns out many carefree picnic-style lunches for the ladies. Often singing to herself as she works, Marie brews tea leaves for the iced tea and makes various items from scratch, including deviled eggs, coleslaw, biscuits, corn bread, pimento cheese sandwiches, tomato sandwiches, cold cuts, sliced fruit, and pies and cakes. Dinners prove more elaborate and demonstrate Marie's special ingenuity in the kitchen.

Ida and Marie share a secret they carefully conceal from Miss Annie and the other cottage guests. Edward possesses a blazing temper. When Ida triggered his anger over some insignificant matter during the second week of their marriage, he bombarded her for hours with a torrent of angry words. Yet she loves her difficult husband and learns to live with his explosive personality, even blaming herself for not pleasing him and arousing his horrid behavior.

Ida takes a cue from Melina Rorke, whose partly fictionalized autobiography, *The Story of Melina Rorke* (1938), portrays her journey from young aristocratic English womanhood to international fame. The author faces an uphill battle as a widowed mother at the age of fifteen but finds great fulfillment nursing thousands of men in South Africa during the Boer War. In 1902, King Edward VII summons Melina Rorke to Buckingham Place and pins the Royal Red Cross on her for brave service tending the sick and wounded.

An article in the *Advance* on May 26, 1938, describes her as a woman who understands men. The article highlights remarks she made to an interviewer in New York City. Melina Rorke characterizes men as "polygamous by nature." Accordingly, women must "cater to them continually—without letting them know they're being catered to, of course." She portrays men as "much weaker—more dependent than women." Moreover, she warns that "they are full of deception" and "can lie to a woman without batting an eye. I've heard them do it time and time again." Perhaps Ida disagrees with Melina Rorke's characterization of the adult male as more dependent and less honorable than the adult female, but she and innumerable other women of the day wholeheartedly subscribe to her pronouncement that wives should cater to every wish of their husbands.

Sailing Thorny Seas. Ida believes her nurturing love and the forthcoming birth of a baby will pacify Edward, for she still fails to comprehend the futility of trying to outflank the snares of destiny. She will learn her dreadful fortune step by step, tempest by tempest. In the meantime she much admires the sentiments expressed in the haunting song "Believe Me, If All Those Endearing Young Charms." The celebrated Irish poet Thomas Moore had composed the words and set them to a traditional Irish air in the early nineteenth century. His song promises eternal love despite the battering effects of age or illness. Ida had selected the piece as one of the solos for her wedding and thus joined many other young brides in defying the tradition of singing only sacred poetry set to music during Christian marriages. The words mirror her unseasoned idealism at the time and her unswerving commitment to marital fidelity. Often after Edward leaves in the morning for Dunstan Supply Company, Ida plays the melody on her piano and nimbly sings the lyrics:

> Believe me, if all those endearing young charms
> Which I gaze on so fondly today
> Were to change by tomorrow and fleet in my arms
> Like fairy gifts fading away.
> Thou wouldst still be adored, as this moment thou art,
> Let thy loveliness fade as it will
> And around the dear ruin, each wish of my heart
> Would entwine itself verdantly still.

It is not while beauty and youth are thine own
And thy cheeks unprofaned by a tear
That the fervour and faith of a soul can be known
To which time will but make thee more dear.
No, the heart that has truly loved never forgets
But as truly loves on to the close
As the sunflower turns on her god when he sets
The same look which she'd turned when he rose.

About the Author

A gifted educator and writer, William E. Dunstan serves as a visiting scholar at the University of North Carolina at Chapel Hill. His comprehensive professional journey includes remarkable achievements as an archivist, historical editor, author, college administrator, public lecturer, and award-winning teacher. He has taught at Brevard College, Carnegie Mellon University, North Carolina State University, and the University of North Carolina at Chapel Hill. The *Chronicle of Higher Education* hailed him as an innovative scholar and author with a deft hand for crafting appealing literature. His previous publications include *The Ancient Near East*, *Ancient Greece*, and *Ancient Rome*.

Made in the USA
Lexington, KY
13 December 2013